INTERNATIONAL EDUCATION
AT THE CROSSROADS

WELL HOUSE BOOKS

INTERNATIONAL EDUCATION AT THE CROSSROADS

Edited by
Deborah N. Cohn
and Hilary E. Kahn

INDIANA UNIVERSITY PRESS

This book is a publication of

Indiana University Press
Office of Scholarly Publishing
Herman B Wells Library 350
1320 East 10th Street
Bloomington, Indiana 47405 USA

iupress.org

Manufactured in the United States of America

First printing 2021

Cataloging information is available from the Library of Congress.

ISBN 978-0-253-05390-9 (hardback)
ISBN 978-0-253-05391-6 (web PDF)

For Peter and Jahdee, and for our children, Noah J., Skylar, Noah S., Benjamin, and Danny, and the international futures that lie ahead of them.

CONTENTS

Crossroads 4: Internationalization in Practice

Intersection

Crossroads 5: Agencies, Mechanisms, and a Nation

PREFACE

IN NOVEMBER 2019, WHEN WE submitted the manuscript for this book to Indiana University Press, like all our authors, we were hopeful about international education at the crossroads. Now, just a few short months later, we are in the midst of the COVID-19 pandemic. Across the globe, schools and universities in the brick-and-mortar sense are shuttered, while we as educators are scrambling to honor our educational mission through virtual means—and to tend to the human needs and anxieties of our students, our colleagues, and, indeed, ourselves. Travel restrictions have imploded international mobility, research has come to a screeching halt, and by March of 2020, K-20 school closures had affected over 90 percent of all enrolled learners across the globe.[1]

To say that this is a blow to international education is a severe understatement. We have been forced to dismantle, piece by piece, all the various structures we have carefully developed to sustain our work. We had to reorient ourselves, our staffs, and all those we serve and with whom we collaborate to a completely new ethos where we are now implementing policies and practices that go against everything in which we believe. The scale of displacement and disruption is staggering, the financial ramifications are unfathomable, and the prejudice this has stirred is alarming. Online platforms that intend to bring together faculty, students, and communities across time zones and national boundaries are revealing the digital divides that separate those who have access to technology from those who do not. Stoked by racist attempts of defining COVID-19 as an Asian virus, and perpetuated by systemic social disparities, discrimination and xenophobia are on the rise and more blatant than ever.

However, the work we do is never more critical than now, and we must not let this global pandemic alter our resolution to understand the world, break down boundaries, learn languages, create partnerships with institutions and communities, and encourage mobility of people and ideas. We cannot retreat into self-isolation, even while the walls of our homes currently lend us a sense of security. We can learn from this. And we still have reasons to be hopeful. We can consider how to better internationalize at home, how to engage faculty, how to more meaningfully and equitably utilize technology, and how to do international education in ways that are more sustainable for the future of our earth. We can develop mechanisms so we are not as vulnerable to the winds of change. We can devise means of more equitably sharing educational resources. We can continue to come together to solve global problems, even when world politics, economics, and pandemics threaten to pull us apart.

As we note in our introduction, the symposium that gave rise to this volume considered "the need for new narratives and models within what we all agree is a rapidly changing sociopolitical and educational landscape." This landscape changed even more quickly than we could have envisioned when we wrote these words, yet we still remain at a turning point, "a historical global moment that is in some ways recasting the social role of education as well as redefining international engagement with potential political, cultural, and economic impact." The 2020 presidential election, too, has intervened between the submission and publication of these chapters. We are hopeful that this will change some tides, but many of these pressing concerns will still need to be addressed. The ideas that this book espouses—the need to be global, to share skills that will prepare our students for international engagement, and to understand the links that bridge and divide one's communities and the world we now live in—remain crucial and are all the more urgent today.

We heard from a few of the authors as we hurriedly wrote this preface, and while we cannot predict what the full contours of the world and its educational systems will be when this book is released, we remain confident in the relevance and, indeed, urgency of international education as we move toward the next set of crossroads.[2]

Deb and Hilary
March 30, 2020

Notes

1. UNESCO Institute for Statistics, "Global Monitoring."
2. Thanks to Caroline Levander for pointing us toward the UNESCO statistics and to Caroline, Hannah Buxbaum, Brian T. Edwards, Safwan M. Masri, Kris Olds, Patrick O'Meara, Kathleen Sideli, and Eva Egron-Polak for sharing their thoughts with us.

Bibliography

UNESCO Institute for Statistics. "Global Monitoring of School Closures Caused by COVID-19." UNESCO. Accessed June 11, 2020. https://en.unesco.org/themes /education-emergencies/coronavirus-school-closures.

ACKNOWLEDGMENTS

LIKE ANY INITIATIVE IN INTERNATIONAL education, this volume rests on the collaboration and involvement of many. We are grateful that Indiana University president Michael McRobbie invited us to be co-chairs for the university's first bicentennial symposium, International Education at the Crossroads. The inclusion of this symposium in the bicentennial series speaks to the university's long-standing investment in and commitment to this field and to how, indeed, the university views global and international studies as a vital part of its past and future alike. The Office of the Bicentennial provided us with a superb team to support the conference and this volume, and director Kelly Kish went out of her way to help us throughout this endeavor. Patrick O'Meara was particularly helpful during the planning process, and we are grateful for his decades of commitment to international education at Indiana University and beyond. There is no question that the conference would not have been possible without the sustained support of Jeremy Hackerd, Drew Norris, Brittany Terwilliger, Lynn Waugh, Tawana Green, Emily Stern, Rachel Kucera, Sarah Jacobi, Lynn Schoch, and Emily Abshire. We are also thankful for the editing support of Margaret Schnabel, Jeremy Reed, Meize Guo, and the Center for the Study of Global Change, which greatly helped us wrap up this volume.

Initial ideas for the conference were also aided by conversations with the Department of Education International and Foreign Language Education (IFLE) team as well as the Title VI stalwart and advocate Miriam Kazanjian. We thank Miriam, Cheryl Gibbs, and Tim Duvall, from IFLE, for their guidance from early on. We are also grateful for the advice and support of Indiana University assistant vice president for federal relations Doug Wasitis, who is incredibly committed and knowledgeable about Title VI and other federal funding that supports international education. We are privileged to have received advice and encouragement from such committed and knowledgeable champions of international education.

There are a few speakers and moderators from the original conference who are not included in this volume. We thank Lee Feinstein, Hannah Buxbaum, Russell Valentino, Gil Latz, Michael Hamburger, Eric Hirschberg,

Sam Eisen, and Diane Auer Jones for contributing their expertise and insight to the original conversation.

Of course, acknowledgments are not complete without thanking our families, who keep us grounded. Our spouses, Peter and Jahdee, and our children, Noah J., Skylar, Noah S., Benjamin, and Danny, have been patient and caring as we planned, edited, talked, and worked for a number of years on the conference and now this volume. Lastly, we thank all the contributors to this volume, whose voices and understandings are the foundation for what we hope is a conversation that carries international education onward for the next sixty years and beyond.

We hope that this collection reminds all of us why we do what we do, why we are dedicated to an internationalized education, and why we need to continue to serve our communities, states, and the nation by providing access to high-quality and accessible language instruction, in-depth knowledge of world regions, and global competencies for all.

INTERNATIONAL EDUCATION
AT THE CROSSROADS

INTRODUCTION

Hilary E. Kahn and Deborah N. Cohn

IT WAS A DIALOGUE BETWEEN two colleagues at a crossroads that sparked this volume, which itself is a meeting of the minds and a far-reaching exchange of ideas that transcends boundaries and brings together a multitude of leading voices to reflect on the past, present, and future of international education. Those two colleagues are the two of us, Hilary Kahn and Deb Cohn, who come from different backgrounds and have engaged in different ways within the field of international education. Even though we have been pursuing our work in dissimilar ways, we recognize that we share a core value in our professional and personal pursuits, which is to provide more meaningful internationalized opportunities for learning, teaching, research, and service across the entire educational pipeline, from pre-K to career, from scholarship to practice.

While our academic backgrounds are different—one of us is a scholar of Latin American literature and American (in the broadest sense) cultural history and one is an ethnographer and visual anthropologist; one has been actively involved in the internationalization of higher education while the other researches the institutional history of international education and foreign language study in the United States during the twentieth century—we are also not easily categorized. We are equally area and global studies scholars, and both of us are as interdisciplinary as they come, though profoundly affected by the academic fields in which we were trained.

While our scholarly points of positionality give us unique perspectives, we have learned that we are both international educators to the core even if our approaches and ideas about international education do not always intermingle. We see this divergence as an advantage, one we continued to build on when we were asked to be co-chairs for Indiana University's bicentennial symposium International Education at the Crossroads in 2018. We quickly realized that the symposium, and now this publication, also needed to be a meeting of the minds.

The primary impetus for this symposium was the sixtieth anniversary of the National Defense Education Act (NDEA), through which emerged the Department of Education Title VI funding that continues today to underwrite the dramatic and transformative expansion of language and area studies at all levels of education across the United States. Indiana University has long been a leader in Title VI programs, which have helped lay the foundation to make Indiana University one of the most internationalized universities in the country. Indiana University would not be the powerhouse it is in international education without Title VI, though we also recognize that Title VI is not the only model or source of federal or philanthropic funding for international education. We know there are many resources, approaches, voices, and global perspectives in the broader field of international education, some of which may or may not be familiar to or align with the US Department of Education's Title VI programs. We also firmly believe that all stakeholders would be best served if we brought them together to collectively take stock of international education.

Therefore, we brought together experts in language, area, and global studies with policy makers, international education leaders, and others to discuss the future of international education in the changing and increasingly global landscape of higher education. The symposium thus explored international education within diverse educational and practical contexts and considered the need for new narratives and models within what we all agree is a rapidly changing sociopolitical and educational landscape. Ultimately, the symposium looked to the future more than the past and aimed to define novel approaches that address the collective responsibility, broad need, and potential impact of advancing international education beyond the sixtieth anniversary of the NDEA. And we did so in Indiana, the Crossroads of America.

We were firmly in the cross-section of the United States, and we were and still are at a historic global moment that is in some ways recasting the social role of education as well as redefining international engagement with potential political, cultural, and economic impact. International education is not only at a crossroads itself, but many of the voices at the conference and now in this volume also suggest that it is in fact being practiced in the crosshairs. We are indeed at a turning point, so our conversations started at the various crossroads currently faced by the field and then looked to the future. What can international education do to set the course for the next sixty years? What are the needs and priorities of international education in the twenty-first century? How is international education an academic imperative and why? What are the responsibilities of those of us in higher education to foster global learning opportunities for all?

It is not at all coincidental that we asked these critical questions in the middle of the country, at the crossroads, landlocked and away from the coasts, because that is also the future of international education. The need to be global, acquire skills for international engagement, understand the connections between the world and one's community, and be prepared to live, work, and succeed in a world of difference is as important in Indiana as it is in New York or London or Beijing. Rural or urban, local or global, at age sixteen or sixty, people all over the world need the skills, knowledge, and attitudes provided by a global education.

Breaking down binaries was in fact a goal for the conference and has continued to guide our conceptualization of this volume. Thus, readers will find that the authors are deliberately rethinking paradigms and challenging dichotomies and other categories that we often rely on for meaning in international education. This rethinking includes trying to break through some of the major absences and gaps in the internationalization of higher education today. For example, why are area studies and language instruction not given more attention as essential components in internationalization, which tends to prioritize the mobility of students and partnerships? This question is particularly vexing when we know that employers and nations recognize this knowledge as critical for developing needed skills in a range of careers and national contexts. Also, for the United States, what can Title VI programs and other federal agencies learn from other global and diverse perspectives and practices of international education, as well as from one another? How do we overcome the tension that continues to exist between interdisciplinary programs and global studies and disciplines, language and literature departments, and area studies?

If we all have the same goals—like we (Deb and Hilary) realized we did—shouldn't we continue to talk and determine new directions together? Shouldn't we collectively and globally produce new knowledge and practices of implementation? Shouldn't we work together to leverage these crossroads and pave a path for international education for years to come? Shouldn't we use this moment to think about area studies, global studies, language studies, and international education in a global context and through new lenses? And lastly, shouldn't we all be allies rather than adversaries? For us, the answer was clear. So we decided to use this opportunity to reinspect, reorganize, diversify, and reenergize the field of international education in an intellectual and pragmatic way. We felt we had a responsibility to do so. This is just the beginning, though. It is up to all of us to keep this conversation going.

How the Book Is Organized

Like any work that is trying to challenge boundaries, we struggled with how to organize the book. We ultimately decided to organize it around main thematic *crossroads*, which are connected by *intersections*. While all the contributions speak across all themes, the intersections are broad statements about the current and future landscape of international education.

The first crossroads explores diverse perspectives of international education in a global context. Readers may wonder why we need to qualify the global component of education that is intentionally international, but areas of the world, including the United States, often define their own approaches and needs in international education in very specific, nationalistic, and nonglobal terms. We feel it is imperative to bring these voices together, as this is the foundation on which innovative practices can be implemented and sustained. Quite simply, we need to ensure that processes of internationalization in higher education are in fact global—that is, that they are engaging with different world approaches to international education. However, we also openly admit, primarily due to the fact that the anniversary of a lynchpin US federal program anchors this volume, that the authors pay particular attention to international education in the United States.

All of the authors in this volume are answering two questions: Why international education today? Why international education tomorrow? They are responding to these questions from their particular positions and professions in the field as well as from various scales of application, from campuses, to nations, to the world. We do not want to fall prey to homophily, so we encourage the authors to speak about idiosyncrasies and the current world realities that require us to think about international education as a way of bringing different agendas together for a common future, as well as of advancing the impact that universities the world over can have. We want the voices in this volume to be as constructive as they are critical and to have general global impact, as much as having particular significance within specific campuses, university partnerships, curricula, and educational and political systems.

The next two crossroads delve into the current and future role of area studies, global studies, and language learning. In the United States, institutional capacity for this component of international education has been built by the Department of Education with Title VI programs and other US federal agencies, but this area seems to have been eclipsed in institutional internationalization by attention to student mobility (basically, international students coming in and domestic students going out to study abroad). While partnerships, international student services, faculty research and mobility, and curriculum internationalization are also priorities in the field, it seems that area studies and language learning are no longer central or, at some universities and associations, even in the conversations around internationalization at all. This is a gap that needs to be addressed and one that we focus on in this book. This deep knowledge of regions, cultures, politics, and languages matters, and it needs to be more central in discussions about international education.

This does not mean that we cannot be critical about global and area studies or that we cannot call for improved techniques and infrastructures for language instruction. It does not imply that we cannot use this opportunity to think about how Title VI programs must continue to evolve to meet current needs and challenges. In the second crossroads, readers will encounter the significant impact that Title VI has had on area studies and language learning in the United States, as well as recognize the ontological limitations when area studies are qualitatively defined in opposition to global studies. The goal of this conversation is to demonstrate the critical role of area studies and also to encourage a robust conversation between global studies and area studies. They cannot exist in a vacuum, and they do not exist as zero sums. They represent a now worn-out binary in need of dissection. The wider field of international education also needs to be in this discussion, and area and global studies are critical in broader conversations around internationalization.

The third crossroads involves an extensive overview of language learning in the United States that, quite frankly, validates the importance of the Department of Education's Title VI programs as well as the Department of Defense's National Security Education Program's sustained support of critical language instruction. The authors also consider language learning in provocative ways that may or may not intersect with traditional approaches. In so doing, we anticipate that the interlacing of these perspectives will push all of us to expand our ways of thinking about the practices and parameters of language learning, bilingualism, and second-language acquisition, as well as the relationship between language, identity, and place.

All the contributions vigorously defend language learning within curricular, institutional, state, and national (US) contexts. Many invoke insights and recommendations from *America's Languages: Investing in Language Education for the 21st Century*, the 2017 report commissioned by the American Academy of Arts and Sciences and prepared by the Commission on Language Learning, three members of which have contributed to this volume (Dan E. Davidson, Brian T. Edwards, and Rosemary G. Feal). This section provides far-reaching and diverse perspectives on language learning, which include the consideration of heritage language learners, the perils of monolingualism and benefits of bi- and multilingualism, high-impact language pedagogy, language revitalization, and how institutions of higher education can realistically sustain the teaching of low-enrolling languages of critical national need. The need for collaboration is clearly called for, and authors speak about how essential it is for federal agencies to work together and to see their respective programs as complements rather than competitors. They also call for more collaboration across and within academic departments and for more productive alliances between those scholars who pursue literature and those who pursue languages. The responsibility of higher education to reach out and partner with schools and communities to advance language learning and internationalization along the entire pre-K–to-career pipeline is also encouraged. Voices not regularly heard in discussions on international education are contributing to this rethinking of language learning. For example, lessons emerge from the revitalization of indigenous languages and culture, as well as from heritage language learners, which provide a needed reminder that language and culture are indivisible and never apolitical.

"Internationalization in Practice" is the fourth crossroads, in which authors break down tensions between practice and scholarship and consider the many contexts in which internationalization is put into practice. These authors, who represent global and institutional perspectives, demonstrate the applicability of international education and also discuss the importance of cultural, linguistic, and area studies training for students, scholars, practitioners, and global intellectuals, who will put these skills into practice in a variety of ways. The contributors discuss how international education and interdisciplinary training in area studies prepare individuals to have global impact and how employers are demanding employees with such global literacies. They think critically about how internationalization is deployed and practiced within institutions of higher education and about how international education must be equitable and inclusive. As we consider internationalization in practice, we cannot do anything but consider global learning as an imperative—for the future of education, economic prosperity, social well-being, and, quite frankly, world peace.

The volume's final crossroads includes perspectives from Washington, DC, and outlines how different US federal agencies uniquely contribute to the landscape of international education. We were proud that we could bring so many of these voices together at the 2018 conference, from the Department of Education, Department of State, and Department of Defense, along with key associations dedicated to international education in the US context. It was clear how these federal agencies have unique roles to play in creating a smarter, more secure, and global nation. Whether the stakeholders are the military, diplomats, policy makers, schoolteachers, students, undergraduates, businesses, or the media, the United States needs to support, sustain, and fight for the federal programs that help us do what we do better and help us prepare ourselves and our future generations for the complicated, interconnected, and clearly global world in which we live, work, and learn.

Indiana University: An Homage at the Crossroads

Indiana University (IU) accepted its first student from outside the United States in 1857. IU professor Elmer Bryan traveled to the Philippines in 1901 to assist in developing teacher education. Since then, Indiana University has actively demonstrated its commitment to international education. During

World War II, in partnership with the US military, the American Council of Learned Societies, and other organizations, IU became a pioneer for instruction in Central Asian, Slavic, and Turkish languages that were rarely taught in the United States at that point. This both provided the university with an opportunity to further strategic national interests and attracted international students and faculty to the university and thus was a means of bringing the world to Indiana. The appointment of Leo Dowling as international student adviser by the university president Herman B Wells in 1943 was also a demonstration of IU's early trailblazing. More so, Wells's involvement with the development of the Marshall Plan, his contributions to conversations that led to the United Nations, and his deep commitment to international partnerships and student and faculty mobility put IU in the vanguard of internationalized institutions and in the field of international education itself.

Indiana University's involvement with language education and international studies, as well as, ultimately, with Title VI, escalated with the addition of William Riley Parker to its faculty in 1956. Parker, a Milton scholar, came to IU from the Modern Language Association (MLA), where he had served as executive secretary since 1947. In this capacity, Parker, who had little facility for languages but a pressing belief that the study of modern languages was critical to protecting US national interests, had spearheaded a campaign to expand and improve the teaching of foreign languages, which was at an all-time low across the nation in both quantitative and qualitative terms.

In the years following World War I, the isolationist attitude that marked US politics also had a direct impact on language education: even as high school enrollments climbed overall, the number of students studying languages plummeted dramatically. The onset of World War II highlighted the shortsightedness of the neglect of language education in no uncertain terms, as soldiers and diplomats found themselves unable to communicate with either enemies or allies on the battlefields or in war rooms. The lesson was short-lived, though, and after the war, language enrollments at the high school and university levels continued to drop, leaving the nation once again without the capacity to respond to crises that would inevitably arise around the world. (Language study in elementary schools was a moot point as, by 1951, languages were only taught at this level in fifty-seven communities across the entire United States.[1]) Indeed, in 1954, on the eve of Sputnik,

Russian was only taught in eleven of the nation's twenty-seven thousand public and private high schools and in one hundred eighty-three colleges and universities across the United States.[2]

In 1952, Parker founded the Foreign Language Program at the MLA. Over the next few years, the initiative, which he spearheaded until his move to Bloomington, revolutionized, revitalized, systematized, and professionalized the study of foreign languages in the United States. The program's efforts also laid the foundations for the expansion of language study through Title VI of the NDEA—and, in 1959, at President Wells's instigation, Parker took a leave of absence from IU and went to Washington, DC, as the first chief of the NDEA Language Development Program.

For six months, Parker commuted between DC and Bloomington, simultaneously planning and implementing Title VI initiatives and informing his colleagues about the new program. Indiana University was successful in the earliest rounds of competition and also led the way in developing new language-study and teacher-training programs. In 1962, Parker chaired a task force that prepared a ten-year plan for strengthening language instruction in Indiana high schools that was the first of its kind in the nation. The university thus committed itself to training Indiana residents as citizens of the world, in an effort to ensure that the Crossroads of America became a crossroads for international education as well.

Over the years, IU's engagement with international education has evolved to meet the changing international landscape and to prepare our students to understand and contribute to the increasingly diverse and interconnected world. It need not be said that IU's international engagement, for example, is grounded more on mutual sustainment, collaboration, and community orientation than when Elmer Bryan first traveled to the Philippines at the beginning of the last century.

Yet, even with this extensive history, Indiana University would not be the university it is today without the NDEA and Title VI. Indiana University Bloomington has been a leader in Title VI programming for years and currently teaches over seventy languages, most of which are less commonly taught languages of critical national need. Title VI built this capacity and infrastructure, which in effect made it possible for the campus to host many other federal programs, such as the Department of Defense Language Flagship Programs and the Department of State's Youth Entrepreneurship Livelihood Program. Indiana University is thus a perfect example of how the efforts of these federal agencies are complementary rather than competitive and a model for how we may continue to work collectively to build the infrastructure for international education across all the crossroads, from coast to coast and from campus to classroom.

There is not a one-size-fits-all approach to international education, and Title VI has allowed Indiana University and many other institutions across the country to build their capacity to serve a wide array of unique stakeholders. Whether working with students and faculty from a Research 1 university, a historically Black college or university, a tribal college, or a community college; providing professional development opportunities to high school language teachers or guidance counselors; helping businesses better understand the global marketplace; providing international resources to the media; or engaging communities across our states, Title VI allows universities to serve a wide swath of people, institutions, and sectors, on the coasts and at the crossroads, in urban and rural communities, in classrooms and newsrooms.

The multiple National Resource Centers (NRCs), Language Resource Centers (LRCs), Foreign Language and Area Studies (FLAS) Fellowships programs, and the Center for International Business and Education Research at Indiana University Bloomington have collectively had significant impact across the Crossroads of America, by reaching thousands of Indiana elementary and secondary school teachers and students through professional development and educational activities, by training hundreds of university and college faculty and administrators, and by serving thousands of individuals across the state through global programming and language instruction. These programs also expand the impact of international education, ensuring that it is not an elite, majority-focused initiative but one that is accessible to *all* students. This strong foundation built by Title VI is not only reserved for the Indiana University Bloomington campus; it has enabled innovative partnerships, often funded by other federal agencies, with the military, businesses, and community colleges.[3] Additionally, in 2016, Indiana University received funds from the Department of Defense's Language Flagship Program to develop a state-strategic plan for world language learning and global competencies to strengthen the educational pipeline and provide access to global skills and career training for students and today's workforce. Indiana University could not have had this type of impact were it not for Title VI and for the many state partnerships and collaborations that have been built on the legacy of international education it represents at Indiana University.

Notes

1. Parker, *The National Interest*, 8.
2. Ibid., 7.
3. For example, in 2020, IUPUI (Indiana University–Purdue University Indianapolis) received a Title VI Undergraduate International Studies and Foreign Language award in collaboration with Ivy Tech Community College to build global pathways and internationalize first-year experiences at both institutions.

Bibliography

Parker, William Riley. *The National Interest and Foreign Languages.* 3rd ed. Washington, DC: US Government Printing Office, 1962.

Intersection

1

THE IMPORTANCE OF INCREASING OUR INVESTMENT IN INTERNATIONAL EDUCATION

Michael A. McRobbie

INDIANA UNIVERSITY'S PROUD HISTORY OF internationally focused education goes back more than one hundred years. This history stems, in part, from a long-standing recognition that the best university education instills an understanding of the world outside of the boundaries of the United States: of the history (ancient or modern), cultures, religions, politics, economies, institutions, art, literature, and, of course, languages of other countries.

Such an understanding is even more important today, when the world is more interconnected than ever and when there is hardly a discipline or profession that is not affected, to a greater or lesser degree, by globalization. Not only is this educational dimension a matter of practical necessity, but it is increasingly being demanded by students. Indeed, of all that a quality university education comprises, we believe that international literacy and experience ranks at the very top and that the world in which our students will live will require more, not less, knowledge about the world.

As such, we continue to work to expand IU's world-class international faculty; to welcome a large and diverse international student body, whose members are valued for the diversity in thought and culture they bring to our campuses; to increase the number of students who study overseas, where they will gain vital knowledge and understanding of other countries and cultures; and to develop new international alliances with governments and institutions. We are also working to dramatically expand our foreign languages curricula. IU now offers instruction in approximately seventy world languages each year—more than any other university in the country.

All across IU, in every school and in every discipline, the importance of the international dimension of a college education is underscored. It is mandated as part of our general education curriculum and stressed in various basic and advanced forms on all IU campuses. This is designed to help provide our students with courses of study that will give them greater understanding of the world and to support research and scholarship on some of the most important global developments that will help policy makers and business leaders make better and more informed decisions.

We were pleased to host the Indiana University bicentennial symposium International Education at the Crossroads at a time when all of us are seeking to equip students with the skills they need to succeed in an interconnected world—a world where change is an inescapable constant and the ability to communicate effectively across countries and cultures will be increasingly critical to the economic strength and security of our nation. IU looks forward to continuing to help lead the dialogue about the current environment of global and international studies, identifying paths forward for increased engagement in global activities and speaking out when appropriate about the critical role international education will play in ensuring a safer and more prosperous world.

To this end, I invite you to read my recent commentary, which originally appeared in *Education Dive* as "President Speaks: Colleges Must Prioritize Foreign Languages," encouraging colleges and universities to strengthen their investments in foreign language education and pursue innovative approaches to foreign language acquisition, such as the Indiana Language Roadmap.

In 1979, the President's Commission on Foreign Language and International Studies used some very powerful words in characterizing America's insufficient understanding of global affairs.

"Americans' incompetence in foreign languages is nothing short of scandalous," the commission concluded, adding that "the United States requires far more reliable capacities to communicate with its allies, analyze the behavior of potential adversaries and earn the trust and the sympathies of the uncommitted."

Nearly four decades after the release of the commission's "Strength Through Wisdom" report, our world has never been more interconnected.[1] Here in my home state of Indiana, about one-fourth of our $359.5 billion gross domestic product comes from international trade.[2] More than 8,000 companies export their products around the globe from locations in Indiana, and we have more than 800 foreign-owned businesses that employ some 200,000 Hoosiers.[3] Our towns and cities are also becoming increasingly diverse and multicultural; more than 8 percent of Indiana residents speak a language other than English, and more than 275 languages are spoken within homes across the state.

Indiana is representative of the globalization that is occurring all across the US. And yet, our country still faces a major deficit in our ability to understand and work with other people around the planet because we cannot effectively communicate with them. Ours remains a major—if not "scandalous"—foreign language deficit at a time when markets are rapidly becoming more global, when interdependencies among countries are becoming greater and when our national security challenges are becoming grander and more complex.

A sobering new report by the Modern Language Association indicated US colleges and universities slashed a staggering 651 foreign-language programs during a recent three-year (2013 to 2016) period, a stunning statistic that likely reflects, in part, the impact of the Great Recession and that coincides with a sizable drop in the number of students enrolling in foreign language courses.[4]

The loss of these programs is extremely troubling. It suggests that we fail to recognize how critical strong language competence is to our economic competitiveness and national security. It also shows how quickly we can forget the lessons we learned at other key points in our country's history, such as in the days after the terrorist attacks of 9/11, when we saw a resurgence of focus on foreign language and cultural studies programs as critical to our nation's security.

As the American Academy of Arts and Sciences' Commission on Language Learning concluded in a 2017 report, English continues to be the primary language of international business and diplomacy, but proficiency in that language alone will not meet our nation's strategic needs in a truly global society.[5] There must be a renewed investment in language education, the commission decided, and not just in moments of urgency, such as supporting Russian studies during the Cold War and increasing instruction of certain Middle Eastern languages after 9/11.

Fortunately, there is a serious movement toward a more forward-thinking strategy when it comes to the foreign language acquisition needed for the US to maintain its position as the world's leading economic, political and military power, and for its states to compete nationally and internationally.

Bipartisan federal legislation, co-sponsored by Sen. Todd Young (R-Indiana) and Sen. Tammy Baldwin (D-Wisconsin) and reintroduced in Congress earlier this year, would reauthorize Title VI of the federal Higher Education Act, providing a strong framework for continued support of university-based programs that develop US expertise in languages and international studies and ensure there are globally ready graduates who will serve as future US diplomats, business leaders and national security professionals.[6]

Since 2017, the Indiana Language Roadmap, an initiative led by the Center for the Study of Global Change in Indiana University's Hamilton Lugar School of Global and International Studies, has been developing a plan to make quality world language instruction and global learning available and affordable for all Hoosier residents.[7] This project is being supported by the Language Flagship, a key initiative of the National Security Education Program within the US Department of Defense, and it reflects input from the business, government, health care and education sectors across our state. In support of national and state needs, Indiana University continues to teach more than 70 foreign languages each year.

These and other local, state and national efforts are all highly encouraging. Still, much work needs to be done to encourage more students to pursue language degrees, to become foreign language instructors themselves and to engage in cultural studies. As the world shrinks, we need to train our students in Mandarin, Korean and Russian, as well as in less commonly taught languages such as Pashto, which is widely spoken in Afghanistan.

Finally, we need to do a better job of raising awareness in our communities of the economic, political and societal benefits of increased language skills and global competencies. Indeed, this is one important area where we all need to be speaking the same language.[8]

Notes

1. Reinhold, "Panel Urges."
2. Perry, "How Important."
3. International Trade Administration, "Indiana Exports."
4. Johnson, "Colleges Lose."
5. Commission on Language Learning, *America's Languages*.
6. Young, "Young and Baldwin."
7. Center for the Study of Global Change, "Indiana Language Roadmap."
8. Originally published in *Education Dive* on April 8, 2019.

Bibliography

Center for the Study of Global Change (Indiana University Bloomington). "Indiana Language Roadmap." Accessed October 2019. https://global.indiana.edu/research/indiana -language-roadmap/index.html.

Commission on Language Learning. *America's Languages: Investing in Language Education for the 21st Century*. American Academy of Arts and Sciences, February 2017. https:// www.amacad.org/publication/americas-languages.

International Trade Administration. "Indiana Exports, Jobs, and Foreign Investment." International Trade Administration, Department of Commerce. Last modified February 2018. https://legacy.trade.gov/mas/ian/statereports/states/in.pdf.

Johnson, Steven. "Colleges Lose a 'Stunning' 651 Foreign-Language Programs in 3 Years." *Chronicle of Higher Education*, January 22, 2019. https://www.chronicle.com/article /Colleges-Lose-a-Stunning-/245526.

Perry, Mark J. "How Important Is International Trade to Each U.S. State's Economy? Pretty Important for Most U.S. States." *AEIdeas* (blog of the American Enterprise Institute), March 9, 2018. https://www.aei.org/carpe-diem/how-important-is-international-trade -to-each-us-states-economy-pretty-important-for-most-us-states.

Reinhold, Robert. "Panel Urges Stress on Foreign Tongues." *New York Times*, November 8, 1979. https://www.nytimes.com/1979/11/08/archives/panel-urges-stress-on-foreign -tongues-carter-unit-proposes-programs.html.

Young, Todd. "Young and Baldwin Reintroduce Bill to Ensure American Students Remain Globally Competitive." Press release, February 8, 2019. https://www.young.senate.gov /newsroom/press-releases/young-and-baldwin-reintroduce-bill-to-ensure-american -students-remain-globally-competitive.

CROSSROADS 1

INTERNATIONALIZATION IN
A GLOBAL CONTEXT

2

INTERNATIONALIZING EDUCATION AS WE MOVE DEEPLY INTO THE TWENTY-FIRST CENTURY

Mary Sue Coleman and Kenneth M. Coleman

INTERNATIONAL EDUCATION INVOLVES STUDENTS AND scholars coming to the United States from other countries, as well as US students and scholars going abroad. It also involves taking a global perspective in classrooms, field experiences, and labs—whether those venues are located in the Unites States or abroad.

The internationalization of higher education has accelerated rapidly in recent decades. Where do we stand now in the United States?

Coming to America

There is no question that the world is coming to the United States to study in record numbers. According to the Institute of International Education, more than one million international students studied in the United States in 2017–2018.[1] That figure is nearly double the numbers from a decade earlier and comprises more than 5 percent of the total enrollment in our schools. About half of these international students are undergraduates, whose families generally pay the full cost of attendance, and about half are graduate students, who are most often funded by federal or private research grants.

Our success as a nation is due in no small part to our ability to attract the very best students and faculty from the United States and the world. According to the most recent annual analysis by NAFSA: Association of International Educators, the 1,094,792 international students studying at US colleges and universities during the 2017–2018 year contributed $39 billion to our economy and supported more than 455,000 jobs.[2]

Our country's economic competitiveness and global leadership would be impossible without the extraordinary flow of international talent that has been drawn to the United States for many decades by US values—including, importantly, the value of academic opportunity. For the United States to remain a global leader, we must continue to sustain a pipeline of human capital. Human capital drives our research institutions, which generate the ideas from which innovative entrepreneurs create the "next big thing" that will have significant economic, geopolitical, and even humanitarian impacts. Innovation and creativity are the new bedrock of economic success, and international education feeds both. Think Sergei Brin, Larry Page, and Google—an emigré from Russia and a student from Michigan, brainstorming together at Stanford to create a technology and a brand that have transformed economies fundamentally, never to be the same again.

To be sure, not every international student or scholar will prove to be a Sergei Brin. But somewhere in those 1,094,792 international students studying in the United States in 2017–2018, there may be another—or even two or three. If so, the United States and the world may well prosper from these students' interactions with scholars from the US heartland or the Pacific Northwest or New York City. Those who come to the United States to study or do research will find platforms from which it is possible to transform the world.

Going to the World

To confront the economic and security challenges that face the United States, we must educate our own students about the world outside our borders. Many of the challenges that face the United States are global in nature—climate change, food security, superbugs and pandemics, automation in industry, artificial intelligence, cybercrime, and terrorism, to name but a few. To face these challenges, we must produce a workforce with skills in foreign languages, multiple cultures, international law, and international relations.

This workforce must be embedded in sectors, industries, and disciplines that we haven't previously thought of as international. Engineers who can speak Mandarin, Spanish, or Hindi are increasingly as important as diplomats who understand those languages. Fortune 500 CEOs increasingly must have as thorough an understanding of some aspects of international law as do federal trade representatives. Members of the armed services are increasingly called on to use language and cultural skills in places like Afghanistan and Iraq.

Perhaps more importantly, to enjoy and appreciate the world in which we and others live, we must experience it firsthand. To savor the world we must engage with, not cower from, the Other. The liberal arts belong in all of higher education, from medicine to engineering to the social sciences; no discipline is exempt from the need to understand how diverse human populations see, perceive, think, honor, and enjoy life. To be educated is to escape, at least in part, from the parochialism from which we all start. No one knows enough about the Other. One point of higher education is to encounter and to come to respect some dimensions of cultural otherness.

Challenges to International Education

Although international education offers these benefits and more to our country, its robustness is threatened in several ways in the current economic and political environment. A future in which our nation is deeply engaged with other economies and cultures is threatening to many people. More than a few US citizens are terrified that the industries in which they and their families have worked for decades will be replaced. This fear is not without reason, as job loss is very real in some industries—although the cause is as likely to be automation or an emergent consensus favoring green energy as jobs being moved abroad.

Our current national rhetoric has turned inward, toward closing our borders and toward draconian measures to mitigate perceived economic and security threats from abroad. More troublingly, such perceived threats can often manifest in a personalized manner. Students and scholars become seen as "agents of the Other."

Some of the proposals that have been discussed by officials—including cutting off students from China and other Asian nations completely—would be a disaster for research institutions, such as Indiana University and other members of the Association of American Universities, which collectively constitute the United States' best research universities. While security issues matter greatly, the United States has long managed to balance the collaborative openness necessary for science and innovation with the requirements of national security.[3] If cool heads prevail, the United States will continue to do so.

Solutions in International Education

When it comes to protecting and enhancing international education for the future, the first priority is to tell the story—to the public and to policy makers—of what international education does for our nation. We must be able to continue attracting and welcoming the best and brightest from around the world.[4] They must continue to study here, because so many of them stay, become entrepreneurs, build companies, and make—or contribute to—the discoveries and innovations that build our economy for the future.

We also need policies at the state and national levels to help address US citizens' fear of this new economy, which fuels some of the xenophobic attitudes we see. We need education and job-training programs that go to the places—the coal-mining towns in West Virginia, the steel and auto workers in Pennsylvania and Ohio and Michigan—where new economic opportunities are most needed yet where the fear of a globalized economy may be most pronounced. Indiana University has initiatives that can help on this front, such as the Sustaining Hoosier Communities Initiative of the Center for Rural Engagement.

But what can individual campuses do to encourage the preservation and growth of international education in the United States? Indiana University surely has a plethora of international programs. After discussing some overall principles for international education, we will mention programs with which we have had personal involvement.

At the structural level, schools should allocate organizational and program resources in ways that intentionally advance each school's international education program. For instance, each institution should have a high-level administrator responsible for international engagements and a strategic plan to conduct and enrich them. This plan should encompass careful evaluation of how the school allocates its resources, with regular review of the plan's effectiveness.

During my presidency at the University of Michigan (UM), my colleagues and I took the position that creating a "UM campus abroad" would not promote the type of international engagement we desired. Instead, we codeveloped the UM-Shanghai Jiao Tong Joint Institute. Michigan and Shanghai Jiao Tong University came together to create China's first comprehensive university-to-university partnership with degree-granting programs where students studied alternately on both campuses. To be successful, these kinds of joint ventures require deep engagement by faculty on both sides, continuous monitoring by leaders from each institution, commitment of both leaders to be on the governing board, and continuous evaluation of the model permitting the evolution thereof. A current dean reports that, after more than a decade, "the flow of students has never been better. If anything, they want us to do more (joint research) than we are able to accommodate."[5] But the Michigan solution may not be the solution for other institutions that have different histories and patterns of engagement.

For students at both the undergraduate and graduate levels, we should encourage international travel, study abroad, in-class international activities, and specific programming for international students. This includes providing resources for these activities to enable a significant portion of the student body to participate. For instance, the Ross School of Business at Michigan declared that every single student had to have an international experience, and other programs follow similar precepts. Many donors—individual and corporate—now express a significant interest in helping fund such programs, and institutions should consider cultivating those resources.

For faculty, we need to maximally encourage not only international travel and study but also connection with their international students. This includes encouraging and even incentivizing opportunities for international sabbaticals, jointly funded international teams for research projects, and participation in international meetings. Promoting and rewarding all these activities sends important signals. Further, research universities should encourage faculty advisers to connect with the home countries of their international graduate students. One particularly effective program sponsored by the Fulbright Commission funds US dissertation advisers to travel to the home countries of international students to assess what sort of career skills are necessary to help students from those countries succeed. This model could be expanded well beyond the borders of the Fulbright program to improve graduate education at large.

Reaching out beyond our campuses is also crucial—both to prepare precollege students for international education and to help the broader public understand the value of such educational programs. For instance, partnering with local K–12 schools to establish international education programs is one avenue for outreach. This is especially important in a time when many public primary and secondary schools simply do not have sufficient funding even for foreign-language programs. We should build on Title VI's language resource centers programs, which provide grants to strengthen foreign-language instruction in K–12 schools. We should also support other forms of outreach that go beyond K–12 education, including establishing international community education programs in parts of the country that may be suspicious of global engagement.

The bottom line is that we face significant challenges to the future of international education. But with careful attention to public policies that balance security concerns with scientific advancement, to structural reforms to universities' departments and programs, and to new forms of outreach, we can ensure a healthy future for robust international education in the United States—so we continue to reap the benefits of our university system's long-standing global leadership. The United States can continue to play the role it has long played in international education—the place where people want to study and conduct research and the source of inquisitive and appreciative visitors to other countries.

Notes

1. Institute of International Education, "Enrollment." See the International Student Enrollment Trends, 1948/49–2017/18 tab.
2. NAFSA: Association of International Educators, "Economic Value Tool."
3. Coleman, "Balancing Science and Security."
4. Illustrative of the collaborative and international nature of scientific progress, see Sundermier, "Better Night's Sleep," which illustrates how researchers from the University of Southern California, the University at Buffalo, Stanford, the University of North Carolina at Chapel Hill, Arizona State, the University of Lille (France), and the US Department of Energy studied the function of melatonin in sleep disorders, type 2 diabetes, and certain cancers. Many of the scientists in this project came to the United States from other countries, including, but not limited to, Argentina, France, Russia, and Sweden.
5. Jun Ni, personal communication to Mary Sue Coleman, October 17, 2018.

Bibliography

Coleman, Mary Sue. "Balancing Science and Security." *Science* 365, no. 6449 (July 12, 2019): 101.

Institute of International Education. "Enrollment." Accessed March 25, 2020. https://www .iie.org/Research-and-Insights/Open-Doors/Data/International-Students/Enrollment.

NAFSA: Association of International Educators. "NAFSA International Student Economic Value Tool." Accessed March 25, 2020. https://www.nafsa.org/policy-and-advocacy /policy-resources/nafsa-international-student-economic-value-tool.

Sundermier, Ali. "How to Build a Better Night's Sleep." Association of American Universities. Last updated May 23, 2019. https://www.aau.edu/research-scholarship/featured -research-topics/how-build-better-nights-sleep.

3

WHAT'S HAPPENING TO THE WORLD?

Patrick O'Meara

IN 1957, THE SOVIET UNION successfully launched Sputnik, and the United States responded with an accelerated space race, as well as increased investment in scientific research and teaching. Because of the fear of Soviet hegemony, the United States was also jolted into an understanding that it had to affirm its leadership in the new and challenging postcolonial world. The need for specialists with proficiency in less commonly taught languages and in area studies led to partnerships between universities, government agencies, and foundations. The challenge was tangible, and the enemy was clearly defined. Since then, generations of language and area specialists have continued to meet the need for specialized international skills and knowledge, relevant research, and the education of students for academia, government service, or the professions. This has not been static; changing political, economic, and social conditions have constantly called for new thinking, but this core academic mission remains essential.

However, many of the current challenges the United States faces are diffuse and do not appear as immediate or as clear cut as the watershed event of Sputnik. There are now leaders and policy decisions that have negative impacts on hundreds of millions of lives and the potential to warp the future. Cross-cutting, international research is urgently needed to examine the global significance, ideological underpinnings, and long-term implications of these new challenges. In 1957, it was the Soviet Union. Today, in different parts of the world, democracy and democratic institutions are under assault, and populism and authoritarianism are on the rise. At times, there is a domino effect, as leaders copy one another in bypassing their constitutions, stifling opposition, muzzling the press, hampering civil society, and denying human rights. Their primary goal is to entrench personal power and to foster narrowly defined interests. In such countries, the phenomenon of "fake news" is legitimized and increasingly employed by regimes

25

and interest groups. Questioning the validity of uncomfortable or threatening facts results in doubt and discord and in a lack of trust in established knowledge and the power of differing viewpoints. Unaware that they are being manipulated, gullible followers readily accept populist misinformation; this has become one of the greatest threats to democracy and political debate.

The United States and the West have historically been advocates for open and fair political systems. Currently, rather than strongly advocating for reforms through funding initiatives or exerting pressure, realpolitik seems to have become the lode star of many major Western powers in their relationships with countries where there are gross violations of human rights, politically motivated murders, corruption, and stifling of the press and opposition. They frequently choose to ignore such transgressions, and the perpetrators are allowed to go about their business with impunity.

On the global level, increasing religious intolerance, fundamentalism, terrorism, and violence are on the ascendancy. Xenophobia and the harsh treatment of political and economic migrants are major current concerns. These disturbing trends are often studied as discrete phenomena, but they should also be seen in the broader global context, as well as in relation to the decline of democracy and the resurgence of authoritarianism across regions and continents.

The significance of international alliances and organizations is now also being undermined. The United States has been a principal actor in the founding and support of important international organizations, such as the United Nations, NATO, the International Monetary Fund, and the World Bank, as well as a major force in multinational agreements on trade, climate, and arms control. The US presence in such organizations is now either diminishing, or there are threats of its withdrawal. This is not just a US issue but one with far-reaching ramifications. It must be seen in the context of Russia and China becoming increasingly influential in international economies and security. We are seeing, once again, a division of the world in line with what appeared to be a declining concept, that of spheres of influence; Israel and Palestine, Syria, Ukraine, and Venezuela have become more intransigent and part of this new international power struggle. Relapsing into trade wars, tariffs, walls, boundaries, and other retrogressive measures fuels neoisolationism and contradicts the tendency toward greater global commitments and perspectives. Continuing in-depth and intrinsic research on Russia, China, and other world areas remains essential, but there are fundamental contextual changes that call for different levels of analysis.

Climate change is not only a topic for personal discussions and news reports but an increasing and evident reality in daily lives throughout the world. The legitimacy accorded to climate-change skeptics is an area of particular concern, especially as the validity of scientific findings is undermined by corporate interests or conservative agendas—all while the issue of global warming grows more urgent every day. Climate change must be seen as part of the larger configuration of democracy, authoritarianism, fake news, and international alliances and organizations.

The salience of globalization also calls for reconsideration. On the positive level, globalization has led to transformations in modes of communication, exchanges of ideas and perspectives, trade, and the eroding of barriers and boundaries. Internet access, Facebook, and cell phones have not only changed countless lives but have also had enormous implications for education, knowledge distribution, and personal communication, and they have influenced, positively and negatively, political change. In this era of threats and challenges, these modes of communication will become ever more crucial. At the same time, global investment has often exploited cheap labor and demonstrated a lack of concern for the environment. Global researchers must now widen the sphere of their scholarship to address current pressing concerns. The underlying cultural, economic, and political assumptions implicit in globalization must be part of addressing the troubling and fundamental changes that are now occurring across regions and continents.

As in 1957, this is another watershed moment. These are but a few of the current directions that should be part of academic and political agendas. In his 2018 undergraduate commencement address on the Indiana University Bloomington campus, President Michael McRobbie raised a number of relevant and significant issues about the role of universities in the current context:

> We have witnessed in recent years, a disturbing and increasingly widespread casual attitude toward the truth. We have seen rampant attacks on established knowledge and open hostility to verifiable facts. We have seen a fundamental rejection in some quarters of dispassionate rationality. And we have seen political upheaval around the globe driven by wild claims and spurious statistics.
>
> But as a great educational and research institution, for nearly 200 years, Indiana University has stood—and will always stand—for truth, unembellished by artifice or equivocation.

This de-valuing of expertise and experience has all too often led to a distrust of scientists and a rejection of basic science. Citizens and policy makers in the United States and elsewhere have cast doubt on established scientific understanding, sidelined scientific evidence, or skewed scientific advice on the basis of political and economic concerns.[1]

What will it take to widen the international discourse? Will an increased awareness of a perceived crisis, such as Sputnik, be necessary, or will the leadership from philanthropic organizations, associations, academic administrators, and farsighted political leaders come to the realization that new forms of interdisciplinary, interregional, and international scholarship are called for? In the immediate moment, there is a tendency to regard seemingly overwhelming political challenges as chronic. At times, history has proved the contrary. Policies can be repealed, political leaders replaced, and organizations reenergized. Such changes can only come about with awareness of options, fallacies, and perils. Perhaps this is where universities should now start the process of changing the intellectual discourse. They should also find ways to increase popular awareness of the inherent dangers of what is happening to our fundamental rights and freedom.

Note

1. McRobbie, "In Pursuit of Truth."

Bibliography

McRobbie, Michael A. "In Pursuit of Truth." Indiana University Office of the President, May 5, 2018. https://president.iu.edu/speeches/select-speeches/2018/2018–05–05-undergraduate-commencement.html.

4

GOING, GOLDEN, GONE?

Internationalization's Past, Present, and Future

Robin Matross Helms

I'VE HAD A LOT OF conversations in the last couple of weeks about Karin Fischer's recent article in the *Chronicle of Higher Education*, "How International Education's Golden Age Lost Its Sheen." The article highlights recent worrisome trends in internationalization, including declining international student numbers, and contrasts them to the momentum of earlier years in such areas as study abroad and establishing branch campuses abroad. It raises the question of whether enthusiasm and support for international activity will continue in the current geopolitical climate.

As Fischer's pieces always are, the article comprises a thoughtful discussion that incorporates data and a variety of points of view. But based on the reactions I've heard, I'm worried that its more subtle points have been lost behind the "golden" headline.

The Past: "Has Internationalization Only Been Skin Deep?"

The article's characterization of circa 2013 as internationalization's "golden moment" centers on international students flocking to US campuses, while institutional leaders traveled the world signing memoranda of understanding and setting up outposts. To a degree, data from the American Council on Education's (ACE) *Mapping Internationalization on U.S. Campuses: 2017 Edition* reinforce the golden moment characterization—nearly three-quarters of institutions reported that internationalization had accelerated on their campuses. And particularly when it comes to student mobility (both inbound and outbound) and international partnerships, the time, energy, and resources devoted to internationalization efforts—as reported in our survey—underscored this assessment.[1]

But let's take a closer look at the golden age. Yes, institutions were making money from incoming international students. But as ACE's *Mapping* data illustrate, we weren't doing such a great job of supporting those students beyond their first weeks on campus. Orientation—yes. Ongoing programs to help them fully integrate into the classroom and institutional life? Not so much. What about outposts abroad? Certainly, there are high-profile examples, such as New York University in Abu Dhabi and Shanghai and others cited in Fischer's article, but of the *Mapping* survey respondents, only around 5 percent maintained a physical presence abroad. And as Fischer points out, *Mapping* respondents ranked curriculum internationalization and faculty development as their fourth and fifth priorities for internationalization, behind education abroad, recruiting international students, and partnerships abroad. And indeed, new research by ACE and the National Survey of Student Engagement shows that curricular and faculty initiatives have the greatest impact on student global learning. But while there were some improvements between 2011 and 2016, data on actual activity reflected a relative lack of attention to these areas.[2]

So just how golden was the golden age? Golden in the sense of revenue, sure. But golden in terms of what we accomplished? As Fischer implies in her conclusion, that's not so clear. In the *Mapping* survey, we asked institutions *why* they were seeking to internationalize, and the number one reason was "to prepare students for a global era." With our collective focus on mobility and comparative lack of attention to what was happening on campuses to engage *all* students and faculty in our global endeavors, how much progress we made toward accomplishing our goals is questionable. Golden is, perhaps, in the eye of the beholder. But students and faculty are (or should be) the beholders who matter most, and their interests were not necessarily the drivers of our pre-2016 golden-era internationalization efforts.

The Present: "Some Colleges Are Retrenching, while Others Try to Sustain a Global Footprint"

As Fischer points out, stagnating numbers of international students have captured the headlines, along with controversies over Confucius Institutes, widespread foreign language program closures, and an array of issues surrounding foreign outposts. She describes the mood at the winter meeting of the Association of International Education Administrators as "somber," as participants reflected on the current state of the field.

Among the institutions I work with in ACE's Internationalization Laboratory, I have seen something else. The Internationalization Laboratory cohort meeting in February 2017 was characterized by consternation and angst, but even as the policy roller coaster of the last two years was picking up speed, there was also a sense that we would get through it. Yes, the word *demoralizing* was used, but so was the word *energizing*—and there was perhaps a feeling that our work was more important than ever. The energizing sentiment may have been rooted in a sense of opportunity to change things up and redirect, a chance to correct some of the missteps of the so-called golden age. Reflecting on the 2016 *Mapping* data and prospects for the post-election future, ACE's report (written in spring 2017) notes, "Some institutions may turn their internationalization focus inward, with increased attention and resources devoted to on-campus curricular, co-curricular, and faculty development initiatives—exactly what is needed to advance progress toward comprehensive internationalization in ways that an exclusive external orientation and on-going emphasis on mobility will not allow."[3]

Though my evidence is anecdotal, I have been impressed by what I've seen along these lines on many campuses since then: great creativity in leveraging international partnerships to support students protected under the Obama-era Deferred Action for Childhood Arrivals policy; enhanced support for international students in the visa application process; efforts to formalize global elements of general education requirements; collaborative online international learning (COIL) picking up steam as a way to bring opportunities for international collaboration and connections to more of our students; in short, a new or renewed focus on the activities that matter most when it comes to student learning.

Granted, Internationalization Laboratory institutions are not necessarily typical of US higher education. They have leaders who understand internationalization and have committed time and resources to a strategic, comprehensive approach. But these institutions keep coming. We continue to fill a new Internationalization Laboratory cohort each year—and the 2019 cohort is on track to fill well ahead of schedule. Momentum continues.

The Future: "The End of an Era Doesn't Necessarily Mean That Things Regress. Maybe They Just Change"

Fischer notes that internationalization "is about equipping people to understand and adapt to a more tightly interdependent world" but that "educating global citizens . . . may not play well with the America First crowd."[4] True, the need to respond to a globalized world may not resonate in the current political climate. But globalization itself? The train has left the station. The world *is* increasingly interdependent, and our students need to be prepared for that reality.

Take my husband. Like many Washingtonians, he is a government contractor. He works for a private consulting firm whose primary client is the Federal Aviation Administration. His firm's specialty is aviation weather—how weather events affect planes and how policies respond to and mitigate these effects.

Well, weather is a borderless phenomenon. If different countries enact different policies surrounding weather events, passenger safety is potentially compromised. Thus, part of my husband's work is to convene an international community of experts and policy makers to hash this all out. He is a US citizen working for a US government agency on US policy. But in his work, he is called on to navigate cultural and linguistic differences, understand underlying political tensions and complexities, and build consensus on controversial international issues. This is—and will continue to be—the reality for our students, whether we, collectively as a nation, like it or not.

So we in higher education need to keep at our internationalization work. But we also need to be smart, deliberate, and articulate about what we're doing and why. As Hans de Wit and others have argued, we cannot think of internationalization as an end in and of itself. Fischer cites Joanna Regulska, vice provost and associate chancellor of global affairs at the University of California, Davis, as an internationalization leader who is thinking in this vein: "Rather than talking about internationalization as a goal in itself, [Regulska] sees it as a way of helping to achieve the university's mission. She casts international education as serving a goal that colleges are increasingly embracing: student success."[5]

Like Regulska suggested to Fischer, in the Internationalization Laboratory, we encourage participants to start their internationalization planning by asking how international efforts and activities further the overall strategy and goals of their institutions. This includes those that overtly reference global activity and also broader priorities, such as diversity and equity, employability of graduates, and top-quality research production.

We also need to do a better job of connecting with our local communities and tying our internationalization efforts to their needs. As I write this, I am on a plane to Duluth, Minnesota, where ACE and the Council for Regional Economic Competitiveness are convening a group of local economic development, business, and higher education leaders for a conversation about how to attract global talent to the region and build its international profile. We need more of these conversations and collaborations in more of our communities.

Finally, we need to be part of the global conversation about higher education internationalization. Yes, we're dealing with a lot here in the United States, but there's a whole world out there that we can learn from. Some places, such as the United Kingdom, are facing similar challenges. How are they meeting them, and what can we adapt from their approaches? And let's not reinvent the wheel when it comes to good practices—Australia, for example, has made great strides in supporting international students, while researchers the world over are finding ways to collaborate on cutting-edge projects. There is a lot of expertise that we can tap to further our efforts, even—or particularly—when the going is tough.

In Fischer's article, my mentor and dissertation advisor Philip Altbach states, "The era of internationalization might be over, or on life support."[6] I respectfully and collegially disagree. Admittedly, I'm a glass-half-full kind of person. But I really do believe that if we do it right, the golden age of internationalization is not, in fact, behind us but rather is yet to come. So let's get back to work—golden moment or not, our students can't afford for us to stop now.

Notes

The material in this chapter is © 2019 American Council on Education. Reprinted with permission.

1. American Council on Education, *Mapping Internationalization.*
2. Kinzie, Helms, and Cole, "Glimpse of Global Learning."
3. American Council on Education, *Mapping Internationalization.*
4. Fischer, "International Education's Golden Age."
5. Ibid.
6. Ibid.

Bibliography

American Council on Education. *Mapping Internationalization on U.S. Campuses: 2017 Edition*. Washington, DC: American Council on Education, 2017. https://www.acenet.edu/Research-Insights/Pages/Internationalization/Mapping-Internationalization-on-U-S-Campuses.aspx.

Fischer, Karin. "How International Education's Golden Age Lost Its Sheen." *Chronicle of Higher Education*, March 28, 2019. https://www.chronicle.com/interactives/2019-03-28-golden-age.

Kinzie, Jillian, Robin Matross Helms, and James Cole. "A Glimpse of Global Learning: Assessing Student Experiences and Institutional Commitments." *Liberal Education* 103, no. 2 (Spring 2017). https://www.aacu.org/liberaleducation/2017/spring/kinzie_helms_cole.

5

THE GLOBALIZATION OF INTERNATIONALIZATION?

Elspeth Jones and Hans de Wit

OVER THE PAST DECADES, MOST scholarly and public attention with respect to internationalization in higher education has focused on the Western world. As Majee and Ress note, "very little research has aimed to understand and conceptualise internationalisation efforts in the context of the historical particularities of the postcolonial condition."[1] For several years we have written about whether the concept of internationalization of higher education has itself become globalized.[2] Are institutions, countries, and regions simply mimicking the priorities of Anglo-Western forms of internationalization, or are distinctive forms of the concept emerging that better reflect local needs and priorities? In this chapter, we reflect further and summarize some key points, by which we hope to raise awareness of alternative approaches in different global contexts.

With an increasing number of countries and types of institutions around the world engaging in the process of internationalization, our work considers the impact on policy and practice of new perspectives coming from voices and regions that do not normally have a strong presence in the discourse. Our concern is to emphasize that internationalization should no longer be considered in terms of a Westernized, largely Anglo-Saxon, and predominantly English-speaking paradigm. Indeed, we go further and identify, "the need to learn from other non-western national and cultural contexts—to understand the full extent of internationalization as a phenomenon and what we can learn from each other in order to benefit students, employers and nations."[3]

We see rapid changes in international higher education, which have only increased in range and complexity over the past decade. Global competition for talent, growing complexity in cross-border activity, branch campuses, and the creation of global professionals and citizens are issues that are becoming essential parts of the language of university leaders in all parts of the world. Notions of importing and exporting countries are being turned upside down as students choose study destinations in countries that were once seen as only sending students to the West to study. Global mobility flows are increasingly complex, offering new opportunities for those able and willing to access them. Non-Western countries are emerging as key players and beginning to challenge the dominance of Western discourse on internationalization. There are increasing expectations of employers for cross-culturally capable graduates, ideally with international experience, to meet these demands.[4]

Scott has argued that "under the impact of accelerating globalization . . . a new paradigm of international education might emerge that is both more threatening and more helpful."[5] Certainly, the world is facing strong threats to the underlying values of cooperative internationalization. Rising populism, nationalism, and xenophobia, at a time when political instability has led to increasing migration, all contrive to make the jobs more difficult of those who view internationalization as far more than simply a neoliberal or market-driven concern. On the other side of the political divide, the need for higher education to address global societal challenges, summarized in the Sustainable Development Goals of the United Nations, implies a global agenda. Balancing and integrating local needs with global demands is a major challenge for higher education institutions in the context of ongoing massification on the one hand and the demand for a global knowledge economy on the other. What are the implications of this changing worldwide panorama for internationalization and the call for a more localized approach to internationalization?

In 2012, we wrote that "a globalized interpretation of internationalization requires a more nuanced approach to its delivery than has hitherto been the case," and suggested a range of factors that needed to be taken into account, including:

- geographical variation in social and economic needs resulting in differentiated local and regional responses;
- ethical issues in global engagement and sustainability of practice; and
- the importance of careful consideration of the local context and culture when engaging in cross-border activity.[6]

In 2014, we argued that a globalized view of internationalization requires us to:

- Put political and economic rationales in context by measuring the things which are important, not simply those which can be measured.
- Exploit the globalization of internationalization by learning from partners and from diversity of policy and practice.
- Remember the link between international and intercultural; internationalization of curriculum, teaching and learning, at home as well as abroad, should be a key priority.
- Understand the transformational potential of internationalization and the link with employability and citizenship—enable students, faculty, and support staff to benefit from this.
- Practice what we preach; learn from internationalization research and practice in other parts of the world.[7]

If we can seize the potential of globalized internationalization, resisting the "increasing trend to view internationalisation as a marker of institutional reputation or as a proxy for quality,"[8] we can better realize its benefits for students and the wider university community.

One of the main risks is that internationalization continues to be perceived as strengthening the dominance of the existing powers in international higher education: regions, nations, and institutions.[9] Will new regional alliances become an alternative for the European Union and the United States, and will the creation of new post–Cold War blocks of political and economic influence provide a new focus to higher education institutions and national higher education systems? Will institutions from Asia, Latin America, and Africa be able to compete as world-class universities in ranking and branding? Will successful forms of south-south cooperation emerge as an alternative to current unequal north-south partnerships?

Internationalization in higher education certainly has become a broader global concept than its dominant perception in the developed, in particular English-speaking, world. The number of articles, books, and reports on the internationalization of higher education; the active role of national governments, higher education organizations, and institutions; and the international education associations in emerging and developing countries illustrate this increasing importance. It is also reflected in Global Surveys on Internationalization by the International Association of Universities (IAU).

But at the same time, we see a trend toward the homogenization of activities, approaches, policies, and strategies, similar to those in the traditional industrialized world. As de Wit, Rumbley, Craciun, and their co-authors observe in a report for the World Bank on national tertiary education, internationalization strategies and plans of low- and middle-income countries largely copy the Western paradigm in focusing strongly on mobility, on reputation and branding, and on south-north relations.[10] This is, to a great extent, driven by economic rationales, increased competitiveness, and the dominance of the Western university model. Rankings exacerbate this, along with the numerical indicators used to measure internationalization: numbers of international students, international scholars, and mobile students and staff, as well as the number of internationally co-authored publications. These indicators tend to drive governments and institutional leaders in higher education to focus (a) on increasing these quantitative targets and (b) on policies for realizing them, such as teaching in English, tuition-fee policies, exclusive focus on research, and so on. Little space is left for innovative ideas for internationalization, embedded in the local and institutional context.

To counter the perception of homogenization, the book we edited with Gacel-Ávila and Jooste presented a number of approaches to internationalization that were embedded in specific regional, national, or institutional contexts.[11] Embracing this kind of diversity led Egron-Polak and Marmolejo to write that "the concept of 'emerging voices' in the new higher education landscape should be comprehensive and inclusive in scope. It is not only one single, unified voice, nor does it always come from the same cluster of countries or from the same type of institutions."[12]

Several key themes were identified in the book. We now consider three of these, which respond to views that the majority of internationalization follows similar patterns the world over.

Internationalization in School Education

It would seem obvious to suggest that internationalization should be fundamental to education at all levels, yet the discourse has largely neglected internationalization in primary and tertiary education. In fact, internationalization at those levels has evolved substantially, but this has largely been ignored in the debate on the internationalization of higher education until fairly recently, and, indeed, de Wit observed that "higher education has to realise that internationalisation starts not only at the university but before that and they should support and collaborate with the other levels of education, take advantage of this development and build their own strategy on it."[13] Rizvi points to an internationalization approach that is important for both developing and developed countries: "While issues internal to higher education are well-researched, seldom examined are the questions of the ways in which the schools sector prepares students for international higher education, as well as the implications for universities of the attempts by schools to internationalize their policies, programs and practices."[14] According to Rizvi, this underlines the need for universities to develop closer and more direct links with schools and school systems around the world. Internationalization is not the exclusive domain of higher education and can only reach full potential if it is aligned with and built on other levels of education.

Internationalization and Social Responsibility

Another dimension of higher education internationalization that has been rather ignored concerns the social role and responsibility of higher education. Egron-Polak and Marmolejo argue (in this volume and elsewhere) that the United Nations' 2030 Agenda for Sustainable Development may offer a new framework within which internationalization of higher education could evolve.[15] They conclude that

> Higher education institutions already contribute, in a variety of ways, to goals such as those of the 2030 Agenda and have done so for decades. They collaborate to build capacity in partner institutions in many disciplines, they internationalise their curriculum with the aim of instilling in graduates a global consciousness; they have focused on developing learning outcomes linked to global citizenship; undertake research on sustainable lifestyles and alternative economic models, develop new health policies and practices that expand access to treatment, train teachers at home and internationally, etc. However, these valuable activities are often somewhat marginal in the overwhelming focus of internationalisation strategies on attracting more international students, on finding partner institutions that enjoy a strong international reputation, on building partnerships according to self-interest due to pressure to show impact at home, focusing on research that has the greatest potential to raise both individual and institutional status and others.[16]

In two recent contributions to *University World News*,[17] Brandenburg, de Wit, Jones, and Leask argue that there is a need for institutions to consider their role in supporting internationalization for society, a concept described by them as follows: "Internationalisation of Higher Education for Society (IHES) explicitly aims to benefit the wider community, at home or abroad, through international or intercultural education, research, service and engagement."[18] Thematic examples of internationalization of higher education for society include its contribution in relation to the refugee crisis facing the Middle East and Europe and lessons for similar crises elsewhere, its role in helping to rebuild postconflict countries, and the enhancement of social inclusion.[19]

Immigration Patterns and Refugees

Streitwieser, Miller-Idriss, and de Wit argue that

> Universities' reception of refugees ought to be understood within broader higher education internationalization frameworks and global engagements, because receiving countries' efforts to help refugees maintain and acquire high-level skills during periods of crisis and displacement will have a significant and ongoing impact on the recovery and reconstruction efforts of sending regions once the conflict ends. While developing countries are usually the primary senders and receivers of refugees, the crisis that began in Europe in 2015 has changed that pattern once again.[20]

They state that such an understanding will not only solve the immediate problems of the individuals concerned but will also help to ensure that these individuals have the skills and knowledge needed for reconstruction when political stability has returned. They believe that the Syrian refugee crisis has helped to showcase on a grand scale, arguably unprecedented in modern times, how university internationalization can be connected to broader issues of global stability in the short and longer term. Ergin, de Wit, and Leask refer to this as forced internationalization, stating that, "whereas in the past, internationalization of higher education has primarily been voluntary and part of deliberate institutional (and in some cases governmental) policy, this emerging form of internationalization is forced."[21]

International Dimensions of Higher Education in Postconflict Settings

The world is faced with an increasing number of postconflict settings: Afghanistan, Colombia, Iraq, South Africa, South Sudan, Sudan, and Syria, to mention some key current ones. Heleta argues that universities from the developed and emerging world need to play a crucial role here, through collaboration and provision of assistance: "Despite the enormous challenges facing post-conflict countries, rebuilding and gradual internationalisation of higher education need to be considered as priorities by local and international actors. Students in these countries deserve quality and relevant education that prepares them for global engagement and functioning."[22]

Internationalization and Social Inclusion

There are some interesting examples of how internationalization can be used as a means to enhance the social inclusion of traditionally disadvantaged populations in the Latin American and Caribbean region. This includes women living in rural areas struggling to set up their own business as a means of subsistence. Ramírez Sánchez, Cáceres Seguel, and Pinto Baleisan showcase the experience of a group of women entrepreneurs who were able to consolidate their marketing strategies and make innovations in their products thanks to the internationalization program of the Viña del Mar University, Chile.[23]

Social responsibility and global citizenship development are increasingly present in higher education internationalization discourse, in particular for developing countries. Here it appears that higher education shows a more focused acknowledgment of the social mission of universities than in the developed world, where the notion of society has become more market focused and such terms as *workforce development* and *employability* dominate the agenda of higher education and its internationalization.

Regional Trends in Internationalization

Until relatively recently, internationalization trends in different parts of the world have tended to follow traditional models. Student mobility from developing regions to more developed economies and transnational education (or international program and provider mobility) delivered by Anglo-Western institutions have been the main area of focus. However, a number of other trends have begun to emerge in recent years. For example, there has been an increase globally in the number of programs delivered through the medium of English in order to attract students who do not speak the local language. Alongside this, improving perceptions of institutional quality in countries previously seen as sending students rather than receiving them have disrupted traditional global student flows. Education hubs in East and Southeast Asia, as well as dominant destination countries in the Middle East and parts of Africa and Latin America, are now creating opportunities for wider participation in international education than ever before. Some other notable trends were described in de Wit, Gacel-Ávila, and Jones.[24]

As far as the Latin America and Caribbean region is concerned, Gacel-Ávila, Bustos-Aguirre, and Celso Freire noted short-term mobility as an innovative strategy that has been gaining importance in the past ten years, expanding international opportunities for students.[25] However, regional economic and political instability, along with a lack of effective long-term planning and implementation, have begun to undermine efforts and progress made.

Abouchedid and Bou Zeid's study of the Middle East and North Africa (MENA) also presented key obstacles, such as that many institutions in the region lack the important physical and financial resources required for internationalization.[26] There is inadequate government funding for public universities and overdependence on student fees in private institutions. Internationalization requires a commitment from higher education leaders that should be reflected in policies, mission statements, and strategic plans, but in reality, only a few universities mention internationalization in their mission statements, they argue. Cooperation exists only as piecemeal initiatives taken by some higher education institutions (HEIs) on an individual basis. The region lacks a regional qualification framework to facilitate transferability of credits and mobility of students across the diverse HEIs of the area. Student mobility is also challenged by security problems and political instability in the wider MENA region and by visa problems for students wishing to travel to Europe and the United States. Privatization policies that allow the establishment of foreign institutions are mainly motivated by political and commercial considerations at the expense of quality in terms of curricula, faculty qualifications, and research facilities, which greatly limit the involvement of HEIs in the regional internationalization process.

Klemenčič writes about institutions in peripheral locations and argues that, for them, "the imperatives for internationalisation are magnified by the limited 'organic' intake of talent and the high salience of international networks and graduates with international competences to aid economic development and growth."[27] For such institutions, a deliberate internationalization strategy is indeed a necessary ingredient of their own modernization and institutional capacity building, with regional cooperation a particularly desirable option, since it potentially helps strengthen the regional relevance of partner institutions and their collective international status and visibility: "Universities in peripheral countries may not be the most desired international partners of institutions in the educational hot spots, but they are often preferred partners to other institutions in the peripheral neighbouring countries."[28] However, Klemenčič argues, the reality is that, for peripheral universities, the internationalization of higher education is often associated with modernization, or catching up with internationalized peers in more developed higher education hubs, and this sense of catching up is precisely what can prompt universities into the uncritical imitation of other institutions or internationalization agendas.

For the Caribbean region, Rampersad describes the University of the West Indies (UWI) as illustrating the use of internationalization as an engine of national and regional development.[29] UWI's strategy highlights how information and communication technology can facilitate entry to new markets and engender demand for programs in which the university enjoys a strong reputation and has market appeal. Furthermore, Rampersad identifies the strategies of expanding research links with traditional partners that are leaders in their field and of aggressively pursuing relationships with counterparts in regions offering new opportunities for growth and development. He notes that these are especially valuable where historical and cultural links can be leveraged.

These cases reflect a dynamic and broad regional approach to internationalization. It is clear that while student mobility is an important activity, other dimensions may be even more so. Regional and subregional integration and cooperation emerge as needing greater prominence in the analysis of internationalization in higher education.

Similar approaches can be found at the national level in emerging and developing countries, several of which are investing in higher education and in world-class universities in an attempt to move up in the rankings—their primary driver for internationalization. This means that national interests prevail above institutional autonomy and initiative, and the danger of uncritical imitation is high.

A number of alternative lessons can be learned by observing institutional initiatives in internationalization. According to Hagenmeier, internationalization in a postcolonial context must affirm awareness of local identity, cultures, and languages.[30] Critical for success, he argues, is the strengthening of the university's role as a catalyst connecting indigenous knowledge, language, and culture to the wider world, for the mutual benefit of local communities, international stakeholders, and the university. His view of a conceptual link between Africanization and internationalization, which affirms rather than jeopardizes the university as an African university embedded in indigenous communities, is in line with Knutson's call to problematize internationalization through indigenous world views in the Canadian context.[31]

Some Reflections

So, to return to the question in our title, it is true that internationalization has become increasingly a global phenomenon. However, our view is that internationalization strategy, far from becoming globalized in the sense of homogenization, continues to be developed beyond traditional understandings. Engaging with the different political, economic, social, and historical factors in regional contexts can offer new insights for those who choose not to imitate Anglo-Western models. Some of the issues to be taken into account in these emerging contexts include:

- potential tensions arising from past colonial influences of different kinds;
- local identity, cultures, and languages;
- institutional values, including the local social role of higher education;
- increasingly competitive operating environments;
- finding the right institutional balance between local, national, regional, and global objectives;
- questions of sustainability; and
- recognizing potential contributions to addressing global challenges.

In summary, how can institutions operate successfully in their local, national, and regional contexts, making a meaningful and responsible contribution to the society they are part of, while also meeting internationalization objectives? Will they take a competitive direction or the route toward a more socially responsible approach?

The competitive route is difficult, requires substantial public and private investment, and can increase the social divide. As de Wit, Hunter, Howard, and Egron-Polak and Ilieva and Peak observe, both in the developed and the developing world, the main point of policy and action in internationalization still focuses on mobility, in particular student mobility, and quality assurance of that process is weak.[32] De Wit, Hunter, Howard, and Egron-Polak also point to the fact that this focus on mobility is not inclusive but, rather, elitist, only reaching a small minority of students and academics.[33]

The more socially responsible approach is also not easy and it, too, requires substantial public and private resources, but it is more socially inclusive and in the long run will result in a tertiary education sector with higher quality. This approach implies paying greater attention to internationalization of the curriculum at home. It should align with other levels of education and better address the international dimensions of social responsibility. The examples we have highlighted manifest both the opportunities and the obstacles that such an approach faces.

De Wit and Leask argue that, "Aligning the practice of internationalization with human values and the common global good, requires that we first challenge some of our long-held views about what it is to 'be international' as a university, a teacher, a student, a human being. This requires pushing the boundaries of our own and others' thinking, focusing on people and ensuring that they develop and demonstrate the institution's espoused human values."[34]

We hope that this chapter may provide food for thought for readers in more developed, Anglo-Western countries as well as in developing and emerging environments. It is crucial that we take account of different contexts in our understanding and approach, considering internationalization in a more nuanced fashion than has been done previously. As Aw correctly remarks, "the work of internationalization is complex, multifaceted and fraught with power relations. The need to examine carefully the role of culture, access, knowledge and relevance in internationalization practices, policies and initiatives, cannot be understated."[35] We have attempted here to further such examination, in order to stimulate reflection, understanding, and action toward innovative, sustainable, ethical, and socially inclusive conceptualizations of internationalization.[36]

Notes

1. Majee and Ress, "Colonial Legacies," 4.
2. See Jones and de Wit, "Globalization of Internationalization" and "Globalized Internationalization"; de Wit, Gacel-Ávila, and Jones, "Voices and Perspectives."
3. Jones and de Wit, "Globalized Internationalization," 50.
4. Jones and de Wit, "Globalized Internationalization."
5. Scott, "Future Trends," 55.

6. Jones and de Wit, "Globalization of Internationalization," 39.
7. Ibid., 29.
8. Jones, "Internationalisation and the Student of the Future," 210.
9. Egron-Polak, "Internationalization of Higher Education."
10. De Wit, Rumbley, et al., "International Mapping."
11. De Wit, Gacel-Ávila, and Jones, "Voices and Perspectives."
12. Egron-Polak and Marmolejo, "Higher Education Internationalisation," 14.
13. De Wit, "School Internationalisation," 1.
14. Rizvi, "School Internationalization," 18.
15. Egron-Polak, "Internationalization of Higher Education"; United Nations, "Transforming Our World."
16. Egron-Polak and Marmolejo, "Higher Education Internationalisation," 17.
17. Brandenburg et al., "Internationalisation in Higher Education" and "Defining Internationalisation."
18. Ibid.
19. De Wit, Gacel-Ávila, and Jones, "Voices and Perspectives."
20. Streitweiser, Miller-Idriss, and de Wit, "Higher Education's Response."
21. Ergin, de Wit, and Leask, "Forced Internationalization," 10.
22. Heleta, "Higher Education," 41.
23. Ramirez Sánchez, Cáceres Seguel, and Pinto Baleisan, "Internationalization Strategies."
24. De Wit, Gacel-Ávila, and Jones, "Voices and Perspectives. "
25. Gacel-Ávila, Bustos-Aguirre, and Celso Freire, "Student Mobility."
26. Abouchedid and Bou Zeid, "MENA Region."
27. Klemenčič, "Internationalisation in Universities," 101.
28. Ibid., 105.
29. Rampersad, "Internationalisation."
30. Hagenmeier, "Innovative Approaches."
31. Knutson, "Internationalization and Indigenization."
32. De Wit, Hunter, et al., "Internationalization of Higher Education"; Ilieva and Peak, "Shape."
33. De Wit, Hunter, et al., "Internationalization of Higher Education."
34. De Wit and Leask, "Towards New Ways," 1.
35. Aw, "Foreword," 1.
36. This chapter draws on several of our published works, including a chapter with Jocelyne Gacel-Ávila in de Wit et al., *Globalization of Internationalization.* Her contribution to that chapter is gratefully acknowledged.

Bibliography

Abouchedid, Kamal, and Maria Bou Zeid. "Internationalization in the MENA Region: A Case Study of Higher Education." In *The Globalization of Internationalization: Emerging Voices and Perspectives*, edited by Hans de Wit, Jocelyne Gacel-Ávila, Elspeth Jones, and Nico Jooste, 73–78. London: Routledge, 2017.

Aw, Fanta. "Foreword." In *Globalization of Internationalization*, edited by de Wit et al., xxi–xxiii. London: Routledge, 2017.

Brandenburg, Uwe, Hans de Wit, Elspeth Jones, and Betty Leask. "Internationalisation in Higher Education for Society." *University World News*, June 6, 2019. https://www.universityworldnews.com/post.php?story=20190414195843914.

———. "Defining Internationalisation in HE for Society." *University World News*, June 29, 2019. https://www.universityworldnews.com/post.php?story=20190626135618704.

De Wit, Hans. "School Internationalisation: Whose Opportunity?" *University World News*, August 14, 2015. https://www.universityworldnews.com/post.php?story=20150811193137804.

———, Jocelyne Gacel-Ávila, and Elspeth Jones. "Voices and Perspectives on Internationalization from the Emerging and Developing World: Where Are We Heading?" In *Globalization of Internationalization*, edited by de Wit et al., 221–33. London: Routledge, 2017.

———, Jocelyne Gacel-Ávila, Elspeth Jones, and Nico Jooste. *The Globalization of Internationalization: Emerging Voices and Perspectives*. London: Routledge, 2017.

———, Fiona Hunter, Laura Howard, and Eva Egron-Polak. "Internationalization of Higher Education." Study for the European Parliament, Committee on Culture and Education, Brussels, July 2015. http://www.europarl.europa.eu/RegData/etudes/STUD/2015/540370/IPOL_STU(2015)540370_EN.pdf.

———, and Betty Leask. "Towards New Ways of Becoming and Being International." *University World News*. Last modified July 28, 2019. https://www.universityworldnews.com/post.php?story=20190722112900397.

———, Laura Rumbley, Daniela Craciun, Georgiana Mihut, and Ayenachew Woldegiyorgis. "International Mapping of National Tertiary Education Internationalization Strategies and Plans (NTEISPs)." *CIHE Perspectives no. 12*. Boston: Center for International Higher Education, 2019.

Egron-Polak, Eva. "Internationalization of Higher Education—An Introduction." *IAU Horizons* 17, no. 3; 18, no. 1 (2012): 15. https://www.iau-aiu.net/IMG/pdf/iau_horizons_vol.17_no.3_vol.18_no.1_2012_en.pdf.

———, and Francisco Marmolejo. "Higher Education Internationalisation—Adjusting to New Landscapes." In *Globalization of Internationalization*, edited by de Wit et al., 7–17. London: Routledge, 2017.

Ergin, Hakan, Hans de Wit, and Betty Leask. "Forced Internationalization: An Emerging Phenomenon." *International Higher Education* 97 (2019): 9–10.

Gacel-Ávila, Jocelyne, Magdalena Bustos-Aguirre, and José Celso Freire Jr. "Student Mobility in Latin America and the Caribbean: Latest Trends and Innovative Programs." In *Globalization of Internationalization*, edited by de Wit et al., 61–72. London: Routledge, 2017.

Hagenmeier, Cornelius. "Innovative Approaches to Internationalisation in Rural South Africa: the Case of the University of Venda." In *Globalization of Internationalization*, edited by de Wit et al., 169–81. London: Routledge, 2017.

Heleta, Savo. "Higher Education and its International Dimensions in Post-Conflict Settings." In *Globalization of Internationalization*, edited by de Wit et al., 40–49. London: Routledge, 2017.

Ilieva, Janet, and Michael Peak. "The Shape of Global Higher Education: National Policies Framework for International Engagement." Report for British Council, London, 2016. https://www.britishcouncil.org/sites/default/files/f310_tne_international_higher_education_report_final_v2_web.pdf.

Jones, Elspeth. "Internationalisation and the Student of the Future." In *Possible Futures: The Next 25 Years of The Internationalisation of Higher Education*, edited by Hans de Wit, Fiona Hunter, Linda Johnson, and Hans-Georg van Liempd, 206–10. Amsterdam: European Association for International Education, 2013.

———, and Hans de Wit. "Globalization of Internationalization: Thematic and Regional Reflections on a Traditional Concept." *AUDEM: The International Journal of Higher Education and Democracy* 3 (2012): 35–54.

———, and Hans de Wit. "Globalized Internationalization: Implications for Policy and Practice." *IIE Networker* (Spring 2014): 28–29.

Klemenčič, Manja. "Internationalisation of Universities in the Peripheries." In *Globalization of Internationalization*, edited by de Wit et al., 99–109. London: Routledge, 2017.

Knutson, Sonja. "Internationalization and Indigenization: Transforming Canadian Higher Education." In *The Future Agenda for Internationalization in Higher Education, Next Generation Insights into Research, Policy, and Practice*, edited by Douglas Proctor and Laura E. Rumbley, 28–37. London: Routledge, 2018.

Majee, Upenyu S., and Susanne B. Ress. "Colonial Legacies in Internationalisation of Higher Education: Racial Justice and Geopolitical Redress in South Africa and Brazil." *Compare: A Journal of Comparative and International Education* (October 17, 2018): 463–81. https://doi.org/10.1080/03057925.2018.1521264.

Ramírez Sánchez, Carlos, César Cáceres Seguel, and Carolina Pinto Baleisan. "Internationalization Strategies and Social Inclusion: The Experience of Women Entrepreneurs in Rural Areas of the Region of Valparaiso, Chile." In *Globalization of Internationalization*, edited by de Wit et al., 50–57. London: Routledge, 2017.

Rampersad, David. "The Internationalisation of Higher Education in the Caribbean." In *Globalization of Internationalization*, edited by de Wit et al., 89–98. London: Routledge, 2017.

Rizvi, Fazal. "School Internationalization and Its Implications for Higher Education." In *Globalization of Internationalization*, edited by de Wit et al., 18–25. London: Routledge, 2017.

Scott, Peter. "Future Trends in International Education." In *Possible Futures: The Next 25 Years of the Internationalisation of Higher Education*, edited by Hans de Wit, Fiona Hunter, Linda Johnson, and Hans-Georg van Liempd, 52–56. Amsterdam: European Association for International Education, 2013.

Streitwieser, Bernhard, Cynthia Miller-Idriss, and Hans de Wit. "Higher Education's Response to the European Refugee Crisis: Challenges, Strategies, and Opportunities." In *Globalization of Internationalization*, edited by de Wit et al., 29–39. London: Routledge, 2017.

United Nations. "Transforming Our World: The 2030 Agenda for Sustainable Development." Sustainable Development Goals: Knowledge Platform. October 21, 2015. https://sustainabledevelopment.un.org/post2015/transformingourworld.

6

WHY INTERNATIONAL EDUCATION

Recent Past, Present, and Future

Eva Egron-Polak

I WOULD LIKE TO BEGIN my chapter with a personal anecdote. After I completed sixth grade, my family sought and received political asylum from Canada. We were, in the summer of 1968, among the first group of refugees to leave what was at that time Czechoslovakia. Upon arriving in Canada, I was placed into eighth grade in a very small village, with a population of two thousand, in southern Ontario, where my parents were settled by Canadian government services. I quickly realized the importance of languages: in Czechoslovakia I had been forced to learn Russian until sixth grade, and my parents forced me to learn German after school. During the flight that brought us from Europe to Canada, we and all the other travelers were asked by a public announcement: "Where would you like to disembark: Montreal or Toronto?" My parents looked at one another and said, "We'll get off in Toronto." Why? My father had encountered American soldiers during World War II liberation and so had learned a few words, such as *yes* and *no*, in English. Neither he nor my mother had any knowledge of French.

Because Toronto was English speaking, then, we disembarked there and embarked on a life where I had to learn English. At home, my parents often used German as a secret language that I could not always follow. This made me decide to learn French so that they could not follow my conversations. And that is how I have ended up living and working for the past seventeen years in France at the International Association of Universities.

I will examine here why international education is important and look at it from an international, global perspective. I would also like to address the Title VI program, which offers a perfect case study of how rationales for international education policy adjust over time to respond to specific needs and interests. Title VI is a US initiative that initially served to build domestic capacity in international education that was needed for security reasons. It was at least partially sparked by the race to space and the launching of Sputnik, as well as, in large measure, by the need for US expertise in diplomacy and outreach to build strategic alliances for the nation. The program evolved over time, but its genesis can be found in these circumstances.

Similarly, let me briefly outline the genesis of the International Association of Universities (IAU), of which I spent the last seventeen years as secretary-general, and which provides me with a global perspective on this topic. The IAU was created by about 150 university presidents who came together in 1950 in Nice, France, to commit to building peace through higher education cooperation. This post–World War II period was the genesis of many organizations, including the United Nations and its agency for education and scientific cooperation, UNESCO. To this day, the IAU is still housed at UNESCO.

During this period, following on the very destructive and turbulent war years, international education, including the knowledge of languages, cultures, and traditions, was seen as an important national resource and, increasingly, as a way to build mutual respect and tools that could be used for socioeconomic development abroad. As many developing nations began to obtain their independence, international education became instrumental in development assistance and humanitarian aid.

Eventually, as diverse approaches to such development cooperation and international cooperation in education were crafted and deepened, the scope and definition of international education itself was broadened. It was not just languages, area studies, and human resource development through scholarship programs. International academic mobility of all kinds intensified; international research gained prominence; and, generally speaking, international education became a broader and more substantial activity.

In the higher education community, there was real enthusiasm and a general sense that this was a positive activity in which to engage, valuable in itself—a positive way to change the world for the better and a manifestation of global solidarity.

Is this still the case today? As in the post–World War II era, the world is experiencing a very turbulent political, economic, and geopolitical context. There is no longer a bipolar system, as there was during the Cold War. Rather, we are faced with a highly interdependent, quickly changing, and multilateral landscape in a globalized world. The political climate around the world is changing rapidly as well—and not for the better, for the most part. We see growing nationalism, protectionism, and populism. In many parts of the world, there is strong anti-Western sentiment, rising xenophobia, and unprecedented migrations of people. We also see new actors wielding tremendous economic and political power, such as nongovernmental organizations, nonstate actors, and private companies. Within an environment of uncontrolled and incredibly fast communications capacities, we see the value of knowledge, expertise, and science being questioned. It is not surprising, then, that there is also a shifting set of rationales for international education.

In the current era, international education has come to be known more as internationalization, and this process, as a policy or strategy, has become a far more central instrument or lever for international relations among nations and world regions. It is not only more central to the university but is also now part of and discussed within trade policy and national security policy and is seen by decision makers as central to innovation, economic development, and competitiveness. There is no doubt that for many countries, education has been viewed as an export industry that brings in major revenues. It is also a tool for exerting political will and can be used as an instrument of soft diplomacy. This was exemplified in the dispute between Canada and Saudi Arabia that started in August 2018, when Canada's foreign minister posted a tweet protesting the arrests of several Saudi women human rights activists in Saudi Arabia.[1] One of the arrested women had relatives in Canada. The Saudi government found the tweet offensive and intrusive. The diplomatic war between the two countries that ensued saw the Saudi Arabian leadership using scholarships and student mobility to demonstrate its discontent with what they perceived as interference in domestic affairs, and they knew full well what a tremendous impact their decision to stop allowing Saudi scholarship holders to study in Canada would have on Canadian higher education institutions.

International collaboration among higher education institutions is also a means to foster greater economic, cultural, and political regional integration. This is of course most evident in the European Union, but it is being replicated in many other regions. There are regional developments in Asia, in Latin America, and in Africa using higher education as a means to create stronger links and strengthen integration, and the European experience is often used as the model. Nevertheless, national interests are still very strong as economic competitiveness at national or regional levels is built on being internationally connected in the knowledge society. Moreover, and increasingly so in aging industrialized nations, international collaboration and internationalization are seen as ways to secure the future capacity for knowledge creation. Recruiting international students from around the world is often the only way to maintain active and productive academic departments in many sectors in the Anglo-Saxon countries. The demographic trends in these countries make current higher education unsustainable, so attracting international talent into universities is also a strategic way of securing future resources.

These developments have made aspects of international higher education so important that few institutions would state that this is not a priority. Yet, at the same time, there are more and more voices raised that question the benefits of internationalization and ask whether this process brings the goals and objectives that it had promised. Indeed, in a recent article, Jane Knight and Hans de Wit, well-known scholars and promoters of internationalization, asked specifically whether internationalization in the university is achieving its objectives.[2]

To question whether internationalization is indeed a positive trend is not at all a negative phenomenon. In my view, one of the reasons for this questioning is because international education, area studies, language studies, internationalization of the curriculum in various disciplines, and other aspects have dropped much too low on the list of priorities in the policy discourse, where internationalization has become almost synonymous with student mobility and with the recruitment of international, fee-paying students becoming a top priority. The revenue thus generated is often simply replacing funds lost through cuts from the public purse. At times, the large number of international students admitted is seen as reducing available spaces for domestic students. That is one of the main reasons why there is a backlash in some countries and communities to the whole process of internationalization. It is seen as too commercially driven.

These criticisms and negative commentaries have led to a new, or renewed, conversation about the need to focus on curriculum and more generally on the process of internationalization at home, which covers not only curricular changes but also the extracurricular activities and more generally the ethos of the institution and thus touches all students, not simply those who can go abroad. As well, there is a growing call for making internationalization more inclusive, and some efforts are underway to avoid elitism. It would be highly undesirable for internationalization to be another means to exacerbate gaps and social injustice. In this regard, we are seeing a diversification of partner countries and partner institutions, moving away, to some extent, from the well-trodden tracks of cooperation that almost exclusively take place between universities in industrialized countries, leaving aside many institutions in the developing world. Projects involving universities in developing nations are usually focused only on capacity-building activities, which tend to be too often a one-way learning process rather than the kind of collaborative partnerships where mutual learning takes place. Yet it is this mutual learning that is needed for internationalization to flourish and benefit all.

For future developments, and when considering institutional collaborations beyond Europe and North America or Australia, it is crucially important to expand boundaries, not to focus only on the BRICS (Brazil, Russia, India, China, and South Africa) but to really diversify our partners, because there is much to learn from partners who are different and experiencing distinct contexts and challenges. This is a far more enriching process. Further, the approaches to internationalization are diversifying. Technology is clearly an instrument for doing more and reaching more broadly in international work. Mobility models are diversifying, with shorter and shorter trips abroad. Such short mobility schemes have the potential to be more inclusive, but they need better preparation and coordination and must be integrated into the curriculum. In addition, there is a growing trend around the world to see both international students and diverse local communities as real sources of potential for learning about other cultures. They are our neighbors; they are present in our daily life. Successful interaction with local communities that engages students and research in purposeful learning can significantly enrich a university's international programs. As the former president of the University of Amsterdam, Sijbolt Noorda, once said so rightfully, "What we need is internationalization by bus, not internationalization by plane."

There is also a growing concern about the fairness of international relations in higher education, the values that underpin them, the way that international relations are conducted, and the need for a more ethical approach to these relations, because they are not always taking place on a level playing field. The power relations between partners in higher education international cooperation are not always balanced, and extreme care is required to be true partners.

Contributors to this volume were asked, in our reflections, to look at the future trends of internationalization. Allow me to set my sight only as far as tomorrow; the future is much too unpredictable. So let us look toward tomorrow and recall that the end of World War II acted as an impetus for many developments to prevent the threat of war—a way to avoid further violence. These developments included the Title VI program in the United States and, on the world scene, the creation of such organizations as the United Nations, UNESCO, and, of course, the International Association of Universities. These were all instruments to promote collaboration and understanding among peoples and countries. They were a response to a global threat.

What is the greatest peril to humanity today, and, most especially, what threatens all of our tomorrows? The failure to meet the UN Sustainable Development Goals (SDGs) is perhaps the most pressing threat. These seventeen goals, agreed upon by all UN member states, encompass all of the global challenges that must be met. And universities have a global responsibility to be central actors. This is not easy to do. Often, the voice of higher education is not loud enough or coordinated enough—or when we speak truth to power, our interlocutor simply hangs up. However, as institutions for the creation and dissemination of knowledge, universities must be forceful concerning their central place in this discussion. The SDGs can provide a new, global framework to build bridges between disciplines and knowledge systems and, certainly, can become a solid platform for partnerships and collaborations. Universities have experience in bringing expertise from various disciplines to resolve issues and challenges. Experience in international collaboration and projects also helps universities realize the importance of being sensitive about the specific economic, political, and cultural contexts in which the issues are being addressed. Thus, they are partners of choice in collaborative efforts to meet the sustainable development challenge that is threatening the future of humanity.

Regarding the question of whether international education is at a crossroads, my response would be both yes and no. International education is more central to learning and to research today than ever before. So the crossroads is only about which way to go to increase, deepen, and travel even further on this path. Being internationally savvy and sensitive is not a luxury for a few experts or for those few who are interested in international issues. It is a necessity for all of our students to be open to the world and to have some understanding of how the world affects us and how what we do affects the world. In each and every way that international education is carried out, it is essential to recognize that learning can be mutual and enriching, no matter where the collaboration takes place and with which communities. In international collaboration in higher education, it is imperative to stop considering other universities in other countries as rivals or enemies. They are not; higher education is not a business just like any other. Finally, universities have a responsibility to contribute to the narrowing of gaps between the rich and the poor, at home and globally. By the exemplary fashion in which they conduct themselves and their international relations, universities have to teach all graduates not to see the world as "us and them," because those dichotomies bring mistrust and fear. We are all neighbors, living and (ab)using one planet, and it is essential that we instill this sense of shared and collective responsibility to meet future challenges.

Notes

It was an honor to be invited as one of the panel members in a session tasked with considering the future of international education. I am grateful to the organizers for the enriching experience and thank most particularly Drs. Deborah Cohn and Hilary Kahn.

1. Stephenson, "Future Still Uncertain."
2. Knight and de Wit, "Internationalization of Higher Education," 2–4.

Bibliography

Knight, Jane, and Hans de Wit. "Internationalization of Higher Education: Past and Future." *International Higher Education* 95 (Fall 2018): 2–4. https://doi.org/10.6017/ihe.2018.95.10715.

Stephenson, Grace Karram. "Future Still Uncertain for Saudi Students in Canada." *University World News*, November 9, 2018. https://www.universityworldnews.com/post.php?story=20181107072128708.

Intersection

7

THE BROADEST POSSIBLE EDUCATION

The Future of Global and International Studies

Jonathan F. Fanton

ONE OF THE GREAT CHALLENGES of higher education in the twenty-first century is how to adapt most effectively to a world that is, increasingly, at our fingertips—in some ways smaller and in other ways more difficult to comprehend—at a time when our campuses, our research teams, our businesses, and our communities are becoming more international with every passing year. As Indiana University president Michael McRobbie has written, "The best university education instills an understanding of the world outside of the boundaries of the U.S.: of the history, cultures, religions, politics, economies, institutions, languages, art, and literature of other countries. Such an understanding has never been more critical to humanity and to building a respectful, responsible, and engaged global community."[1]

Here, I will share some observations drawn from my experiences as president of the American Academy of Arts and Sciences and from the Academy projects that have touched on the theme of "international education at the crossroads."

I begin with background about the American Academy and its mission.

The Academy was founded in 1780, during the American Revolution, by John Adams, John Hancock, and sixty-one other scholar-patriots who understood that the new republic would require new institutions to gather knowledge and advance learning in service to the public good. Modeled after the great learned societies of Europe, the Academy was created to be a venue for intellectual exchange and a forum for the discussion of new ideas.

It is important to note that the Academy has never been an exclusively American enterprise. Our founders were far too worldly and prescient for that. Although its name and early mission emphasized the importance of the arts and sciences for the United States, it has always operated according to a firm conviction that knowledge is not limited by national borders and that international collaboration is indispensable to human progress.

As a wartime diplomat, John Adams knew firsthand the value of such collaboration. The first two international members to be elected to the Academy were his French counterparts: the ambassador and foreign minister with whom he worked to secure French support for the American Revolution. Since then, the Academy has elected international members in every field, including many whose names you will recognize—Lafayette, Euler, Gladstone, Ruskin, Darwin, Einstein, Nehru, Anna Freud, Boulanger, Goodall, and Mandela, to name a few. And the Academy's work—the projects and studies to which our members dedicate their time and share their knowledge and expertise—has frequently been international in its aims and its emphasis.

Today, the Academy pursues a range of projects that offer valuable insights into the evaluation of "the future needs and priorities of international education in a changing and increasingly interconnected world" that was undertaken by the International Education at the Crossroads symposium.

The project with the most obvious relevance is our Commission on Language Learning. In 2014, a bipartisan group of members of Congress asked the Academy to undertake a new study of the nation's language education needs. In their letters, they requested that the Academy provide answers to the following questions: How does language learning influence economic growth, cultural diplomacy, the productivity of future generations, and the fulfillment of all Americans? What actions should the nation take to ensure excellence in all languages as well as international education and research, including how we may more effectively use current resources to advance language attainment?[2]

In response to this request, the Academy created the Commission on Language Learning. Chaired by Paul LeClerc, former president of Hunter College and the New York Public Library, the Commission included distinguished language scholars and social scientists, representatives of the military and the US State Department, a federal judge, and many others.[3] The Commission's final report, *America's Languages: Investing in Language Education for the 21st Century*, was published in 2017. It offers concrete recommendations to improve access to as many languages as possible, for people of every age, ethnicity, and socioeconomic background.

The title of the report, *America's Languages*, refers to an important historic fact about our nation and one of its great strengths. As stated in the report's introduction: "Linguistic diversity is deeply embedded in our history.

The English we speak is only one of many European, Native American, African, and Asian languages that have been spoken on the North American continent. This diversity is a cherished part of our nation's past, a fact of our present, and a key to our future: a valuable asset in our relations with other nations and cultures and a benefit to our children as they grow up in an interconnected world."[4]

And yet we have neglected this competitive advantage for far too long. About 20 percent of all US residents speak a language other than English at home. But very few speak, write, and read proficiently in that language. In fact, current research suggests that only 10 percent of the US population speaks a language other than English proficiently. And we lag far behind many nations of the world. So, while English continues to be the preferred language for world trade and diplomacy, there is an emerging consensus among leaders in business and government, teachers, scientists, and parents that proficiency in English alone is not sufficient to meet the nation's needs in an interconnected world. We are wasting our resources when we fail to develop the languages that immigrants bring with them or that our students study in middle and high school and then abandon when they get to college. And we are beginning to see the adverse effects of this neglect.

For example, 40 percent of business leaders who responded to a recent poll by Shirley J. Daniel, Fujiao Xie, and Ben L. Kedia reported that their businesses had failed to reach their potential due to international language barriers.[5] We also know that our foreign service and security agencies continue to seek language expertise for diplomatic, military, and cultural missions around the world—deep expertise, including an understanding of nuance, so that nothing is lost in translation. There are many other benefits of a more robust language education as well, including the development of important habits of mind and the cultivation of new and valuable perspectives on the world. We are also beginning to understand that there may be cognitive enhancements for speakers of more than one language, like improved executive functioning, memory, and problem-solving ability, as well as a greater resistance to dementia and Alzheimer's disease. Given all of these findings, we can and must improve access to languages for everyone.

As our report concludes, there is "much to gain by participating in a multilingual world, and so much to lose if we remain stubbornly monolingual."[6]

America's Languages offers five basic recommendations, all focused on increasing the number of US citizens who speak a language other than English:

1. Increase the number of language teachers at all levels of education so that every child in every state has the opportunity to learn a language in addition to English.
2. Supplement language instruction across the education system through public-private partnerships among schools, government, philanthropies, businesses, and local community members.
3. Support heritage languages already spoken in the United States, and help these languages persist from one generation to the next.
4. Provide targeted support and programming for Native American languages as defined in the Native American Languages Act.
5. Promote opportunities for students to learn languages in other countries by experiencing other cultures and immersing themselves in multilingual environments.[7]

Each of these recommendations is then elaborated on and made concrete with pilot initiatives, model programs, and other suggestions selected by the Commission for their scalability, efficiency, and cost-effectiveness. Our report has been the inspiration for a new federal bill, the World Language Advancement and Readiness Act, introduced by David Price and cosigned by Don Young, Leonard Lance, and sixteen of their colleagues in the US House of Representatives. The act proposes three-year competitive grants to support local and state school districts to establish, improve, or expand innovative programs in world language learning.

The report was also an important influence on the Senate Labor, Health and Human Services, Education and Related Agencies Bill. It now includes a proposal for new and increased funding for Native American language immersion programs and a feasibility study for the creation of a new, national clearinghouse for best practices, curricula, and expertise in the preservation of native languages. The report has also been used in deliberations about the Senator Paul Simon Study Abroad Act, the Esther Martinez Native American Languages Preservation Act, and the Biliteracy Education Seal and Teaching (BEST) Act.

America's Languages also endorses more equitable opportunities for study abroad, since deep immersion in other cultures helps us understand the interests and outlook of other countries and how US policy affects our friends and competitors. Our report advocates resource-sharing consortia like the Big Ten Academic Alliance, which uses distance-learning technologies to provide instruction in more languages to more students enrolled in the alliance institutions. And it calls for more funding for Title VI centers, such as those in the Hamilton Lugar School of Global and International Studies at Indiana University Bloomington. For sixty years, Title VI language and national resource centers have provided so much of the scholarship, the research, the teaching tools, and the practical training that we need as a nation to engage the world around us effectively and knowledgeably. The centers have been important to our diplomatic and business interests, certainly, and they have also supported our efforts to live full and happy lives as citizens of the world. They are a critical national resource and should be maintained and enhanced for future generations.

The most important takeaway from the *America's Languages* report may be the one highlighted by Leon Panetta, former secretary of defense, in his op-ed published in the *San Francisco Chronicle*, supporting our recommendations. Secretary Panetta wrote:

> In times of great national security challenges, such as those we face today, as well as in times of great opportunity, such as the opening of new international markets, we find ourselves scrambling for people who can speak, write, and think in languages other than English. . . . Because it is difficult to find such people immediately, we are at a disadvantage. Language acquisition is a marathon, not a sprint. By the time we educate and train the experts we need to help us address a particular language gap, we are often too late. The crisis has shifted. Others have captured the new market.
> As a matter of public policy, this is a terribly inefficient way to operate.[8]

That is why *America's Languages* concludes by advancing "a wiser, more forward-thinking strategy . . . to steadily improve access to as many languages as possible," and not to wait until a specific need presents itself.[9]

So the first observation that I can offer, drawn from an Academy project, is that the best strategy for responding to an unpredictable and ever-changing world is also the broadest strategy. As individual students, we may aim for a depth of knowledge, the acquisition of a particular expertise. In the case of languages, we may strive for fluency as speakers, writers, and thinkers in a language other than English. But as institutions, and certainly as a nation, we should strive for breadth in our offerings, for mirroring the variety of the world at large in the courses we make available to our undergraduates and the expertise we provide to our graduate students. We cannot afford, particularly in international education, to chase intellectual fashion or focus on the latest global conflict to the exclusion of other regions, cultures, and languages. As a matter of educational and public policy, coverage—the ability to teach and learn about every region and culture—is the wisest goal and the best way to prepare ourselves for a rapidly changing world and an always-uncertain future.

The Commission on Language Learning follows up on the work of the Academy's Commission on the Humanities and Social Sciences, which produced its influential report, *The Heart of the Matter*, in 2013. That commission included over a dozen college presidents and many distinguished professors, business leaders, and a few household names, including George Lucas, Yo-Yo Ma, the actor John Lithgow, and Supreme Court Justice David Souter. They began their report by asking a simple question: "Who will lead America into a bright future?"

And the answer is, as stated in the report,

> citizens who are educated in the broadest possible sense, so that they can participate in their own governance and engage with the world. An adaptable and creative workforce. Experts in national security, equipped with the cultural understanding, knowledge of social dynamics, and language proficiency to lead our foreign service and military through complex global conflicts. Elected officials and a broader public who exercise civil political discourse, founded on an appreciation of the ways our differences and commonalities have shaped our rich history. We must prepare the next generation to be these future leaders.[10]

As promised in this preamble, the report advocated a broad education for all Americans, an education rich in the humanities and social sciences as well as the STEM fields. It included an entire section that listed ways to "equip the nation for leadership in an interconnected world," most prominently the promotion of language learning and study abroad. It also called for a new "national competitiveness" effort, a public-private partnership to help support education in international affairs and area studies.[11]

But *The Heart of the Matter* was not limited to the topics that commonly fall under the category of international education. It placed a value on all of the humanities and, in fact, on every academic discipline—sciences, social sciences, and humanities alike—as vital to the development of knowledgeable and intellectually flexible world citizens. The Commission understood that while we all find particular specialties in our chosen professions, we should be able to thrive outside of our careers as well, as citizens and community members, parents, church members, and volunteers in organizations helping people both at home and abroad. *The Heart of the Matter* report acknowledged that over a lifetime, we often find ourselves in need of more information and experience than our professional training can provide, and it offered a broad, liberal arts education as the remedy.

And so here is a second observation, this one drawn from *The Heart of the Matter*: our personal goal, as lifelong students, should be to attain a breadth of knowledge that allows us to take full advantage of opportunities as they arise and also to respond to challenges. *The Heart of the Matter* postulated that we can prepare ourselves for the future, even if we cannot predict what the future will look like, through the pursuit of a well-rounded education—before, during, and after our college years.

By now I hope that you are beginning to see in my remarks echoes of the Academy's founders, who set before us a vision of "cherishing every art and science." It is a hallmark of the Academy's work and the fundamental assumption that drives everything we do: that by cultivating every discipline and honoring every intellectual pursuit and profession, we are preparing ourselves and our nation for success in the face of uncertainty—both challenges and opportunities.

This is not a new thought, of course. It is a founding principle of the modern university. But it is an ideal that appears to be under some threat today, especially at public colleges and universities around the country, when cost cutting has become associated with the cutting of curricula— especially with the cutting of the humanities and related social sciences. I have no doubt that the trend will persist until we effectively combat the popular fallacy that the disciplines of linguistic and cultural analysis—history, literature, languages, global studies—are less practical, less rigorous, less lucrative, and therefore less valuable than the hard sciences. We cannot submit curricula to this kind of cost-benefit analysis. We cannot predict which disciplines will be considered valuable in the future, and any attempt to try is always and necessarily shortsighted. Knowledge does not conform to disciplinary boundaries, language barriers, or national borders—so neither can the pursuit of knowledge.

This connects to my third observation. All of us who are involved in some way in academic life—as students, faculty, and even learned societies like the American Academy—have new and valuable opportunities to form scholarly partnerships beyond our borders and to engage in more international collaborations. We should pursue such partnerships because they enhance the pursuit of knowledge. I also believe that such an international approach is, increasingly, a necessity in many fields. For example, the

Academy's 2014 report on basic scientific research, *Restoring the Foundation: The Vital Role of Research in Preserving the American Dream*, notes that many of the most transformative scientific discoveries of the last twenty-five years—like the Human Genome Project, the research into subatomic particles currently underway at CERN, and the operation of the Hubble Space Telescope—are all the work of multinational collaborations.[12] Conversely, our language commission report reminds us that we have missed some important opportunities by remaining insular and focused only on scholarship produced close to home. For example, in 2004, Americans and other English-speaking scientists were late in recognizing the severity of the avian flu epidemic because initial research on the disease was published in Chinese-language journals. I suspect that we are missing opportunities to address other challenges as well but perhaps fewer and fewer as technology improves and our networks reach across continents and oceans.

I offer three observations about the future of international education, all drawn from Academy work over the past five years.

First, as a nation, we should create a cadre of experts for every region, culture, and language—because we cannot predict how and where our lives will intersect with the rest of the world.

Second, as individuals, we should seek a well-rounded education in the sciences, social sciences, and humanities—including a familiarity with other cultures, languages, and histories. That kind of education is the best preparation for a changing world, no matter what your job may be or where you may live. It is also the best preparation for a life well lived, with an understanding of the world that surrounds us and an appreciation of our differences and commonalities, across international, cultural, and linguistic boundaries.

And third, as scholars and researchers, we should cultivate new relationships with colleagues from other countries, because knowledge has no borders and because other nations and cultures have so much to contribute to our own understanding of how the world works.

The challenge, of course, is how to sustain such an ambitious agenda with limited resources. Expertise is expensive. So is a broad-based education. And so are international partnerships.

As president of the American Academy, I met dozens of leaders in business and international relations, in science and medicine, in government, and in the arts who understand that their own efforts—as professionals, as citizens, even as parents—depend on a vast and ever-growing body of knowledge about the world around us. All of these sectors are sustained by the kind of education I have described today, and all can play a role in supporting our pursuits. It is critical that we find new ways to engage businesses, civic organizations, and others outside of academia in the education of future generations.

For example, in support of our *America's Languages* report, the Academy released a document called "Bridging America's Language Gap." The call to action is signed by over 150 organizations and thirty-five leaders who urge greater support for languages in order to maintain and enhance American global leadership, including Norman Augustine, retired chair and CEO of Lockheed Martin Corporation; Ruth A. Davis, former director general of the US Foreign Service; the documentary filmmaker Ken Burns; Robert Haas, chair emeritus of Levi Strauss & Co.; Melody Barnes, former director of the White House Domestic Policy Council; Rush Holt, CEO of the American Association for the Advancement of Science; and many others.

In one sense, "Bridging America's Language Gap" is a tool for future advocacy on behalf of language educators. It offers proof that a wide range of people and organizations consider language education to be critical to the future of the nation, and it presents that support in a way that policy makers find persuasive. But in another sense, the petition is a model for future action. It is itself a collaborative act, a vehicle through which the sectors can work together to support a vision of US education that is international at its very core.

I think that is a very hopeful message for all of us in academia. If approached in the right spirit and for the right reasons, people from every walk of life will help support the work you do. They understand its value, intuitively if not in its particulars. They will lend their names and reputations to the cause and possibly other kinds of support as well—not just financial but mentoring opportunities, internships, and on-the-job training. The benefits of such collaborations are too important to ignore.

And so, in conclusion, I believe we all need to think broadly about international education and the way it improves so many aspects of our lives and to remember that we have friends at every level of American society who are ready to help us prepare the next generations for lives that will be even more worldly than our own.

Notes

1. McRobbie, "Importance of Global Literacy."
2. Commission on Language Learning, *America's Languages*, 40.
3. Two members of the commission, Dan Davidson and Brian Edwards, also participated in this symposium, and they, along with a third member of the commission, Rosemary Geisdorfer Feal, have contributed chapters to this volume.
4. Commission on Language Learning, *America's Languages*, 5.
5. Daniel, Xie, and Kedia, "2014 U.S. Business Needs."
6. Commission on Language Learning, *America's Languages*, 6.
7. Ibid., x.
8. Panetta, "Americans Are Losing Out."
9. Commission on Language Learning, *America's Languages*, 30.
10. Commission on the Humanities and Social Sciences, *The Heart of the Matter*, 17.
11. Ibid., 12.
12. Committee on New Models, *Restoring the Foundation*.

Bibliography

Commission on Language Learning. *America's Languages: Investing in Language Education for the 21st Century*. American Academy of Arts and Sciences, February 2017. https://www.amacad.org/content/Research/researchproject.aspx?i=21896.

Commission on the Humanities and Social Sciences. *The Heart of the Matter: The Humanities and Social Sciences for a Vibrant, Competitive, and Secure Nation*. Cambridge, MA: American Academy of Arts and Sciences, 2013. https://www.amacad.org/content/Research/researchproject.aspx?d=286.

Committee on New Models for U.S. Science & Technology Policy. *Restoring the Foundation: The Vital Role of Research in Preserving the American Dream*. Cambridge, MA: American Academy of Arts and Sciences, 2014. https://www.amacad.org/restoringthefoundation.

Daniel, Shirley J., Fujiao Xie, and Ben L. Kedia. "2014 U.S. Business Needs for Employees with International Expertise." Paper presented at the Internationalization of U.S. Education in the 21st Century: The Future of International and Foreign Language Studies conference, College of William & Mary, Williamsburg, VA, April 13, 2014. http://www.wm.edu/offices/revescenter/globalengagement/internationalization/papers%20and%20presentations/danielkediafull.pdf.

McRobbie, Michael A. "The Importance of Global Literacy and The Role of the University as a Gateway to the World." *Huffington Post*, November 11, 2015. https://www.huffpost.com/entry/the-importance-of-global-_1_b_8534416.

Panetta, Leon. "Americans Are Losing Out Because So Few Speak a Second Language." *San Francisco Chronicle*, August 6, 2018. https://www.sfchronicle.com/opinion/openforum/article/Americans-are-losing-out-because-so-few-speak-a-13135901.php.

CROSSROADS 2

LEGACIES OF TITLE VI, AREA,
AND GLOBAL STUDIES

8

IN PRAISE OF TITLE VI

Stephen E. Hanson

IN 2018, WE CELEBRATED THE sixtieth anniversary of the founding of the Title VI programs for the support of teaching and research in area studies, foreign languages, and international affairs managed by the US Department of Education.[1] This was a remarkable milestone, given the persistent attacks on Title VI from both within and outside the academy over the past several decades. Indeed, it seems that virulent criticism of Title VI unites a wide range of constituencies that would otherwise seem to have little in common. Left-wing commentators decry area studies centers and US government support for them as relics of the Cold War era and argue that global studies programs at universities today must reject the regional boundaries and federal priorities of Title VI as outmoded products of US imperialism.[2] Right-wing critics, by contrast, see Title VI as supporting an often radical academic approach to world affairs that is unjustifiably critical of US foreign policy priorities—especially concerning the US alliance with Israel.[3] Within academia itself, advocates of rational choice theory and "big data" approaches to the analysis of international relations view area studies scholars as hopelessly out of date and unscientific.[4] Those of us who have consistently defended the value of an in-depth understanding of the polities, economies, and cultures of diverse world regions as a core element of US higher education have often found ourselves fending off attacks from all these opposing groups simultaneously.

The questions thus naturally arise: What is the likelihood that Title VI of the Higher Education Act in its present form will survive in the decades ahead? Is there any chance that we will be in a position to commemorate the centennial of Title VI in 2058? I must at the outset confess my personal bias concerning this issue: I have benefited from Title VI support over the course of my entire academic career. As a graduate student at the University of California, Berkeley, studying the Soviet Union in the 1980s, a summer

Foreign Language and Area Studies (FLAS) Fellowship allowed me to take my first trip to Saint Petersburg (then Leningrad) to gain fluency in the Russian language. As a junior scholar at the University of Washington (UW) in Seattle in the 1990s, I benefited greatly from the contacts and resources generated by Title VI National Resource Center grants to what is now the Herbert J. Ellison Center for Russian, East European and Central Asian Studies (REECAS) of the Jackson School of International Studies. During the 2000s, as director of REECAS at the University of Washington, I relied on the Title VI programs to support faculty colleagues across multiple academic schools and departments, dozens of graduate students obtaining regional expertise (including a number of foreign area officers from the US Army and Air Force), and members of the Seattle community with a personal interest in the postcommunist region. Now, as vice provost for international affairs and director of the Reves Center for International Studies at the College of William & Mary, I continue to rely on faculty whose regional expertise and language training are the direct result of Title VI funding to the universities that granted them their graduate degrees. For well over three decades, I have seen firsthand just how much good these programs do.

I would even make the case that without the continuation of Title VI funding for global and regional studies centers at US universities, the field of Russian, East European, and Eurasian studies as we know it would likely have been eviscerated after the end of the Cold War. Those of us who began our careers in this field in the 1990s can well remember the ubiquity of the then-dominant view that the expertise of "former Sovietologists" had become irrelevant with the collapse of the USSR. In a decade in which the United States had emerged as the sole world superpower, when powerful new forms of information technology promised to usher in a new global order of democracy, prosperity, and peace, and influential scholars declared that the end of communism meant the "end of history" itself, it was certainly a challenge to defend the continuing value of seemingly arcane knowledge of Russian, East European, and Central Asian histories, languages, and cultures.[5] By the end of the 1990s, pundits were openly declaring that "Russia [was] finished"—doomed to sink into perpetual marginality in global geopolitics as a result of systemic corruption, demographic crisis, and military ineptitude.[6] And after the horrifying terrorist attacks of September 11, 2001, public attention shifted inexorably to the Middle East. In such an environment, the prospect of obtaining significant Title VI funding for the study of

Russia and its neighbors became one of the few incentives that could some-times still persuade skeptical university administrators to maintain institu-tional support for teaching and research about the postcommunist region.

Today, of course, it is obvious to everyone—including Francis Fuku-yama—that the collapse of the Soviet Union did not bring about the end of history. Russia has emerged once again as a significant actor in world affairs, invading the territory of its neighbors Georgia and Ukraine, inter-vening forcefully in Syria, and utilizing disinformation to sow discord in a number of previously stable Western democracies. As during the Cold War, informed observers worry about the lack of sufficient expertise in Russian, East European, and Central Asian studies in US foreign policy-making cir-cles.[7] While the continuation of Title VI support, along with the generosity and foresight of foundations like the Carnegie Corporation, has provided a lifeline to a new generation of specialists on postcommunist affairs over the past three decades, concerns continue to be raised about the future sustain-ability of the field.[8] Title VI funding thus remains a vital foundation for the development of expertise on Russia, East Europe, and Central Asia—as it has been for the past six decades.

The broader lessons here go well beyond the postcommunist region. The precarious fate of Russian, East European, and Central Asian studies after the collapse of the Soviet bloc illustrates a larger problem: US foreign policy priorities tend to shift quickly in response to recent developments, while genuine expertise in regional affairs takes decades to nurture. As a result, we are usually woefully unprepared when new threats to national security emerge in understudied parts of the world. Contrary to realist theories of international relations, it is typically not rivalry among established great powers but rather the impact of previously marginal movements in neglect-ed regions that poses the greatest challenge to US national interests. Few in the presidential administration of Woodrow Wilson expected Vladimir Lenin's Bolsheviks to emerge victorious after the fall of czarism in March 1917, yet this tiny group of radical revolutionaries created a regime that ulti-mately challenged US interests on every continent. Germany after its defeat in World War I, too, was thought to be fatally weakened for the foreseeable future, but by the 1930s, the initially marginal Adolf Hitler and his Nazi Party emerged as the greatest threat to democratic values and human rights the world has ever known. At the time of the 9/11 attacks, there were almost no specialists in Afghan affairs in academic or government settings; as a result, the US government was left scrambling to find capable speakers of Dari, Pashto, and other regional languages. Similarly, only a paltry number of fluent speakers of Arabic were stationed in the US Embassy in Baghdad during the US invasion of Iraq in 2003.[9] In sum, the historical record clearly shows that US policy makers will always need a corps of experts on every world region—especially those not (yet) in the headlines. For this purpose, stable Title VI funding serves a vital national security interest.

The case for Title VI does not rest solely on its importance for national defense, however. Not only does the cultivation of deep expertise on diverse world regions help to defend the nation against new foreign policy threats, it also helps US citizens take advantage of emerging opportunities abroad. In an increasingly globalized economy, employers and government agencies alike rate knowledge of foreign languages and cultures as a highly desirable skill set for new employees.[10] Study abroad and other forms of cross-cultural immersion have been shown to be positively correlated with academic achievement, personal self-confidence, and, perhaps counterintuitively, increased patriotism as well.[11] The weight of the evidence suggests that deep exposure to diverse global cultures and perspectives really does contribute to the development of a more tolerant and efficacious citizenry.

At this point, no doubt some readers would protest that my defense of our existing Title VI programs is too one-sided in its praise. Surely, such readers might ask, our scholarly understanding has progressed beyond outmoded divisions of the world into discrete cultural regions such as those institutionalized in Cold War area studies programs? Surely globalization has proceeded far enough that we must now study the postcommunist region, Western Europe, East Asia, Southeast Asia, South Asia, the Middle East, Africa, Latin America, and North America not as disconnected units but instead as interconnected entities enmeshed in global flows of capital, labor, migration, and information?[12] Shouldn't we try to move beyond the established Title VI framework so as to redesign federal support for global education to respond to these new global conditions?

Such criticisms of Title VI funding priorities arise out of good intentions. Yet they are fundamentally misguided nonetheless. The reality is that the current array of programs supported by Title VI of the Higher Education Act is remarkably well suited to meet the global challenges and opportunities the United States faces in the twenty-first century. Of course, occasional updating and revision of Title VI program priorities is salutary;

in fact, such updating has gone on continuously over the past six decades. But there is no need for any radical change in the way Title VI is organized.

I would also argue that an unabashed defense of Title VI in its current configuration within the Department of Education well serves both the national interest and the interests of the academic community. This is true for three reasons: first, any alternative would require an unlikely resolution of complex collective action problems; second, Title VI costs the US taxpayer remarkably little, given its demonstrable benefits to the country; and third, Title VI programming is already at the cutting edge of current thinking about how best to reform higher education.

The first reason that the academic community should defend existing Title VI programs is simple: given current political realities, it is almost impossible to imagine building a winning coalition to support any alternative to them. The root of the problem here is that the benefits provided by Title VI—the generation of expertise on global regions and cultures and the acquisition of greater cultural understanding by the broader public—are in essence public goods. No one individual can make a meaningful contribution to the creation of such goods on her or his own, yet once regional expertise and global cultural competence are reasonably well established in a given country, every individual citizen benefits from their existence. As Mancur Olson taught us long ago, the provision of public goods of this type represents a collective action problem: rationally, each individual should choose not to sacrifice her or his own interests to preserve a given public good but should instead become a "free rider" on the efforts of others.[13] This well-known problem in economic theory explains why the provision of public goods does not automatically emerge from market competition but instead typically requires the imposition of special institutional incentives by central governments or other external actors.

The logical conclusion that flows from this analysis is that while it might be relatively easy to destroy the existing institutional framework of Title VI programs in the US Department of Education, organizing a sufficient number of individual politicians, bureaucrats, academics, and citizens in support of any particular alternative would be a daunting task at best. Some radical academic critics of Title VI might prefer, for example, to design global studies programs with an explicitly anti-imperialist intent, but they would find few if any allies in Congress or the federal bureaucracy. Conversely, right-wing critics of Title VI might want to implement more stringent requirements that federally funded area studies centers align with contemporary US foreign policy priorities, but the result would be far less interest and support for area and regional studies by faculty experts at major US universities.

Moreover, the political conditions that allowed for broad bipartisanship in the creation of Title VI after the launch of Sputnik in 1957 are mostly absent today. Political polarization between Republicans and Democrats is at its highest level since the US Civil War, making it almost impossible to pass major bipartisan legislation of any sort, and a broad swath of public opinion is highly skeptical about new taxpayer-funded initiatives in general. In such an environment, it is hard to imagine how a new legislative proposal to design and implement a radically different set of programs to support the dissemination of regional expertise and global cultural competence would gain bipartisan sponsorship, pass both houses of Congress, and be signed into law by the US president. But since Title VI programs provide a public good, they are unlikely to be replaced by the spontaneous workings of the market economy.

This brings us to the second reason why those of us who support the cause of international education should support Title VI without qualification: these programs are remarkably inexpensive. The entire annual budget of Title VI and Fulbright-Hays in 2018, about $72 million, amounts to approximately 0.1 percent of the annual budget of the US Department of Education—which itself amounts to approximately 10 percent of the annual budget of the US Department of Defense.[14] To be blunt, in the rough-and-tumble world of lobbying over major federal outlays on Capitol Hill, Title VI funding is pocket change. And yet this funding has sustained dozens of major centers for teaching, research, and outreach to the community about polities, economies, and cultures in every region of the world; trained generations of experts in academia, business, the US military, and the NGO sector; and exposed countless students in K-12 schools, community colleges, minority-serving institutions of higher learning, and research universities to global perspectives other than their own. It is hard to imagine a greater bargain for the US taxpayer.

Indeed, the fact that Title VI is basically a rounding error in the context of the overall annual US federal budget is itself a serious political problem, since it is much harder to organize lobbying efforts and raise political awareness about such a small set of programs in competition with massive, well-funded lobbyists fighting for their share of (say) federal defense appropriations, farm subsidies, or health care spending. Even within academia itself, some federal relations officers at major US research universities are understandably tempted to spend most of their time and energy defending Pell Grants and research funding from the National Science Foundation and National Institutes of Health rather than focusing on the preservation of Title VI. When academics themselves start attacking Title VI programs as outmoded or reactionary, university administrators become even less interested in lobbying for them. Were it not for the truly superhuman efforts of Miriam Kazanjian of the Coalition for International Education to rally the supporters of Title VI at critical moments, Title VI might well have been eliminated long ago.

That Title VI is inexpensive and that these programs would be hard or impossible to replace politically were they to disappear are not by themselves sufficient reasons to fight for its preservation. What makes the case for Title VI absolutely watertight is that these programs are, simply put, fantastic. They give scholars of all backgrounds the support to gain true fluency in the foreign languages they need for their research as well as deep personal familiarity with the regional contexts they study. They provide a lifeline to teachers of less commonly taught languages—including several that are vital to US national security—that would otherwise almost certainly be unsupported in US university curricula. They help to preserve major university library collections in foreign languages at a time of severe budget cuts for new acquisitions. They afford opportunities for US military officers, future government officials, and business leaders to gain graduate-level training in global and regional affairs. They give students from less-advantaged backgrounds the financial resources necessary to support their university educations and to study abroad. They generate innovative pedagogical approaches and new curricular materials for foreign language and area studies teaching used at K-12 institutions across the country. In countless ways, Title VI programs enrich the nation by making global perspectives accessible to the US citizenry.

In fact, the design of Title VI funding streams responds effectively to several of the greatest contemporary demands for the reform of US higher education. First, Title VI programs are genuinely interdisciplinary. At a time when university administrators around the world are striving to find innovative ways to break down the silos separating faculty and students in different academic departments and professional schools, Title VI's National Resource Centers, Centers for International Business, and Undergraduate

International Studies and Foreign Language grants already represent successful examples of robust interdisciplinary and interschool collaboration. Second, Title VI programs are genuinely diverse and inclusive. From the beginning, Title VI administrators have placed a central emphasis on ensuring that the work Title VI supports is disseminated broadly to a variety of stakeholders, including foreign language and culture programming for primary and secondary schools, joint programs with community colleges and minority-serving institutions, outreach to the business community, and programming on world affairs for interested members of the general public. Third, Title VI programs are—against all odds—still fundamentally bipartisan. At a time when concerns about a perceived lack of ideological diversity within US academia are being raised with increasing intensity, Title VI stands out as a federal program that has attracted congressional support from thoughtful Democrats and Republicans alike since its inception. If one were to tell a group of randomly selected university presidents that a new federal education program might successfully catalyze interdisciplinarity, diversity and inclusion, and bipartisanship simultaneously, most would be highly skeptical. Yet Title VI has been producing all of these outcomes consistently for six decades now.

Can we maintain or even expand federal funding for Title VI programs at the Department of Education in the decades ahead? The analysis above makes it crystal clear that this goal should be a high priority for everyone in the field of international education. It also generates several recommendations for individuals wishing to help support this cause. First, those of us within academia need to recognize that the repeated intellectual critiques of existing Title VI priorities from both left-wing and right-wing authors, as well as from rational choice theorists, have taken a real toll, making it harder over time to rally collective action by faculty, university administrators, legislators, and federal officials in support of these programs. Reasonable criticisms of one or another priority or evaluation tool within the Title VI framework should of course be welcomed—but bashing the entire framework that makes these programs possible is an academic luxury our community can no longer afford. Second, given that the amount of federal money devoted to these programs is so small, those of us in the field of international education should adopt a "big tent" approach to our collective efforts to rally support. Rather than compete for tiny slices of existing funding streams, we should be working together to greatly expand the resources available for this important cause. Title VI, international exchanges, study abroad, foreign language training, and scientific research on pressing global challenges should thus not be seen as competing priorities but rather as complementary activities that all require additional federal, corporate, foundation, and private funding. Finally, even in a world increasingly affected by innovations in artificial intelligence, robotics, and big-data approaches to social science, we should never be shy about trumpeting the value of an in-depth understanding of regional histories, polities, economies, societies, and cultures. Indeed, advances in information technology have only increased the importance of training future graduates to understand and empathize with world views and cultural perspectives other than their own—a uniquely human skill set that computers are unlikely to master for the foreseeable future.[15]

Notes

1. Technically, Title VI of the Higher Education Act is jointly administered with the Fulbright-Hays programs in the US Department of Education. I will simply use the term *Title VI* in the text for convenience.
2. Bale, "When Arabic"; Poblete, *Critical Latin American.*
3. Kramer, *Ivory Towers*; Kurtz, "Taking Sides."
4. Bates, "Area Studies," 166–69; Mayer-Schoenberger and Cukier, *Big Data.*
5. Fukuyama, "End of History?," 3–18.
6. Tayler, "Russia Is Finished," 35–52.
7. Demirjian, "Lack of Russia Experts."
8. Gerber, *Report on the State of Russian Studies in the U.S.*
9. Baker and Hamilton, *Iraq Study Group Report*, 60.
10. Daniel, Kedia, and Xie, "U.S. Business Needs."
11. Sutton and Rubin, "Documenting"; Jones, "Exploring," 682–705.
12. Glover and Kollman, *Relevant/Obsolete?*
13. Olson, *Logic.*
14. Department of Education figures calculated from "2018 Congressional Action Table" from US Department of Education, Budget Office, "Department of Education Fiscal Year 2018 Congressional Action," March 27, 2018, https://www2.ed.gov/about/overview/budget/budget18/18action.pdf.
15. Aoun, *Robot-Proof.*

Bibliography

Aoun, Joseph. *Robot-Proof: Higher Education in the Age of Artificial Intelligence*. Cambridge, MA: MIT Press, 2017.

Baker, James A., III, and Lee H. Hamilton, co-chairs. *Iraq Study Group Report*. New York: Vintage Books, 2006.

Bale, Jeffrey. "When Arabic Is the 'Target' Language: National Security, Title VI, and Arabic Language Programs, 1958–1991." PhD diss., Arizona State University, 2008.

Bates, Robert. "Area Studies and the Discipline: A Useful Controversy?" *PS: Political Science and Politics* 30, no. 2 (1997): 166–69.

Daniel, Shirley J., Ben Kedia, and Fujiao Xie. "U.S. Business Needs for Employees with International Expertise." Report presented at the Internationalization of U.S Education in the Twenty-First Century: The Future of International and Foreign Language Studies conference, College of William & Mary, Williamsburg, VA, April 13, 2014.

Demirjian, Karoun. "Lack of Russia Experts Has Some in U.S. Worried." *Washington Post*, December 30, 2015. https://www.washingtonpost.com/news/powerpost/wp/2015/12/30/lack-of-russia-experts-has-the-u-s-playing-catch-up/.

Fukuyama, Francis. "The End of History?," *National Interest*, July 1, 1989, 3–18.

Gerber, Theodore P. *Report on the State of Russian Studies in the U.S.: An Assessment by the Association for Slavic, East European and Eurasian Studies.* Pittsburgh: ASEES, 2015. https://www.aseees.org/sites/default/files/downloads/FINAL-ASEEES-assessment-report_0.pdf.

Glover, William, and Ken Kollman, eds. *Relevant/Obsolete? Area Studies in the U.S. Academy.* Ann Arbor: University of Michigan Press, 2012.

Jones, Calvert W. "Exploring the Microfoundations of International Community: Toward a Theory of Enlightened Nationalism." *International Studies Quarterly* 58, no. 4 (2014): 682–705.

Kramer, Martin. *Ivory Towers on Sand: The Failure of Middle East Studies in America.* Washington, DC: Washington Institute for Near East Policy, 2001.

Kurtz, Stanley. "Taking Sides on Title VI." *National Review*, December 12, 2007. https://www.nationalreview.com/2007/12/taking-sides-title-vi-stanley-kurtz/.

Mayer-Schoenberger, Viktor, and Kenneth Cukier. *Big Data: A Revolution That Will Transform How We Will Live, Work, and Think.* Boston: Houghton Mifflin Harcourt, 2013.

McGinn, Gail. "Government Needs and Shortages in Foreign Language and Regional Expertise and Knowledge." Report presented at the Internationalization of U.S Education in the Twenty-First Century: The Future of International and Foreign Language Studies conference, College of William & Mary, Williamsburg, VA, April 11–13, 2014.

Olson, Mancur. *The Logic of Collective Action: Public Goods and the Theory of Groups.* Cambridge, MA: Harvard University Press, 1968.

Poblete, Juan. *Critical Latin American and Latino Studies.* Minneapolis: University of Minnesota Press, 2003.

Sutton, Richard C., and Donald L. Rubin. "Documenting the Academic Impact of Study Abroad: Final Report of the GLOSSARI Project." Paper presented at the Annual Conference of NAFSA: Association for International Educators, Kansas City, MO, June 2010.

Tayler, Jeffrey. "Russia Is Finished." *Atlantic Monthly* 285, no. 5 (2001): 35–52.

9

THE POLITICAL ECONOMY OF INTERNATIONAL EDUCATION IN THE UNITED STATES

Kris Olds

ONE OF THE MOST INTERESTING consequences of studying and then working in several countries, before eventually moving in 2001 to the United States, is having your eyes opened to the taken-for-granted dimensions of higher education in the United States. When I moved to Madison, Wisconsin—after being raised in Canada, studying for a PhD in England, and, subsequently, working in England and Singapore—I was warmly welcomed by a large and diverse number of colleagues at the Center for Southeast Asian Studies, one of eight Title VI-supported National Resource Centers (NRCs) at the University of Wisconsin–Madison (UW-Madison) at that time. These centers were part of the International Institute, which was jointly managed by the College of Letters and Science and the Division of International Studies.[1]

After moving to Madison, I quickly learned how vibrant the faculty, staff, and students were and committed to international education, including language, area, and global and international studies. The university's NRCs, some of which were founded with federal government monies in the early 1960s (before they were deemed NRCs), played an integral role in facilitating a vast array of courses at the undergraduate and graduate levels across all of the world's regions. Over sixty languages were taught at UW-Madison when I arrived, including a dizzying array of less commonly taught languages (e.g., Hmong, Khmer, and Burmese), both during regular term and via intensive and high-impact summer language institutes. The people associated with these centers organized and implemented multiple outreach programs at the K-12 level in Madison and beyond, while also contributing to a variety of less visible but nevertheless important forms of public and institutional service, such as hosting visiting diplomats and their staff, helping European Commission officials learn about technology transfer from publicly minded public universities, and using area studies center capacity to help facilitate the global circulation of knowledge via book series, online news platforms, and so on.[2]

The seemingly taken-for-granted dimensions of this array of international education activity, which is matched if not exceeded across the United States in such universities as Indiana University Bloomington and the University of Washington in Seattle, were different from anything that I had experienced at the University of British Columbia (where I completed my BA and MA degrees), the University of Bristol in England (where I completed my PhD), or the National University of Singapore (where I worked for four years before moving to the United States). These three research universities also have strong to very strong international education agendas and capacity, though, for all their strengths, they lacked the sheer breadth and depth of interests and associated programming in the majority or all of the world's regions that was evident at UW–Madison. The University of British Columbia, for example, had very strong Asian studies programs, given the location of the university, export trading relations across the Pacific, and the Pacific Rim developmental agenda of the 1980s, but was lacking equivalent capacities regarding African studies and Latin American studies.[3] The National University of Singapore, in turn, had deep capacity in East and Southeast Asian studies but was lacking capacity in European studies, African studies, and Latin American studies.

So where did breadth and depth in international education come from at UW–Madison in particular and in US public research universities more generally? I would like to suggest that it was enabled by a variety of structural changes in society and economy but that Title VI area studies and language funding played the key difference in driving forward and sustaining international education activities on many US university campuses. And it did so for a remarkably small amount of money—the aggregate equivalent of eleven US college football coaches' salaries, or 18 percent of Cambridge University Press's annual revenue—as I will discuss later in this chapter.[4]

The first factor underlying the breadth and depth in international education on US campuses is historical in nature and generated a path dependency dynamic of gradual areal expansion and deepening with respect to area studies expertise. The majority of the host universities of NRCs have the "DNA" of the public land-grant university. The Land Grant College Act (or Morrill Act) of 1862 enabled public universities in the United States to acquire the material resources and associated public service missions to expand over time and better serve society on a number of levels, including with respect to socioeconomic development. While originally focused at the state scale, public land-grant universities progressively became more involved with respect to research and service at the national and then international levels. The long history of national and then international activity of land-grant universities (like Michigan State University, for example) made them prime candidates for Title VI support after the approval of the National Defense Education Act of 1958.[5]

Second, the breadth and depth of international education at public universities that received Title VI support since 1958 were also indirectly supported via massification and associated investment (a term you hear less and less out of politicians' mouths these days) by US states in their universities. On massification, as noted by the National Center for Educational Statistics, the growth of university enrollment from the 1950s for the next several decades was historically unprecedented as "large numbers of young people entered college and second, public colleges expanded dramatically to meet the demand. College enrollment rose by 49 percent in the 1950s, partly because of the rise in the enrollment/population ratio from 15 percent to 24 percent. During the 1960s, enrollment rose by 120 percent." And even though this growth slowed, enrollment still "rose by 45 percent" in the 1970s.[6]

Such structural change in US higher education ensured that large numbers of faculty needed to be hired, campus infrastructures could be expanded, an abundance of area studies courses could be created, and numerous languages could be taught, though all subject to institutional commitment to international education. This said, similar demographic transitions took place in Canada and, to a lesser degree, in the United Kingdom, where universities also grew and hired additional faculty. The breadth and depth of international education programs and offerings did not, however, grow like they did at US universities. So these demographic structural shifts are not the only explanation for why international education offerings are so broad and deep at public research universities hosting NRCs and foreign language area studies (FLAS) programs.

The National Defense Education Act and Its Legacy of Title VI Programs: Making the Difference

The above structural changes supporting the growth of the faculty base that was in place to take advantage of the emergence of the National Defense

Education Act (NDEA) enabled Title VI funding. As is evident in figure 9.1, funding began in 1958 and only grew by approximately $20 million (in current dollars) from 1958 to 1990—a remarkably small growth level considering that these were the years of the Cold War and Vietnam War. The early years of this program were more focused than they are now and were more tightly integrated into realizing US geopolitical agendas via drawing in and cultivating university-based expertise in area studies.[7] That being said, Higher Education Act Title VI funding was quite limited and at risk of being ended multiple times, especially from 1970 on.[8]

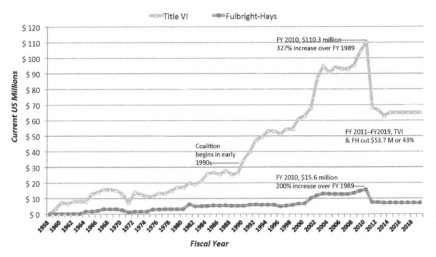

Figure 9.1. Higher Education Act Title VI and Fulbright-Hays funding history (fiscal years 1959–2019). *Source: ©Miriam A. Kazanjian, Coalition for International Education. Reprinted with permission.*

The 1989 to 2010 period was marked by relatively rapid growth in the allocation of US federal monies to support international education. And while there was a significant plunge in funding levels from 2010 to 2013, and funding flatlined to the low $70 millions from 2013 on, the funding continued to make an important difference on multiple US university campuses, including the one I moved to in 2001.

These monies helped fuel the creation and maintenance of area studies centers, language programs, research programs, outreach programs, international partnerships, and so on. For example, Title VI directed funding through 2018 to UW-Madison to train "close to 6,000 Foreign Language

Area Studies (FLAS) fellows" and award "over 5,000 degrees and certificates through NRCs."[9] This is accomplished with a modest annual investment of approximately $4 million per year in the current budget cycle.

Title VI funding, even if widely distributed across dozens of campuses in the United States, has major leveraging power. This federal government funding is purposively complemented by extramural funding and support via other US government departments (e.g., Department of Defense monies for language flagship programs); such private nonprofit institutions as the Rockefeller, Ford, Henry Luce, and Andrew W. Mellon Foundations; research and development agency funding (e.g., the National Science Foundation, USAID); and associated organizations, such as the Social Science Research Council and the American Council of Learned Societies. The funds also blend with university monies provided by state governments' tuition revenue and indirect cost charges, which leads to a complex thicket of revenue that maintains the depth and breadth of international education activity that I took note of when I moved here.

It is genuinely shocking how much international education activity is directly and indirectly supported for a relatively modest amount of money (see fig. 9.2).

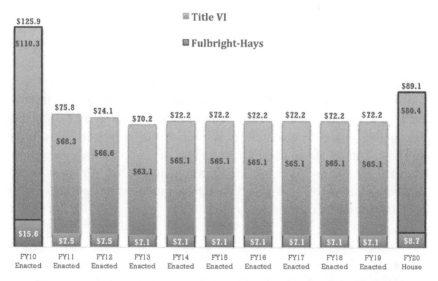

Figure 9.2. US Department of Education Title VI and Fulbright-Hays funding (fiscal years 2010–20) in millions USD. *Source: ©Miriam A. Kazanjian, Coalition for International Education. Reprinted with permission.*

Title VI area studies centers and language offerings are national and international gems; they are amazing strategic resources with respect to knowledge production, teaching, and learning that help the United States better understand the world and better represent the United States via partnerships, joint ventures, diplomacy, and so on. From my now insider-outsider perspective, I would agree that they are "America's foundational programs for international education," as stated by the Coalition for International Education.[10] This sum—$72.2 million, distributed across the entire United States—is equivalent to

- the approximate annual cost of maintaining utilities at UW-Madison,
- the approximate cost of a new student dorm building that provides one thousand beds (two per room),
- the approximate cost of building a 100,000-square-foot academic / light research building,
- the approximate cost of building fifteen hundred elevated parking garage spaces, and
- the equivalent of the aggregate salaries of the top eleven US college football coaches in 2018.[11]

Title VI-funded activity also directly and indirectly supports the internationalization strategies of many US universities, a key strategic agenda that the vast majority of US universities have formalized and prioritized over the last several decades. Title VI-funded activity does this via providing or accentuating capabilities to bring to life the tangible mechanisms that realize internationalization. Internationalization, which can be defined as "an ongoing process of change whose objective is to integrate the institution and its key stakeholders (its students and faculty) into the emerging global knowledge economy," is brought to life via such activity.[12] Or consider this broader definition of "comprehensive internationalization," put forward by NAFSA's John Hudzik:

> a commitment, confirmed through action, to infuse international and comparative perspectives throughout the teaching, research, and service missions of higher education. It shapes institutional ethos and values and touches the entire higher education enterprise. It is essential that it be embraced by institutional leadership, governance, faculty, students, and all academic service and support units. It is an institutional imperative, not just a desirable possibility.
>
> Comprehensive internationalization not only impacts all of campus life but the institution's external frames of reference, partnerships, and relations.

The global reconfiguration of economies, systems of trade, research, and communication, and the impact of global forces on local life, dramatically expand the need for comprehensive internationalization and the motivations and purposes driving it.[13]

Consider the wide array of mechanisms used to entangle US universities with non-US universities and with the societies and economies in which their partner universities are embedded. We hear, for example, about international collaborative degrees (dual and joint degrees), study abroad, branch campuses, massive open online courses, joint advising, joint programs, memoranda of understanding, joint publishing across institutions, and so on. Richard Edelstein and John Douglass created a useful taxonomy of clusters of activity, each with its own modes of engagement:[14]

- Cluster 1—Individual Faculty Initiatives
  - research collaboration
  - teaching and curriculum development
  - academic program leadership
  - sanctioning authority
- Cluster 2—Managing Institutional Demography
  - international student recruitment
  - recruitment of foreign academic and administrative staff
  - visiting scholars and lecturers
  - short courses, conferences, and visiting delegations
  - summer sessions, extension programs, and language-acquisition programs
- Cluster 3—Mobility Initiatives
  - exchange and mobility programs
  - study abroad programs, internships, service learning, research projects, and practicums
- Cluster 4—Curricular and Pedagogical Change
  - incremental curricular change
  - foreign language and culture
  - cross-cultural communication and intercultural competence
  - new pedagogies and learning technologies
  - extracurricular and student-initiated activities
- Cluster 5—Transnational Engagements
  - collaboration and partnerships with foreign institutions
  - dual, double, and joint degrees
  - multisite joint degrees
  - articulation agreements, twinning, and franchising
  - research-intensive partnerships
  - strategic alliances
  - branch campuses, satellite offices, and gateways

- Cluster 6—Network Building
  - academic and scholarly networks
  - consortia
  - alumni networks
- Cluster 7—Campus Culture, Ethos, and Symbolic Action
  - international ethos: changing campus culture
  - engaged leadership

Every single one of these clusters and modes of engagement is furthered, albeit variably, by Title VI-related funding and programs of activity, with Title VI monies acting as the fuel for comprehensive internationalization. This synergy multiplies the impact of Title VI monies and agendas, both for the Department of Education and for the universities on a genuine win-win basis, while rationalizing department expectations for some university-provided cost sharing.

Risks, Stress Points, and International Education Futures

How is it possible that "Title VI/Fulbright-Hays has served as the nation's *primary* Federal supporter of language education" in an era when the "United States today faces unprecedented demand for globally competent citizens and professionals" (my emphasis) and the program's annual budget is equivalent to the aggregate salaries of the top eleven US college football coaches in 2018?[15] This is a disorienting question to consider and reflects, in my opinion, a situation where the capacity of US public universities—especially land-grant universities—to contribute to national development goals is so taken for granted that it has become a national security risk factor.

When a disjuncture exists between policy ambition and programmatic funding level, the monies that are invested matter, and in a major way. Every time there is a battle over the future of Title VI funding for NRCs, Language Resource Centers (LRCs), Fulbrights, and so on, huge waves of concern ripple through US universities that were recipients of past awards.

Moreover, there are a variety of other changes to the system and institutional contexts in which those charged with the core responsibilities of international education and internationalization need to work. Higher education in the United States has undergone major restructuring over the last several decades, and this is in many ways making Title VI funding even more important.

The most important change, by far, is austerity-induced reductions in levels of state government support for universities, including for the US public universities that offer most foreign language and graduate education programming, as well as undergraduate area studies courses and community outreach in the international education area. The US-based Center on Budget and Policy Priorities has captured one aspect of these startling reductions of state support in figure 9.3.

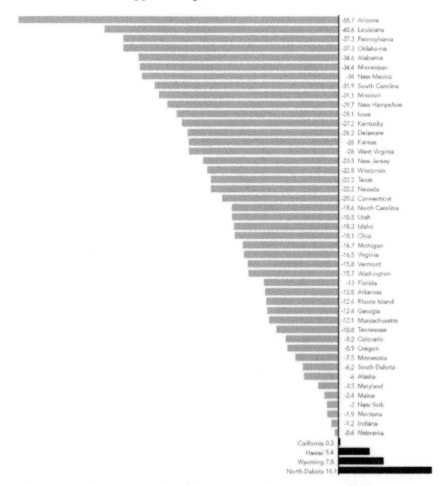

Figure 9.3. State funding for higher education in the United States (percent change per student, inflation adjusted, 2008–18). *Source: Center on Budget and Policy Priorities (CBPP). Reprinted with permission.*

Only two of twenty-three states associated with NRC and FLAS grantees in fiscal years 2018–21 chose not to cut their higher education budgets. The average reduction for all host states was 17 percent (2008–18), with three Title VI recipient states—Arizona, Louisiana, and Pennsylvania—topping this particular austerity chart.

The ripple effects of austerity are plentiful and have been heavily debated and contested across the entire country for the last decade. Effects that are most relevant for international education include the following, though they vary considerably across institutions and are also intertwined on individual university campuses in complex ways.

First, austerity drives the restructuring of departments, especially in the humanities fields, which have historically been the ones most responsible for language education. This restructuring process often involves mergers and the associated fusing of teaching programs and administrative support systems, which destabilize language education units and staff. Positive outcomes of change processes depend on considerable amounts of effort, leadership, trust, and goodwill.

Second, austerity leads to reduced faculty lines, including failure to replace language and area studies faculty who retire or depart for other universities. This decline is intersecting with changes in the professional titles and the nature of employment contracts of language educators. Area studies and language education experts across the country are raising concerns about the attractiveness, stability, and risks associated with language education careers and positions.

Third, austerity reduces course offerings, especially ones that are area studies in nature and are taught on a sufficiently regular basis. This can slow down time to graduation and lead to equivalencies being sought through other effective but less-than-ideal offerings.

Fourth, due to all of the above and reduced student demand, we see a decline, albeit an uneven one, in the teaching of less commonly taught languages, especially in the last decade.[16]

Fifth, austerity enhances competition for graduate students between major research universities that are recipients of Title VI monies, including with funding for FLAS fellowships. Graduate offers in research universities are increasingly "full packages" of funding, but these cannot include multiyear guarantees of FLAS monies, given the nature of FLAS funding restrictions. On a related note, many US universities are seeking to enhance the level and equity of teaching assistant (TA) support, which is to be encouraged, but this can have disruptive workload impacts on the units historically responsible for language education, where workload expectations for TA positions are highly variable.

Sixth, austerity facilitates the loss or reduction of administrative capacity to support the broader organizational units that Title VI–funded centers, programs, and initiatives are associated with.

And seventh, austerity underlies the emergence and implementation of new budgeting models (e.g., performance-based budgeting, activity-based budgeting, responsibility-centered management) that have high potential to structurally penalize departments and programs that have less generative capacity to scale up undergraduate enrollment numbers and credits granted. The degree of delegation of budgets downward from schools and colleges to departments and programs is variable, though the overall structural effect is to devalue language and area studies programming given that course enrollment size tends to lean to the smaller end of the spectrum. School/college/faculty leadership will have an increasing role in shaping the budgetary politics and systems that govern international education in practice, for good and for bad.

The aggregate effect of austerity on international education at US universities is negative, for the most part. Leaving aside the reduction in capacity on the research, teaching, and service fronts, widening cleavages are emerging between well-funded universities and colleges with diverse revenue streams and smaller private and public universities dependent on regional student demand. Given this, the dissolution of Title VI funding would seriously reduce the capacity of universities to function as the foundation for international education at a time when the United States needs to more effectively engage with and better understand the rest of the world.

In my mind, structural changes, such as the ones above, raise the need to have more open and honest discussions about future funding levels for international education, of course, but also about broader intrainstitutional governance matters, given the way higher education is rapidly changing. As I noted, internationalization is a preeminent goal associated with many university missions. But are university presidents and provosts walking the walk, so to speak, or are they relying too heavily upon Title VI funding to do the work for them? On a related note, how much attention is being paid to ensuring that the de facto governance of international education on campus is thought about outside of the units where senior international officers reside? Indeed, in an era where we see the rise of STEM and professional programs, such as business and engineering, one could argue that "international" is far too important an agenda to leave to those designated as in charge of international. But how might the organization and governance of the international be reshaped so as to ensure that it is effectively managed and supported and that the foundational programs that have been built up for decades via public investment are not continually chipped away by benign neglect?

And how might international education be reframed in the context of other aspects of changing higher education? For example, universities are undergoing massive changes as IT systems shift to the cloud, student digital ecosystems are built up, and learning management systems get pushed toward learning management platforms. These provide new opportunities to bring the digitalization agenda into international education, including via the development of shared courses and projects, as well as via open educational resources (OERs).[17] And OERs are digital infrastructures of a sort that can lead to the sharing of expertise, skills, and resources outside of the universities where they are concentrated. The effective implementation of OER strategies, once formulated, could genuinely transform the reach of the Department of Education–funded NRCs, not just regionally but nationally and globally.

In short, the taken-for-granted nature of international education in the United States needs to be redressed in novel new ways, while its advocates concurrently seek more sustained support for what is really a remarkable and foundational program of international educational activities, one all too many people in the United States may take for granted.

Notes

I would like to acknowledge the effective and inspiring roles of Deborah Cohn, Hilary Kahn, and Lee Feinstein at Indiana University regarding the International Education at the Crossroads Symposium, where I was a panelist. This chapter is based on my brief comments at this October 2018 event. And thanks to co-panelists Zsuzsa Gille, Steve Hanson, and Seung-kyung Kim for their thought-provoking comments about the essential role of area and global studies in the changing landscape of higher education. A large number of staff (including retired staff) associated with international education at UW–Madison provided helpful information, as did Miriam A. Kazanjian of the Coalition for International Education. All errors are mine, of course.

1. Organizational nomenclature changed following two linked reviews of UW–Madison's Division of International Studies in 2012 and 2013, the first of which I coordinated as chair of the ad hoc review committee. The Division of International Studies is now known as the

International Division, and the International Institute is now known as the Institute for Regional and International Studies (IRIS). IRIS is currently home to seven Title VI-funded NRCs and eight FLAS Center Fellowship programs.

2. My colleagues and I co-founded the New Perspectives in Southeast Asian Studies book series at the University of Wisconsin Press (which is heavily subsidized by the Graduate School of the University of Wisconsin).

3. Dirlik, "Asia-Pacific Idea," 55–79.

4. Calculated via data presented in https://sports.usatoday.com/ncaa/salaries/ (accessed October 13, 2019) and https://www.cam.ac.uk/about-the-university/view-and-download-the-annual-report (accessed June 4, 2020).

5. Hudzik and Simon, "From a Land-Grant," 159–96.

6. National Center for Educational Statistics, *120 Years*, 63.

7. Rockefeller Foundation, "Area Studies."

8. Ludden, "Area Studies," 1–22. NDEA Title VI funding was reauthorized as Title VI of the Higher Education Act in 1980; see McDonnell et al., *Federal Support*, iii.

9. University of Wisconsin–Madison, "Overview."

10. On the Coalition for International Education, see US Global Competence for the 21st Century, http://www.usglobalcompetence.org/index.html.

11. Calculated via data provided to me by colleagues in relevant administrative units of the University of Wisconsin–Madison (August 2019).

12. Hawawini, *Internationalization*.

13. Hudzik, *Comprehensive Internationalization*, 6.

14. Edelstein and Douglass, "Comprehending," 3.

15. US Department of Education, "Title VI Programs."

16. The most recent language education report at the national scale in the United States is the Modern Language Association's *Enrollments in Languages Other Than English in United States Institutions of Higher Education, Summer 2016 and Fall 2016: Final Report*, June 2019.

17. OERs are teaching, learning, and research materials released under an intellectual property license that allows others to freely use, revise, retain, and/or redistribute the material. OERs may include full courses, course materials, books/textbooks, multimedia, tests and quizzes, software, visualizations, simulations, and any other tools, materials, or techniques used to provide access to knowledge. This description is based on a definition of OER published by the Hewlett Foundation at https://hewlett.org/strategy/open-educational-resources/. I was involved in creating UW-Madison's OER strategy, https://edinnovation.wisc.edu/wp-content/uploads/2015/02/OER-Strategic-Framework-at-UW-Madison.pdf, in 2016, and we are seeing modest gains in the use of OERs in international education. Funding for full-time OER staffing remains a key hurdle to overcome.

Bibliography

Dirlik, Arif. "The Asia-Pacific Idea: Reality and Representation in the Invention of a Regional Structure." *Journal of World History* 3, no. 1 (Spring 1992): 55–79.

Edelstein, Richard J., and John A. Douglass. "Comprehending the International Initiatives of Universities: A Taxonomy of Modes of Engagement and Institutional Logics." Research and Occasional Paper Series no. CSHE.19.12, University of California, Berkeley, Center for Studies in Higher Education, December 2012. https://cshe.berkeley.edu/sites/default /files/publications/rops.edelsteindouglass.inthedtaxonomy.12.12.12.pdf.

Hawawini, Gabriel. *The Internationalization of Higher Education and Business Schools: A Critical Review*. Singapore: Springer, 2016.

Hudzik, John. *Comprehensive Internationalization: From Concept to Action*. Washington, DC: NAFSA, Association of International Educators, 2011.

Hudzik, John, and Lou Anna K. Simon. "From a Land-Grant to a World-Grant Ideal: Extending Public Higher Education to a Global Frame." In *Precipice or Crossroads? Where America's Great Public Universities Stand and Where They Are Going Midway through Their Second Century*, edited by Daniel Mark Fogel and Elizabeth Malson-Huddle, 159–96. Albany, NY: SUNY Press, 2012.

Ludden, David. "Area Studies in the Age of Globalization." *Frontiers: The Interdisciplinary Journal of Study Abroad* 6 (Winter 2000): 1–22.

McDonnell, Lorraine M., Sue E. Berryman, M. Douglas Scott, John A. Pincus, and Abby Robyn. *Federal Support for International Studies: The Role of NDEA Title VI*. Santa Monica: RAND Corporation, 1981.

National Center for Educational Statistics. *120 Years of American Education: A Statistical Portrait*. Washington, DC: US Department of Education, 1993. https://nces.ed.gov/pubs93 /93442.pdf.

Rockefeller Foundation. "Area Studies." Social Sciences. https://rockfound.rockarch.org/area -studies.

University of Wisconsin–Madison. "Overview of the Title VI Program at UW-Madison." Institute for Regional and International Studies. Last modified March 13, 2018. https:// iris.wisc.edu/overview-of-the-title-vi-program-at-uw-madison/.

US Department of Education. "International Education Programs Service: Title VI Programs; Building a U.S. International Education Infrastructure." Last modified January 1, 2011. https://www2.ed.gov/about/offices/list/ope/iegps/title-six.html.

10

AREA STUDIES IN THE LIGHT OF NEW THEORETICAL AND GLOBAL DEVELOPMENTS

Zsuzsa Gille

TITLE VI-FUNDED AREA STUDIES CENTERS have played a crucial role in US social science and humanities scholarship in the last six decades. I would argue that this is not so much despite but rather because of the much-debated geopolitical considerations that motivated the founding of these centers at major public universities. In what follows, I will demonstrate how area studies scholarship developed a synergistic relationship with contemporary theoretical and methodological developments. I will start with a personal reflection, which will then lead me into discussing these synergies in general.

Scholarly Biography

My scholarship and professional career have deeply benefited from Title VI and also from the broader scholarly agenda we call area studies. I have experienced a number of tensions in the last twenty-five years between area studies and my discipline, sociology; nevertheless, I have seen these tensions resolved in productive ways.

I was born and raised in Hungary and emigrated, partly for political reasons, in 1988, just before state socialism collapsed. I defended my PhD at the University of California at Santa Cruz (UCSC) in 1999. UCSC had no sociologists with regional expertise, so I audited courses and attended area studies colloquia at the University of California, Berkeley (UCB) and at Stanford. The Title VI center at UCB was crucial for complementing my training in the region, and it facilitated the mentoring that I received from Michael Burawoy, who, as a professor of sociology and a specialist on former socialist countries, was aware of the challenges of straddling disciplinary and interdisciplinary/area studies. I was thrilled to have him serve later as the chair of my dissertation committee. The courses that I audited and the professors with whom I studied at UCSC were in other disciplines, such as history, political science, and anthropology, and the regular Berkeley talk series featured a wide variety of social sciences. While this interdisciplinary exposure was impactful, Burawoy shepherded my dissertation into a strongly defined and recognizably sociological orientation. My thesis was on the history of the politics of waste in state and postsocialist Hungary. Without such discipline (pun intended), my work would have had less of an impact, and, arguably, my research would have been less fundable and myself a less attractive candidate on the still rather discipline-defined job market.

I was extremely lucky to receive the position that I currently hold at the University of Illinois at Urbana-Champaign, because my position in the sociology department was seeded by the Title VI center, which at that time was called Russian and East European Studies (REES). It was an arrangement whereby Title VI paid 50 percent of my salary for three years, after which the College of Liberal Arts and Sciences and my home department, sociology, assumed the full cost of my employment. In return, half of my courses were to be on the region or to have a significant regional component. The position that I was hired for was advertised with two areas of specialization: global and transnational sociology, and Eastern Europe and the former Soviet Union. This was a perfect match for me. In any other sociology department, I would have had to justify my geographical focus, which in my otherwise strongly domestically focused discipline would have meant framing the region and my chosen site as simply a particular version of allegedly universal sociological claims. This is what anthropologists, for whom studying outside the United States and the West is the norm rather than the exception, call the symptom of "another country heard from."

At the time, REES also wanted to hire somebody in anthropology. This was viewed as a high priority because it was anthropology, and not my discipline, that was at the forefront of what we now call postsocialist studies, where most of the theoretical innovations were taking place in Russian and East European studies. Though they did not manage to hire an anthropologist with a Russian and East European studies specialization until many years later, I think the fact that my work was partly ethnographic and was heavily informed by achievements in anthropology made my scholarly contributions more central to area studies.

The other circumstance that made it possible for me to be offered this position was that, at the time, sociology had just started to make the global-transnational turn in reaction to the many challenges globalization poses for the social sciences—some of which I will discuss below.

Although I was excited, well appreciated by colleagues, and enthusiastic in my new position, I did not have an easy time. I both experienced pressures from my discipline and also felt some suspicion from area studies scholars. From sociology—which even today is a very US-focused discipline—there was pressure to orient myself to the discipline, with the understanding that if I published in journals that were key outlets in Russian and East European studies, or if I primarily presented at area studies conferences, my work would be categorized and ghettoized as fake sociology, which simply provided a little particular story on some larger narrative that sociologists writing about the West had already elaborated upon. My advisor, to this day, steers his students toward disciplinary venues and away from area studies outlets. At the same time, I also experienced suspicion from area studies. Colleagues senior to me in Russian and East European studies, who were renowned scholars and firmly committed to area studies, initially had the misconception that global studies—or even just transnational global sociology—was a project that wanted to do away with territorial and cultural differences, reducing all areas, as it were, to some lowest common denominator, to a small piece of what seemed to be universal and totalizing globalization narratives. Indeed, I must say that the initial academic work in this field, or what I call the first wave of global studies and transnational sociological scholarship, did nothing to allay such fears. It is this period that I turn to next.

Globalism, Postcolonialism, and Poststructuralism

The scholarship on globalization in the early 1990s is rightly called by anthropologists "the era of globalism." Following Anna Tsing, I argue that globalism is the conviction that the scale at which you study processes associated with globalization and the effects of globalization is the highest global, transnational, or supranational scale and not the national, local, or regional scale.[1] Sociology was initially resistant to narrowing its scale of observation and unit of analysis, even if I was not. As a sociologist getting my PhD just as global transnational sociology was beginning to emerge but was not yet recognized as a subdiscipline, the only way that I could conduct non-US sociology was through world-systems theory, the sociology of development, and comparative-historical sociology. During these same years, though, these subdisciplines and methodological paradigms themselves faced very serious challenges. First, in light of the changing function of the nation-state and the ways in which globalization had altered the neat, Russian-doll-esque nesting of the local in the national and the national in the global, the world, or what we call "the social," could no longer be assumed to be organized by nation-state containers—an assumption that we call methodological nationalism.[2] Second, new theories and trends in scholarship—in particular, poststructuralism and postcolonial studies—emerged that challenged the methodological and epistemological conventions of these well-rehearsed sociological subdisciplines.

Postcolonial studies, which took the humanities and the social sciences by storm in the early 1990s, was far from a natural ally to Russian and East European studies. To this day, many scholars in area studies reject applications of postcolonial studies; they think it assumes that the Soviet Union behaved just like any other colonizer toward countries of the Communist bloc, which is clearly not the case. I myself argued against this in two ways. First, applying a theoretical orientation such as postcolonial studies does not require that we prove the ontological analogy between Western European colonization and the Soviet Union's political and economic dominance over Eastern Europe. Second, I found postcolonial studies more relevant for analyzing Eastern Europe's relationship with the West rather than with the Soviet Union, especially after the collapse of state socialism in 1989.[3] However, its theoretical foundations and epistemological inclinations proved fertile for my method of practicing area studies. Said's *Orientalism*, a foundational work for postcolonial studies, inspired two books in Eastern European history that not only still represent the highest quality scholarship but also inaugurated a new paradigm in Russian and East European studies.[4] Larry Wolff's *Inventing Eastern Europe* and Maria Todorova's *Imagining the Balkans* were trailblazers that demonstrated how imaginings and knowledge about the Balkans and Eastern Europe had been shaped by centuries of Western economic and geopolitical interests.[5] As these interests changed, so did the characterization of this region, although always within a narrow set of discursive possibilities. These authors, along with several others, made it legitimate to ask: Who draws the boundaries around their respective regions, with what purpose, and what are the features and characteristics of these regions? As Todorova and many others show, the act of assigning a country or region to the Balkans, or to *Eastern* as opposed to *Central* Europe, directly informs what historical data, what conceptual framework, and even what key topics are mobilized in its study. For example, civil society was a more likely topic for scholars of Central Europe than for scholars studying the Balkans.[6] In consequence, issues of ethnic conflicts have driven more of the scholarship of the latter than of the former. As Wolff demonstrates, the characterization of Eastern Europe that informs these choices dates back to and was deeply informed by the Enlightenment.

You will also recognize in this move, in this direction of inquiry, another theoretical influence: namely, the poststructuralist impulse of interrogating the relationship between knowledge and power and questioning any seemingly natural definition of a social problem, culture, or region. This line of inquiry is not an argument about ideology or political bias but an interrogation of how seemingly objective metrics and methods cannot help but depict a specific region or society as lacking in certain positive, key qualities—whether they lie in the strength of democracy, the freedom of the market, or respect for human rights. Those "failures" then invite foreign interventions that range from the economic to the political or military—and are mostly from the West. The reason is that those variables and categories themselves were shaped by accepting Western societies and certain modern historical trajectories as normal and that, when those norms are used to measure other regions of the world, those regions appear not only different but also inferior. This creates a constant and closed feedback loop between power and knowledge. An example might help illustrate this. The World Values Survey (WVS) compares people's attitudes to various political systems, traditions, and values. Repeatedly, the results show that Western people are the most democratically minded. This is despite the fact that respondents living in unstable democracies or in nondemocratic societies show a strong preference for democracy. However, when respondents agree with certain statements posed by the survey, such as the statement that "having a strong leader who does not have to bother with elections or parliament" is a good way of governing their country, they are labeled as lacking sufficient democratic sentiment. As Åsa Lundgren argues:

> In many of the undemocratic countries or unstable democracies that are included in the WVS, people have experienced various degrees of political unrest, turmoil and civic violence. In many cases the only factor that might be able to contain an outburst of civil violence is a strong, albeit undemocratic,

regime. . . . In such a context people may think that democracy is the best system, in principle, but, given the conditions under which they are living, the rule of a strong leader may be preferred to the extent that it brings stability and physical security."[7]

That is, the survey instrument (i.e., the variables and the way that correlation among them is established, measured, and interpreted) fails to reflect the actual social environment in which people live, so what is measured is not so much values but people's differential needs. Poststructuralism argues that unless the social origins of such variables are reflected in our tools of research, we will not only keep misrepresenting a region and its peoples but will also inadvertently legitimate existing ways of relating to them.

By asking these questions we have already made it necessary to treat geographical areas not just as social constructions but also relationally—that is, as products of the relational matrix in which they are suspended. The matrix for my region is a particular set of East/West and North/South geopolitical relations. Some of these dynamics go back to centuries-long imperial interests. Questions informed by such an understanding of relationality need to go beyond looking into the various global economic, social, and cultural contexts of historical developments and societal trends in our region, because reducing relationality to mere context leaves the arrow between the global and Eastern Europe and Eurasia pointing only in one direction: always from the West or the global as cause and to Eastern Europe as effect. Instead, in the last decade, many postsocialist scholars have started to ask whether, for example, Eastern European state socialism and its collapse might also be constitutive of a global context. This perspective—which, for lack of a better word, we have termed relationality—has been elaborated on and taken up by the new generation of scholars who founded postsocialist studies and whose work continues to be the most innovative in area studies.[8] As an early example, Johanna Bockman and Gil Eyal advanced the interesting argument that neoliberalism was developed and tested in vivo in Eastern Europe.[9] Others inspired and motivated by the call to reinvigorate world-systems theory, such as József Böröcz, have shown how the European Union and its predecessor, the Common Market, have been shaped not just by decolonization but also by the socialist experiment in the eastern part of the continent and in Latin America, Asia, and Africa.[10] Yet others, narrowing their scope of observation, have demonstrated how in actual practices of governance, including the adoption of certain technologies, macroeconomic planning, and microeconomic management (of which Taylorism received the most attention), there appears to be not only more continuity between capitalism and socialism within one country over time but also more dialogue and borrowing among experts across the Iron Curtain. To summarize, it is this critical perspective on area studies scholarship that reinvigorated the study of at least my region of focus. This is also the reason why I think that the top young scholars today now flock to area studies conferences and strive to be published in our main area studies journals.

It is crucial here to appreciate that it is research and scholarship in area studies, funded and encouraged by Title VI, that facilitated a deep understanding—or, as Clifford Geertz put it, a thick description—of our field sites.[11] In return, it was this engagement and from-below research perspectives that alerted us to the initial blind spots of area studies and compelled us to explore how these new theoretical developments—postcolonial studies and poststructuralism—may be made relevant for our collective, regionally focused research endeavor. While it is important to keep in mind that postcolonial studies did not originate in Eastern Europe, and that its application to our region is fraught with many obstacles, most emergent scholars in our area will now admit that we can learn much from that scholarly agenda without claiming that our region was a colony in whatever sense of the term or that it existed in relation to a colonial power. Applying relationality to my scholarly work process, for example—reading about the history and the sociology of the regions where subaltern studies, the critique of Orientalism, and postcolonial studies came from; tracking down even seemingly minute connectivities across national and geopolitical boundaries; and not shying away from multiscalar analysis—informed how I thought about the relationship of my country, Hungary, to the European Union. Reading current news about Hungary's right-wing turn, rising xenophobia, and anti-Western attitudes, I am flushed by regret that I and others like me in my field did not make more of an effort to publicize or translate the findings of our research in that country—findings that had been made possible by this relational, multidirectional (east-to-west, east-to-south) approach and that detected the sprouts of European populism early.

Finally, returning to my disciplinary home, sociology: area studies has renewed that discipline's relevance for the second wave of globalization studies, or what we call "grounded views of globalization." This reflects the recognition that we can understand globalization and transnational social relations much better if we come to the inquiry with a well-informed understanding of what those societies in the region are about historically, culturally, and politically. This perspective informed two collective projects I have had the honor of participating in. One was the Michael Burawoy-led book project *Global Ethnography*, and the other is Indiana University's Framing the Global fellowship, which, in collaboration with Indiana University Press and funded by the Mellon Foundation, resulted in a series of programmatic and trend-setting manuscripts by scholars representing a wide range of disciplines and regions.[12] Global ethnography provides novel methodological and analytical tools for using locally grounded—but not locally limited—case studies for theoretical innovations in globalization studies. The Framing the Global project, following *Global Ethnography* after fifteen years, endeavored to elaborate guiding questions and to model how strategically chosen keywords may be used in various disciplinary and interdisciplinary inquiries to enter "the global," which otherwise may seem a daunting methodological task. Shared by both projects is the recognition that multiple perspectives, even when grounded in the same locale, enrich and make more accurate, rather than dilute, research, whether in area studies or in global studies.

Returning to my professional biography, it is the union of these two theoretical trends with area studies, and my effort to make them speak to each other in new ways, that, I think, led my area studies colleagues to accept me as a real area scholar. I think that my involvement in teaching and curriculum development, some of which was funded by Title VI, also contributed to the dissolution of whatever suspicion toward my approach(es) may have existed. The synergy that I describe above informed not only my research but also my teaching, which I love. While I still teach an area-specific course regularly, if not annually, most of my courses attend to societies that span the globe. However, what I have found fascinating is how deeply my work on Eastern Europe also informs how I teach my students, who study all other parts of the world, including Latin America, East Asia, and various African countries.

A wonderful, even if perhaps unintended, consequence of the Title VI project is that it prepared us well for tackling the challenges that globalization poses for scholarship. Therefore, if we keep working on reinvigorating area studies methodologically and theoretically, its future is bright.

Notes

1. Tsing, "Global Situation," 327–60.
2. Amelina et al., *Beyond Methodological*; Brenner, "Beyond State-Centrism," 39–78; Sassen, *Global City*.
3. See Gille, "Global Postsocialist Condition," 9–30.
4. Said, *Orientalism*.
5. Todorova, *Imagining the Balkans*; Wolff, *Inventing Eastern Europe*.
6. Hann and Dunn, *Civil Society*.
7. Lundgren, "Knowledge Production," 43.
8. Chari and Verdery, "Thinking between the Posts," 6–34; Rogers, "Unbound," 1–15; Gille, "Global Postsocialist Condition."
9. Bockman and Eyal, "Eastern Europe."
10. Böröcz, *European Union*.
11. Geertz, "Thick Description," 3–30.
12. Burawoy et al., *Global Ethnography*; Kahn, *Framing the Global*.

Bibliography

Amelina, Anna, Devrimsel D. Nergiz, Thomas Faist, and Nina Glick Schiller, eds. *Beyond Methodological Nationalism: Research Methodologies for Cross-Border Studies*. London: Routledge, 2012.

Bockman, Johanna, and Gil Eyal. "Eastern Europe as a Laboratory for Economic Knowledge: The Transnational Roots of Neoliberalism." *American Journal of Sociology* 1082 (2002): 310–52.

Böröcz, József. *The European Union and Global Social Change: A Critical Geopolitical-Economic Analysis*. London: Routledge, 2009.

Brenner, Neil. "Beyond State-Centrism? Space, Territoriality, and Geographical Scale in Globalization Studies." *Theory and Society* 28 (1999): 39–78.

Burawoy, Michael, Joseph A. Blum, Sheba George, Millie Thayer, Zsuzsa Gille, Teresa Gowan, Lynne Haney, Maren Klawiter, Steve H. Lopez, and Sean O'Riain. *Global Ethnography: Forces, Connections and Imaginations in a Postmodern World*. Berkeley: University of California Press, 2000.

Chari, Sharad, and Katherine Verdery. "Thinking between the Posts: Postsocialism, Postcolonialism, and Ethnography after the End of the Cold War." *Comparative Studies in Society and History* 51, no. 1 (2009): 6–34.

Geertz, Clifford. "Thick Description: Toward an Interpretive Theory of Culture." In *The Interpretation of Cultures*, 3–30. New York: Harper's, 1973.

Gille, Zsuzsa. "Is There a Global Postsocialist Condition?" *Global Society* 24, no. 1 (2010): 9–30.

Hann, C. M., and Elizabeth Dunn, eds. *Civil Society: Challenging Western Models*. London: Routledge, 1996.

Kahn, Hilary, ed. *Framing the Global*. Bloomington: Indiana University Press, 2014.

Lundgren, Åsa. "Knowledge Production and the World Values Survey: Objective Measuring with Ethno-Centric Conclusions." In *Borders and the Changing Boundaries of*

Knowledge, vol. 22 of the Transactions series, edited by Inga Brandell, Marie Carlson, and Önver A. Çetrez, 35–52. Istanbul: Swedish Research Institute, 2015.

Rogers, Douglas. "Unbound: Connections, Critiques, Comparisons." *Slavic Review* 69, no. 1 (2010): 1–15.

Said, Edward W. *Orientalism*. New York: Pantheon Books, 1978.

Sassen, Saskia. *The Global City: New York, London, Tokyo*. Princeton, NJ: Princeton University Press, 2001.

Todorova, Maria. *Imagining the Balkans*. Oxford: Oxford University Press, 1997.

Tsing, Anna. "The Global Situation." *Cultural Anthropology* 15, no. 3 (2000): 327–60.

Wolff, Larry. *Inventing Eastern Europe: The Map of Civilization on the Mind of the Enlightenment*. Stanford, CA: Stanford University Press, 1994.

11

INTERDISCIPLINARITY AND COLLABORATION

The Future of International Studies and Area Studies

Seung-kyung Kim

WHY DO WE STUDY OTHER peoples, cultures, histories, literatures, politics, and economies? How does studying the Other contribute to our understanding of our own people, culture, history, literature, politics, and economy? Why do we require undergraduate students to study two years of foreign language in order to graduate from Indiana University Bloomington? Why does Indiana University offer more than seventy languages? Why did the Department of Education decide to award the largest number of Title VI grants to Indiana University Bloomington in its most recent grant cycle? These questions are both epistemological and ontological; they are philosophical and empirical; and they are real issues that currently face higher education in the United States.

The study of foreign languages in the United States, as well as area studies more broadly, has been losing ground in recent years. On January 22, 2019, the *Chronicle of Higher Education* reported that colleges have lost "a 'stunning' 651 foreign-language programs in 3 years." While between 2009 and 2013, higher education in aggregate only lost one such program, between 2013 and 2016, more than 650 programs were shuttered. This "stunning statistic," which the *Chronicle* attributes to the delayed impact of the 2008 recession on foreign language programs, shows just how threatened these programs have become as colleges and universities seek to cut costs.[1]

Only 20 percent of K-12 students in the United States study a foreign language, and the percentage is even lower for college students, with only 7.5 percent enrolled in a foreign language course during their entire college career.[2] This percentage has been steadily declining in recent years as more colleges drop their foreign language requirements. Many students in the

United States simply do not perceive studying a foreign language as having any value. As students' interest in languages has dropped, there has been very little pushback by schools and governments to keep language programs going. Just ten states and the District of Columbia require knowledge of a foreign language for high school graduation. In Europe, on the other hand, most countries require that students learn at least one foreign language, and studying a foreign language is thus nearly universal. In South Korea, where I grew up, I had to study English from when I was in middle school until I graduated from college. Currently, students in South Korea begin to learn English in kindergarten. What is it that Europeans and South Koreans perceive that so many US citizens fail to understand?

The United States is a complex case, however, and is both a leader and a foot dragger in the process of globalization. While area studies have been caught up in both the shift away from humanities to STEM fields that emphasize career training and the nativist backlash against globalization, at the same time, the obvious need to understand the interconnected parts of the world has kept area studies programs alive at the country's best universities. In addition, the US government recognizes the importance of area studies with its funding programs. As the Department of Education states on its website, "The current era is one of partnerships, networks, and relations among diverse people in multiple fields and among many nations. In this world, Fulbright-Hays and Title VI emphasize the importance of integrating area expertise with thematic knowledge and forming partnerships across programs, within and across communities. These partnerships enable the widest net to be cast to achieve the broadest possible impact."[3]

Why is it important to know more than one language in the twenty-first century? In "Do You Speak My Language? You Should," an opinion piece in the *New York Times* from March 2019, Bénédicte de Montlaur, the cultural counselor of the French Embassy in the United States, argues for the importance of foreign language learning: "If Americans want the next generation to be active participants in a multilingual world, dual-language and multicultural education is crucial. Government spending on foreign-language education and the education of qualified foreign-language teachers needs to increase. More states need to enforce language-education requirements. Colleges need to recognize the importance of their foreign-language education programs. In turn, more parents, students and teachers need to lobby for language programs."[4]

While teaching language is an essential component of area studies, the defining characteristic of the latter is its interdisciplinary training about a specific area. It is a study of other peoples, cultures, histories, literatures, politics, and economies. Put simply, teaching area studies is about teaching cultural awareness, both of our own country and of other countries. This cultural awareness is what is urgently needed within the current environment of geopolitical, ethnic, and religious conflicts. As the world globalizes, and countries and economies become more tightly integrated, it is increasingly urgent that we have a deep understanding of all the different parts of the world. We need to have tools and methods to understand each other, and area studies provide students with these tools and methods. There are real crises facing the world that need to be dealt with and that can only be solved through the cooperation of groups with very different values and belief systems.

The defining characteristic of area studies is that they provide holistic knowledge about a specific area. Interdisciplinary training is required to develop a full understanding of a region or culture, and with this training, interconnections can be perceived so that "the literature is not just recreational, the history is not just background, the anthropology is not just some customs, the politics is not just current events."[5] Thus, area studies bring everything together in a way that deepens one's appreciation of each separate aspect. This deep understanding of a culture is just what the anthropologist Clifford Geertz described in his famous article about thick description, where he pointed out that superficial observation was not sufficient in order to understand cultural phenomena.[6] The very basic example that he provides is an analysis of the difference between a twitch and a wink, both of which appear identical but are completely different in their meaning; this meaning is also dependent on context.

Area studies have long been an outstanding feature of the education offered at Indiana University (IU). IU's commitment to area studies was reemphasized in 2012 with the establishment of the School of Global and International Studies, later renamed the Hamilton Lugar School after two renowned Hoosier internationalists. It houses the Department of East Asian Languages and Cultures, along with other regionally focused departments, and the Department of International Studies, reflecting the school's vision of strong area studies programs that prepare our students with cultural fluency to enhance their training in social science and policy issues.

The Department of East Asian Languages and Cultures' long history and its deep roots in the humanities have been bolstered by our recent hires in social science (namely, in political science and anthropology), and we are currently hiring an additional social scientist to make our department even more multidisciplinary.

Indiana University's leadership in area studies has been recognized by the US Department of Education's Title VI programs, which have enabled our departments and centers to become even more diverse and international. Over seventy languages are taught here, and students from 150 countries study here. The most recent cycle of Title VI funding was the best ever for IU and the Hamilton Lugar School of Global and International Studies, demonstrating the effectiveness of the school's concerted efforts for revitalizing area studies. This followed the 2014 cycle, when IU uncharacteristically lost many Title VI grants that it had previously held for years.

Another important aspect of IU's educational mission is educating international students. IU educates international students who become scholars and leaders in their countries of origin and scholars and leaders in various disciplines in the United States. The two are no longer separate, as academic fields have also globalized and many scholars teach in multiple locations and often in more than one language.

My own biography demonstrates the importance of educating international students in several ways. I grew up in South Korea, finished my undergraduate education in Seoul, majoring in sociology at Yonsei University, and came to the United States in 1980 as an international graduate student. I studied anthropology at the City University of New York, making the study of Korea the focus of my scholarship. I received my PhD and a graduate certificate in women's studies in 1990. I joined the Department of Women's Studies at the University of Maryland that same year and taught there for twenty-five years, before moving to the Department of East Asian Languages and Cultures at Indiana University as the Korea Foundation Professor and the director of the Institute for Korean Studies in 2016.

Just before I left the University of Maryland, while I was serving as the director of the Center for East Asian Studies, I worked with a small number of faculty and staff to prepare a Title VI grant proposal. Thinking back, I feel that I was foolish to attempt this without the backing of the university since it had little interest in area studies. Despite putting together a very substantive proposal, we were not selected. In 2018, Indiana University received nineteen Title VI grants (eight National Resource Center, eight Foreign Language and Area Studies, two Language Resource Center, and one Centers for International Business Education) from the US Department of Education, confirming its position as a national leader of area studies. This is the result of IU and the Hamilton Lugar School of Global and International Studies doubling down on their commitment to area studies when, across the country, other universities have been cutting back on foreign language and area studies teaching. I am proud to be a member of Indiana University, the institution that is not afraid to forge ahead with its commitment to area studies when others retreat.

My life has been lived between the United States and South Korea, and this has required that I develop a personal understanding of two very different, and constantly changing and interacting, cultures. The impoverished South Korea of my childhood has transformed into one of the world's most economically successful countries, and the overwhelming cultural, political, and military dominance of the United States has evolved into something more complex and nuanced. Living in the United States for more than half of my life has required me to develop a deep understanding of the country and its culture. South Korea has continued to be my professional interest, and I go back often to do my research. Having this bicultural life makes me appreciate cultural differences and the importance of the kind of learning that area studies provide.

To conclude, I would like to return to the issue of essential learning about both area studies and global/international studies and what the fundamental relationship between the two is. How should we teach both dimensions of this relationship in the ever-changing landscape of higher education? Area studies work toward an understanding of the world in two distinct ways. The first is learning to appreciate difference in order to comprehend human potential and limitation. This is where the need to learn about other cultures and languages starts. However, globalization pulls everyone together; the truth is that no one is completely Other anymore. We are all part of the same world, and even the most different cultures are tied together by this fact. Nevertheless, all this interconnectedness has not erased difference and, if anything, has made people more acutely aware of difference. This is where understanding specific cultures, histories, literatures, politics, and economies becomes essential.

Here I would like to invoke some key concepts—deep listening, thick description, and critical reflexivity—that are relevant to the future of area studies and that will, in turn, inform the future of global and international studies. Deep listening requires listening as broadly as possible to what people have to say about their lives. Thick description not only describes human behavior but also situates it thoroughly within its cultural context, so that the behavior becomes fully understandable. Critical reflexivity requires us, as scholars, to think critically about the impact of our assumptions, values, and actions in the context of our work. Through this approach, we can foster greater understanding of the world.

Let me throw out some keywords here: *local*, *regional*, and *global*, or, in terms more often associated with the social sciences, *micro*, *meso*, and *macro*. These are inextricably interrelated: "Without a sustained commitment to research in particular places, it can be difficult to 'hear' beyond traditional interpretative frames or the trendy theoretical line of inquiry of the day. And without grounded, empirical research, international studies scholars can too easily lapse into reproducing hegemonic discourses about regions and places."[7] To strengthen the interdependent relationship between area studies and international studies, let's ask ourselves: What kind of area studies are we advancing, and for whom? And what kind of international studies are we advancing, and for whom?

Notes

1. Johnson, "Colleges Lose."
2. Stein-Smith, "Foreign Language Classes."
3. US Department of Education, "History of Title VI."
4. De Montlaur, "Do You Speak."
5. Kenney, "Area Studies," 2.
6. Geertz, *Interpretation of Cultures*.
7. Koch, "'Critical' Area Studies," 807–14.

Bibliography

De Montlaur, Bénédicte. "Do You Speak My Language? You Should." *New York Times*, March 29, 2019. https://www.nytimes.com/2019/03/26/opinion/learn-foreign-language.html.

Geertz, Clifford. *The Interpretation of Cultures*. New York: Basic Books, 1973.

Johnson, Steven. "Colleges Lose a 'Stunning' 651 Foreign-Language Programs in 3 Years." *Chronicle of Higher Education*, January 22, 2019. https://www.chronicle.com/article /Colleges-Lose-a-Stunning-/245526.

Kenney, Padraic. "Area Studies and the 'False Song of Globalism.'" *NewsNet: News of the Association for Slavic, East European, and Eurasian Studies* 57, no. 1 (January 2017): 2.

Koch, Natalie. "Is a 'Critical' Area Studies Possible?" *Environment and Planning D: Society and Space* 34, no. 5 (October 2016): 807–14. https://doi.org/10.1177/0263775816656524.

Stein-Smith, Kathleen. "Foreign Language Classes Becoming More Scarce." *The Conversation*, February 6, 2019. http://theconversation.com/foreign-language-classes -becoming-more-scarce-102235.

US Department of Education. "International Education Programs Service: The History of Title VI and Fulbright-Hays: An Impressive International Timeline." Last modified January 1, 2011. https://www2.ed.gov/about/offices/list/ope/iegps/history.html.

Intersection

12

GLOBAL EDUCATION FOR GENERATION Z

Brian T. Edwards

IN THE SPRING OF 2018, I was in Madrid. I walked over to El Retiro Park, one of my favorite places in the city, but I found the gate locked. A simple announcement was posted: "Debido a las consecuencias de las condiciones meteorológicas y la urgencia de reparación e inspección del arbolado los jardines del Buen Retiro permanecerán cerrados." My disappointment was intense and immediate.

To my side stood two college-aged students, speaking in US-accented English. One aimed an iPhone at the sign. Curious, I glanced over at the screen. Everything looked as I saw it, except that the announcement was no longer in Spanish—the words on the sign were magically transformed into English. I gasped. The students proceeded to introduce me to Google Translate's optical function.

* * *

For Generation Z, namely those born since about 1997, international travel and language learning operate in a profoundly different framework than for those educated before the digital age. New technologies have collapsed distances between continents; translation machines have erased some of the foreignness of foreign travel. The students at the Retiro did not need Spanish proficiency to understand that winds had forced the park to close for urgent tree pruning or to avoid confusion over whether the gardens would remain closed temporarily or forever (*permanecerán cerrados* may sound permanent to an English speaker, but it is not). Many of us who lived abroad during the analog period wax nostalgic about the experience of dislocation we experienced and wonder whether that sentiment has gone the way of the cabin pay phone and the pocket dictionary. Homesickness is softened by FaceTime or WhatsApp; family, friends, and advisers are merely a Wi-Fi connection away. Eighteen years after Skype was launched and more than a dozen years since the first iPhone, it is time to reframe the question of what a global education should aspire to be.

The full-scale arrival of the digital age has also corresponded to a period of international antagonisms, from the rise in populism in disparate countries and continents to uprisings and struggles for democracy in nations ruled by authoritarian regimes, to the long and intertwined set of conflicts in the Middle East over the past two decades since September 2001. Domestically, the rise of anti-immigrant, anti-Muslim, anti-Semitic, and white nationalist rhetoric in the US public sphere has spiked, with notable effects abroad. According to the Pew Research Center, international opinions of the United States are plummeting, with poor numbers on survey questions about views of the United States and whether it takes into account the interests of other countries. Since 2016 and the vituperative presidential campaign, our international standing has degraded further: Pew surveys find low international confidence in President Trump, exacerbating a downward trend. What is worse, international audiences increasingly view the United States as a menace: in 2018, 45 percent of respondents from twenty-two different countries viewed "American power and influence" as a major global threat, up twenty percentage points since 2013.[1]

Now, we should not assume that President Trump's public personality and speech resonate in the same way abroad as they do domestically. What US Americans on one side of the political spectrum find embarrassing or destructive about the president's rhetoric—or on the other side, what they find refreshing or bold about it—is filtered through domestic contexts that have little meaning outside the United States. Translation studies has long reminded us that messages are always inherently detached from their original referent. In 2017, a year into the forty-fifth president's term, I and other scholars of the Middle East and North Africa tracked responses to the then-new president's utterances and public persona and found varying effects.[2] In Morocco, where I surveyed a range of individuals, President Trump's so-called Muslim ban and his announcement of relocating the US Embassy from Tel Aviv to Jerusalem communicated a message about US priorities and principles much more clearly than his endorsement of the controversial Senate candidate Roy Moore or investigations into his finances and administration the same week, both of which were being discussed and debated intensely in the United States.[3] Simply put, even as technology appears to be flattening the world and screening out linguistic and cultural differences, global disjuncture—a gap in the "meaning" of the United States, how it translates, and what it signifies abroad—is on the rise.

In sum, we have two rapidly shifting contexts: a geopolitical context in which the reputation of the United States is waning and an epistemological context in which machines are learning the previously uniquely human task of moving quickly between languages. In such times, what role should global education play for US college students? For the purposes of my argument, I will address what I view as the two most important components of global education: study abroad and language learning. These are separate, of course, but intertwined; both are dynamic areas undergoing significant pressures and changes.

Study abroad has never been more popular. According to the Open Doors 2018 report, 16 percent of students currently earning bachelor's degrees in the United States will study outside the country during their undergraduate years.[4] But immersion in another language is a harder sell, as if the global popularity of English and the ease of Google Translate excuse students from the difficulty of entering another language system.

The pressures on language learning are massive. Enrollments continue to drop sharply. In 2018, the Modern Language Association reported that college enrollments in world languages had fallen 9.2 percent between 2013 and 2016, following a similar decline (6.7 percent) over the previous four years.[5] Despite the 350 languages currently spoken in the United States (about 150 of them indigenous), a creeping monolingualism is taking over.[6] In the face of machine translation, many students ask: Why would one put in the hundreds—or thousands—of hours necessary to learn another language? And study abroad is no longer exerting the positive impact on language learning that it might. When you can study in Jordan, Paris, or the Czech Republic without learning Arabic, French, or Czech, and make your way around the streets of the tourist districts of the world using only English, why bother at all?

We should rigorously assess curricula and learning outcomes in the educational products that providers and institutions offer our students. Even while study abroad enrollments are up, a 2014 survey of US business executives found a "continuing need for international business education in the U.S." with increased emphasis on intercultural communication, foreign language skills, and international experience.[7] Given the increasing cost of a college education and rise in student debt, students and their parents quite reasonably assess the potential value and career options associated with different undergraduate majors. In addition to changes in technology and geopolitics, we must also account for the dramatically rising costs of higher education, which put pressure on educators to justify the "value" of a liberal arts education.

Bearing these competing pressures in mind, educators have both a responsibility and a series of opportunities for taking leadership in tailoring programs in global studies for a new generation. How might a global education for the digital age, tailored to the new generation, address needs in the workplace and the international sphere at once?

I propose three pillars:

1. Give more attention to the transition between high school and college for language learners and more options for students to develop advanced language skills in college—an embrace of language learning across the K-16 spectrum.
2. Foster a commitment to study abroad experiences that privilege immersion, with an emphasis on using as much target language as possible through homestays, studying in authentic language environments, and enrolling in courses at foreign universities.
3. Expand curricula that examine diverse international histories and societies, activate second-language learning, and seek global competency, which I define as an understanding of the multiplicity, independence, and *interdependence* of peoples and cultures, both when they do and do *not* intersect with the United States.

For many US college students, learning a second language was a core course in high school, but interest in pursuing more advanced skills often drops off once they satisfy a college language requirement, as if French, Spanish, or Latin was merely an entrance ticket to be discarded. But college is the time when students who have worked years to gain skills in a second language can finally start to do interesting things with them.

For languages regularly offered in US high schools, how can we think better about the transition between middle and high school language learning and about what might happen differently in college? The apparent chasm between the study of languages on the K-12 level and in colleges and universities is one most educators glance over only tentatively. Language learning is an intriguing place where younger brains tend to respond more easily than older ones, and innovative school systems are incorporating exposure to language at the primary level in new ways, from daily exposure to Mandarin or Spanish to two-way immersion or bilingual programs. Still, however, most US students are introduced to a second language in middle school (unless they speak one at home, which is true for an increasing number of US high school students).[8] As these students reach high school, the most talented of them can frequently fulfill college language requirements via AP exams and without taking a single language course in college.

We are thus losing many of our most talented language students through our focus on a general basic competency for all students. What would it mean to reverse that focus? Even in the face of weakening college-wide requirements, how might we encourage students who have already demonstrated talents or passion for languages to want to pursue learning further?

The first step is for those college-level programs in the major languages taught in high school—Spanish overwhelmingly, of course—to innovate curricula. We should demonstrate to college students as soon as possible that languages other than English are the purview of all disciplines. Too often, to advance in language study in US universities means only to study a language's literature—a practice that is fine for students attracted to literature, of course, but leaves behind many others. The opportunity to study Spanish or Latin American film and media for communication students, use French-language archives for aspiring historians, or engage with German or Russian political scientists, for example, can activate students interested in pursuing other fields to the idea that their language background may indeed be useful for their majors.[9] Where are the sections of philosophy or political science or environmental studies courses taught in Spanish? The discussion section for French history taught in French? Higher-order courses might take advantage of the obvious fact that all academic disciplines, including STEM fields, are regularly taught in the full realm of languages of the world in universities abroad and that many faculty outside language departments have the capacity to offer a course or a section in their discipline in a language other than English. Engaging with colleagues and courses in universities in other countries—bringing in a Spanish or Arabic philosophy lecture, a French astronomy class, or a German political scientist—could be a Zoom or WhatsApp conference call away. And once we offer students the opportunity to study any of the subjects in a language other than English, we also open up the idea that study abroad may be the purview of social science and STEM subjects and majors.

How do we attract students who have already fulfilled a college language requirement in one language to begin another? Given that many more languages tend to be offered in colleges than in high schools, we should also encourage students who developed advanced skills in French, Spanish, or Latin in high school to start another world language, from languages with massive numbers of speakers like Arabic and Mandarin Chinese to minor or regional languages, such as Haitian Creole or idioms with small numbers of speakers, including Louisiana French and native and indigenous languages, such as Tunica (to use examples of languages we offer at Tulane). Some of this can be done directly by language chairs or college advisers, who could reach out directly to accepted students with AP language tests on their high school transcripts.

A debate on many college campuses is whether language requirements should be maintained or softened. The pressures to ease up on language requirements come from many directions; the expansion of STEM fields is the most obvious, but I have also witnessed colleagues in humanities disciplines argue that colleges should lessen the number of courses undergraduates take in world languages so as to make more space for other requirements, including diversity requirements.

These are all well-taken positions. But I think the debate over language requirements is a red herring. When we show students how international competencies derived from advanced language study open up new professional avenues, when we offer rigorous study abroad opportunities that combine true immersion and a wider array of coursework and professional internships abroad, then more students will find the justifications for pursuing passions in language study beyond basic requirements. This flips the focus from the basic requirement for all to higher-level opportunities for students with a demonstrated capacity and interest for language learning.

Students and parents alike ask me frequently: Which language should I (my child) study? Where should I study abroad? What histories and societies should we learn about? I reply: Do whatever interests you! Follow your interest and your passion, whether it be Egyptian Arabic or American Sign Language, Swahili or Brazilian Portuguese. College is the time to try a new language or go further with the one you learned before you got there. As someone who studied Arabic while pursuing a PhD in American studies in the 1990s and was advised to remove Arabic from my CV when pursuing tenure track positions in US American literature (because it was too confusing to search committees), I'm well aware that the ways in which disparate areas of interest may come together are never predictable or prescribed.

* * *

In his 2018 book *Us vs. Them*, Eurasia Group founder Ian Bremmer notes that the failures of globalism—the "belief in universal interdependence and international exchange that seemed to provide paths to prosperity"—have led to a widespread retrenchment, resulting in various forms of protectionism that provincialize citizens and societies.[10] This isolationism runs counter to the utopian aspirations of the digital age. In 2011, when Facebook was being credited for the Arab Spring and when the young Egyptian Google executive Wael Ghonim was a candidate for a Nobel Prize, the promise of open access to the world's information and the global expansion of social networks seemed to portend a different future.

As we enter the century's third decade, it's time to ask anew what a global liberal arts education should look like. What values should we focus on: our universal similarity or the differences between peoples and societies? Most current definitions of global education focus on the common bonds that unite us. In the era of climate change, global pandemics, and digital media, such interconnectedness is surely our reality.

But there is also value in appreciating disjuncture. Translation machinery may make it harder to recognize the differences in cultural systems around the globe. As inequalities across the world are exacerbated, and the United States takes an increasingly isolationist stance, what benefit is there in smoothing over the disparities and distinctions?

One of the traditional justifications for a liberal arts education is that it prepares you to think and to be a solid citizen, and it teaches you how to learn. As we update those learning objectives for the twenty-first century, let's specify that by embracing a second language, students gain the opportunity to think in another system. Learn how to form vocabulary from the ten forms of a trilateral Arabic root, how to express yourself in the pluperfect subjunctive of Spanish, or how to employ politeness levels in Japanese, and you are not only building massive amounts of synapses but also understanding systems of life and thought.

* * *

One of my favorite words in French is *décalage*, which means both a gap in space and a disjuncture in experience. It is also the French word for "jet lag," that disorienting sensation of your mind being somehow out of sync with your present location. Scholars in the field of translation studies have long taught us that moving between languages is always, in a rich sense, recognizing what is lost and gained in translation.

Recalling the scene that transpired outside the gate of El Retiro Park with which I began, and the embrace of difference in global education that I am suggesting for Generation Z, I take a lesson from Mark Twain. In 1903, Twain came across his great story of 1865, "The Celebrated Jumping Frog of Calaveras County," now published in French translation. He hated it. Twain lamented that the story had lost all of its humor—its lightness. To elaborate for his American audience—and for fun, of course—he translated it back to a heavy, leaden English and published the result.

It's a great lesson about translation but also about global education. To try to update it for the digital age, I decided to translate the first sentence of this section—"One of my favorite words in French is *décalage*"—into French and then aim my iPhone back at the screen to see what would happen. How would Google's optical function translate my own translation back to English?

Google did fine until it got to the last word, *décalage*, which flickered back and forth between "shifting" and "gap," as if the artificial intelligence wanted a hint from me. Google could not decide for itself how to render a word that can mean disjuncture or jet lag, or shift or gap. How perfect an analog, I decided, for the shifting gaps in our global education today. We still have time to get it right.

Notes

1. Gramlich and Devlin, "More People."
2. These appeared in "America First 2.0," a special issue of *MERIP: Middle East Report*, no. 283 (2017).
3. "Timeline of the Donald Trump Presidency (2017 q4)." On December 1, 2017, the former NSA adviser Michael Flynn pleaded guilty to lying to the FBI, and on December 4, Trump endorsed the Alabama Senate candidate Roy Moore, holding a huge rally for him on December 8. On December 6, he announced that the United States would recognize Jerusalem as capital of Israel and move its embassy there, rocking Muslim-majority countries. An Amazigh intellectual in his fifties told me: "Ordinary people hate [Trump] because he has said negative things about Islam. The main thing for them is that he's anti-Arab, anti-Muslim, anti-immigrant" (cf. my essay, "Morocco Dispatch").

4. Institute of International Education, "Open Doors Report."

5. Looney and Lusin, "Enrollments in Languages."

6. See the report of the American Academy of Arts and Sciences' Commission on Language Learning, on which I served, for an argument about the importance of language learning to the nation's future: *America's Languages: Investing in Language Education for the 21st Century.*

7. Daniel, Xie, and Kedia, "2014 U.S. Business Needs."

8. For data, see Commission on Language Learning, *State of Languages.*

9. The University of North Carolina at Chapel Hill has a program called "Languages across the Curriculum" that provides one practical model for implementing this concept; see https://catalog.unc.edu/undergraduate/academic-enrichment/languages-across-curriculum/.

10. Bremmer, *Us and Them.*

Bibliography

Bremmer, Ian. *Us and Them: The Failures of Globalism.* New York: Penguin, 2018.

Commission on Language Learning. *America's Languages: Investing in Language Education for the 21st Century.* American Academy of Arts and Sciences, February 2017. https://www.amacad.org/publication/americas-languages.

Commission on Language Learning. *The State of Languages in the U.S.: A Statistical Portrait.* December 2016. https://www.amacad.org/publication/state-languages-us-statistical-portrait.

Daniel, Shirley J., Fujiao Xie, and Ben L. Kedia. "2014 U.S. Business Needs for Employees with International Expertise." Paper prepared for the Internationalization of U.S. Education in the 21st Century: The Future of International and Foreign Language Studies conference. College of William & Mary, Williamsburg, VA, April 11–13, 2014.

Edwards, Brian. "Morocco Dispatch." *MERIP: Middle East Report* 283 (Summer 2017): 40–41.

Gramlich, John, and Kat Devlin. "More People around the World See U.S. Power and Influence as a 'Major Threat' to Their Country." Pew Research, February 14, 2019. https://www.pewresearch.org/fact-tank/2019/02/14/more-people-around-the-world-see-u-s-power-and-influence-as-a-major-threat-to-their-country/.

Institute of International Education. *Open Doors Report on International Educational Exchange.* November 13, 2018. https://www.iie.org/Research-and-Insights/Open-Doors/Open-Doors-2018-Media-Information.

Looney, Dennis, and Natalia Lusin. "Enrollments in Languages Other Than English in United States Institutions of Higher Education, Summer 2016 and Fall 2016: Preliminary Report." Modern Language Association, February 2018. https://www.mla.org/content/download/83540/2197676/2016-Enrollments-Short Report.pdf.

"Timeline of the Donald Trump Presidency (2017 q4)." *Wikipedia.* Last modified September 10, 2019. https://en.wikipedia.org/wiki/Timeline_of_the_Donald_Trump_presidency_(2017_Q4).

CROSSROADS 3

LANGUAGES

13

PRIORITIES IN LANGUAGE STUDY

Campus Trends, Future Needs

Rosemary G. Feal

FOR THE PAST EIGHTEEN YEARS, I have been studying the landscape for language learning in the United States, both on college campuses and in the larger world of the *language enterprise* (commonly understood to include governmental, academic, nonprofit, and business spheres). In my role as executive director of the Modern Language Association (MLA), I monitored trends and led several projects designed to improve the way languages are delivered. The observations that follow are a result of these years of observation and intervention. I restrict my comments to the diversity of models I have analyzed without citing specific programs or endeavors; it is my belief that mentioning institutions by name would curtail the usefulness of my analysis.

If I had to name the biggest issue on college campuses, I would say it is the two-tiered system that occurs in departments that treat language courses and content courses as distinct entities. The MLA Ad Hoc Committee on Foreign Languages report issued in 2007, "Foreign Languages and Higher Education: New Structures for a Changed World," describes this split and offers ideas on ways to bridge it.[1] The report emphasizes the goal of focusing on advanced literacy and transcultural and translingual competence in all courses. Separating early courses from advanced ones in the academic major can work counter to this objective. Further, the report recommends significant transformations to the paths that lead to a major in a language other than English: "Language departments will need to . . . produce unified, four-year curricula that situate language study in cultural, historical, geographic, and cross-cultural frames; that systematically incorporate transcultural content and translingual reflection at every level; and that organize the major around explicit, principled educational goals and expected outcomes. A curriculum should consist of a series of complementary or linked courses that holistically incorporate content and cross-cultural reflection at every level."[2] The historic challenge facing academic language departments, then, is figuring out how to bridge the two-tiered system and devise an integrated major or minor. It is widely recognized that these challenges can create obstacles for even the most imaginative departments. Decades (and, in some cases, a century) of preexisting structures often trigger inertia. The results might manifest as an ossified tenure system that excludes those who teach lower-division courses; the ad hoc nature of course offerings that occurs when professors (who come and go) choose what they want to teach rather than what students need to learn; a low-tech environment; a lack of pedagogical preparation for all those who teach in a language other than English; and so on. Imagine department chairs who must grapple with these inherited structures and wish to change them. They are often limited to the power of persuasion, given that tenured faculty members cannot be compelled to overhaul the curriculum and its adjacent pedagogical practices. Perhaps department chairs secure internal or external funding that supports the desirable changes, which goes a long way toward building appropriate new structures. The *ADFL Bulletin* presents hundreds of cases of successful practices that can inspire other department chairs.

On campuses today, the teaching of languages frequently involves structures external to the departments, and, in general, this is a good development, with some exceptions I will note below. At the institutional level, obtaining a Language Flagship, administered by the National Security Education Program (NSEP), can transform the teaching of specific languages or support technological innovations. The Language Flagship states its mission as "designing, supporting, and implementing a new paradigm for advanced language education."[3] The Language Flagship partners with institutions of higher education and seeks to "graduate students who will take their place among the next generation of global professionals, commanding a superior level of proficiency in one of many languages critical to U.S. competitiveness and security."[4] Flagship programs are therefore in the so-called critical or high-need languages, which currently are Arabic, Chinese, Korean, Persian, Portuguese, Russian, and Turkish. Dozens of universities are designated as Flagships (and some host multiple Flagship programs). Students may be attracted to study at a Flagship institution when they wish to pursue advanced competence, not just in the language itself but also in a wide array of subjects related to the countries where the language is spoken. It should be noted that not all faculty members or students wish to be affiliated with programs that are linked to national security needs, though in practice on campus, the direct links to the mission of NSEP are rarely salient.

Currently, the most prevalent instituted model for enhancing language studies is a language center. The functions of these centers vary widely. They might take the form of a basic resource center for pedagogy and technology affiliated with a library, a center for teaching development, or a unit reporting directly to an administrator, such as the dean or the provost. Typically, these centers function by attraction: language instructors can schedule the use of classrooms with technology, participate in pedagogic workshops and lecture series, apply for travel or research funds, or receive orientation when they are first starting. The best models are large-scale centers, usually found at major universities. These typically provide grants and travel funding for teaching assistants and lecturers, support research, organize workshops and symposia, host a range of programs for external constituents, and aim to train and support language instructors. They might also receive significant funding from federal or state governmental agencies. A few centers have endeavored to connect with local communities, either through K-12 school systems or heritage learner associations. This type of activity provides significant value both to the communities and to the university. The best models work bidirectionally. That is, students on campus and community members mutually benefit from the shared engagements, and there is no "top-down" teaching or administering going on.

The most successful language centers do not promote any universal approach to language teaching, because each language department likely has its own pedagogic goals and culture and would likely see the attempt at imposing such an approach as a threat. A well-functioning center, then, does not centralize or homogenize the ways languages are taught. To do so might further exacerbate the split between language teaching and upper-division courses in the departments. Should departments transfer the training of lecturers and teaching assistants (but not of tenure-stream faculty) to a freestanding language center, it might be tempting for those departments to view pedagogy and its technology as not particularly relevant to their core mission. In my view, omitting serious attention to language pedagogy at the department level is an error that needs remediation through structural means (for example, collaborations between the center and the departments, and the participation of chairs and directors of undergraduate and graduate studies on an advisory board of the center).

Many language centers (including technology centers) have responsibility for a wide range of less commonly taught languages (LCTLs). Often working with departments where these courses are needed, the centers establish language-learning programs that might include the development of new materials, online or hybrid courses, in-person tutorials, testing, and coordination with international study. Among the advantages of such a model are consistency in LCTL offerings that may go by the wayside if connected only to departments, distributed expertise in the pedagogy of LCTLs, and technological support for the delivery of these languages.

One of the most promising models in today's landscape is a shared course initiative. The most successful ones use high-definition videoconferencing for synchronous instruction. Several institutions can share LCTL classes, which lets them offer several languages that are not otherwise available on their campuses. These courses are not a form of online computer-based instruction. Rather, they are taught live by an instructor at the sending institution, and students at the receiving institution attend a regular class in a designated classroom outfitted with sophisticated videoconferencing technology. At the receiving end, students see teachers and are able to interact via videoconference with them and the other classroom of students. Students register at their home institution through the regular registration process. While a shared course arrangement is expensive to set up and requires administrative coordination, like working with different academic calendars, it offers students an in-person classroom that provides the kind of personalization that makes language learning especially relevant.

Another high-impact structure to sustain excellence in languages is the consortium model. Generally set up to enhance the quality of language teaching and learning on the member campuses, these consortia enhance the strengths of the members' programs. Some consortia sponsor symposia, workshops, campus-based initiatives, and materials development. Individual faculty members and administrators from the member campuses meet from time to time to advance work in the field of language acquisition and teaching. Some consortia are set up to concentrate exclusively on LCTLs. They might collaboratively develop online models of LCTL instruction, conduct research in LCTL proficiency assessment, and work to enhance teacher education and professional development.

One of the most transformational language programs is the intensive summer study model. In the most successful summer programs, students live the language 24/7 and have access to their professors for most of the day (and often during evening events). Their out-of-class activities might include theater and music as well as athletic activities, film-themed evenings, and so on. Some universities offer modified nonresidential summer intensive programs, while others use the intersession period. Universities and colleges that prepare their students for study abroad in an intensive program perform a great service, since an immersive study abroad experience correlates highly to advanced proficiency.

Language study in countries where the target language is spoken continues to set the gold standard for developing the kinds of language skills that help students obtain work using the language or go on to graduate studies. The structure of these programs, however, makes a significant difference as to how far a student can get with advanced competence. Those that offer students precious little besides a few hours of classroom instruction a day with other native English speakers have lower chances of success compared with more immersive styles that require students to speak the language outside of class, provide cultural activities, and so on. The number of students studying abroad has increased over the years (so has the number of undergraduate students enrolled in college-level courses), but the duration of the time spent abroad has been dropping. In 2006–07, 9.8 percent of those who studied abroad participated in programs of eight weeks or less; in 2016–17, the figure doubled (to 18.8 percent). In 2018, 65 percent of students who studied abroad were enrolled in summer programs or those of eight weeks or less. Over half of those students went to Europe.[5]

What these data don't show is the language in which the course work is taught. An increasing trend in study abroad is that US university students hear more English than the local language. A typical example: students study art history in Italy, receiving most of their courses in English, with perhaps one Italian-language course (either required or recommended). A stay in Italy without intensive language study is unlikely to produce any useful level of fluency, though the cultural immersion certainly shouldn't be discounted. Further, students are finding it more burdensome to travel outside the United States because of the cost. High tuition at the home institution coupled with the expenses associated with living abroad and accumulating student debt are several factors that account for the trend. Many nonlanguage majors cite the requirements in their majors as a factor that prohibits going away to study in other countries. Finally, students and their families have been experiencing increased anxiety about the safety of studying abroad, particularly in countries where there have been one-time or sporadic attacks; discrimination against people of color, women, or gay and lesbian students; or other factors (even if the percentage of students who have undergone traumatic events outside the United States may not be greater than what happens on this country's campuses and in local communities).

In this final section, I want to expand on two notions I've mentioned above. The first is the content of language studies on college campuses. As the MLA 2007 report indicates, a successful curriculum in the major (and in the department in general) must move away from the ancient model of courses centered exclusively on literature, translation, and diachronic linguistics.[6] The reality on the ground is that virtually no campus continues to offer this kind of approach to language study. Yet those who cling to the myth that literature is antithetical or irrelevant to proficiency at worst and secondary or arbitrary at best may not have explored the shifts that have taken place in courses grouped under the rubric of literature. The literary-, history-, and genre-based model that many of us learned as undergraduate and PhD students has yielded to new forms of cultural analysis, film and art studies, historicism, place-based explorations like urban studies, and so on. Further, many language departments are hiring specialists in adjacent fields, such as philosophy, anthropology, and history. These professors, either native speakers of the target language or highly fluent, can offer courses that appeal to a wide range of students who want to achieve advanced competence and explore fields that are not literary per se. Those who levy a blanket critique of what language departments are doing to prepare students for a multilingual world need to take a closer look at the diversity and depth of curricula as well as the structures provided for learning (internships, group projects and publications, and community-based service, to name a few).

It is also not the case that most undergraduate language programs teach literary and cultural theory at the expense of all else. Even if theory is foregrounded in a few courses, it can be an intellectual pursuit that makes sense. After all, in a university curriculum, virtually all learning in all subjects is based on theory, whether or not professors make it explicit in their classrooms. The myth that literary theory is the dominant force in language departments is therefore especially pernicious because, at heart, it is an anti-intellectual argument that depicts theory as the enemy of the practical acquisition of language skills. It's impossible to imagine mathematics, physics, or biology without theory; the same holds true of anthropology, sociology, and economics. Why, then, is literature singled out as a field that needs to be exempt from theory (or, at least, a theory that dares speak its name in the classroom)? Granted, the late 1970s and 1980s may have foregrounded theory in such a way that literary texts themselves may have seemed to recede. And yet studying a theoretical text in the language— a text whose syntax, vocabulary, and overall structure convey important meaning—happens to be a useful and productive approach to the literary and cultural realms that are the province of the language major. I could name theorists' names here, yet to do so might provoke some of the knee-jerk dismay that we've seen over the last few decades. As with all fields of study, it is the professor's job to reflect on what students will learn in the class, how the learning will take place and be assessed, and what relations exist between the single course and the larger curriculum. Having worked with thousands of language and literature professors in my role at the MLA, I can say with confidence that amazing transformations have taken place at the departmental level and in the wider sphere of research and publication. One has to get up close and personal to see these things, however, and not many people are afforded the viewpoint that I have been privileged to enjoy.

My second point concerns the optimal delivery of language instruction on college and university campuses. If the sole purpose of language courses is to help students achieve advanced proficiency in everyday communications (oral, aural, reading, writing), why study in a university setting at all? There are many language academies here and abroad and online programs for achieving this sort of fluency. The reasons are fairly straightforward, and I alluded to them in the previous comment. University professors provide the kind of intellectual content that can't be found in language institutes. Unless someone wants a superficial knowledge of culture, only an expert can give a full preparation in history, the arts, literary traditions, race relations, the role of women in society, geopolitics, and on and on. And only in this context can a student fully develop the kind of analytic skills that will become transferable to wider contexts, such as employment in the business, governmental, and nonprofit sectors.

Yet despite what I have just said about the curriculum, I believe that an optimal university language program must look beyond the department level for sustenance. A well-functioning language center is the best model

I've observed, particularly in large institutions. Individual departments would have a hard time cultivating adequate preparation and support for language instructors without some kind of centralized structure. In a department that supports multiple modern languages, such a structure might exist internally. The advantage of a language center, however, is the location of expertise and technology in one place. Further, project-based work that doesn't necessarily connect to the curriculum can distinguish the institution, as can grant or training programs for language instructors. I've seen some remarkable work being done by language centers; I've also seen some centers that, either in their minimalist structure or their competition with departments, fail to provide adequate benefit to the campus.

What's often missing in the model I just discussed is the integration of tenure-line faculty members who teach courses on culture, literature, film, history, and so on. An ideal language center would establish connections to the departmental tenure-line faculty in those fields; an ideal department would make those connections work. Is this asking too much within the current context of cutbacks in the humanities? Quite the opposite: I see such a model as a way to buttress and strengthen language teaching that so many students want for intellectual and vocational purposes. Some of my work as a consultant has been helping universities achieve this kind of vision for the construction and integration of a highly functional language center or an internal structure in the department that accomplishes some of the same purposes.

My vision, as is readily discernible, evidences a kind of optimism for the future of language studies that many people might not share. The relentless focus on enrollments on the part of administrators may miss the bigger picture of what's actually possible to strengthen offerings. A wise combination of hiring and supporting faculty members along with creating the right structures for language delivery and undertaking imaginative, project-based work seems the best predictor of success going forward. The question of mission needs to be addressed at every level of the university, right down to the department. Clarification of mission and the vision to carry it out can transform an ad hoc curriculum and delivery of language instruction into a coherent and creative enterprise. I commend those university citizens who are devoted to this ideal, and I look forward to learning more about the results of their work.

Notes

1. MLA Ad Hoc Committee on Foreign Languages, "Foreign Languages," 234–45.
2. MLA Ad Hoc Committee on Foreign Languages, "Foreign Languages."
3. "Our Mission."
4. Ibid.
5. Institute of International Education, "Duration of Study Abroad."
6. MLA Ad Hoc Committee on Foreign Languages, "Foreign Languages."

Bibliography

Institute of International Education. "Duration of Study Abroad." 2018 Open Doors Report. Accessed April 20, 2020. https://www.iie.org/Research-and-Insights/Open-Doors /Data/US-Study-Abroad/Duration-of-Study-Abroad.

MLA Ad Hoc Committee on Foreign Languages. "Foreign Languages and Higher Education: New Structures for a Changed World." *Profession* (2007): 234–45. https://doi.org/10.1632 /prof.2007.2007.1.234.

"Our Mission." About Us, The Language Flagship. Accessed April 20, 2020. https:// thelanguageflagship.org/content/about-us.

14

ENSURING US NATIONAL CAPACITY IN WORLD LANGUAGES AND CULTURES FOR THE TWENTY-FIRST CENTURY

More Learners, More Languages, Better Results!

Dan E. Davidson

THE 2017 REPORT OF THE American Academy of Arts and Sciences' Commission on Language Learning, *America's Languages: Investing in Language Education for the 21st Century*, has presented a wide-ranging and well-documented view of the United States' current language needs: what language capacities and resources are now in place and how US needs are likely to change in the years to come. Foremost among the Commission's recommendations is the call for "a national strategy to broaden access to language education for every student in the United States as preparation for life and work in the global 21st century," which will include "opportunities for students to travel and experience other cultures, immerse themselves in languages as they are used in everyday interactions and across all segments of society."[1]

Access to a second language, whether a heritage language, a tribal language, a critical language, or another widely spoken world language like German, French, or Spanish, is increasingly associated with social and economic advancement in today's highly interconnected world. The need for connectivity begins with our own communication-based society, where, according to a 2015 Census Bureau report, approximately 21 percent of US citizens five years of age and older speak a language at home other than English. US domestic capacity in language is highly critical for our national security, for the nation's global competitiveness, and for the United States' domestic social cohesion and ability to ensure equal rights and access to opportunity and social services for all groups.

The Federal Role in Supporting Language and Regional Studies

Like so many others in the language and area studies fields over the past decades, I personally benefitted from Title VI support of my graduate studies in Slavic at Harvard in the late 1960s, as well as from the opportunity to undertake intensive language and area studies in Russian as an undergraduate at the University of Kansas. The Title VI centers, taken together, are the central component of US publicly supported research and training in the critical regions of the world. Closely intertwined with Title VI is the Fulbright-Hays Program, which has supported PhD dissertation fellowships in area studies and played a major role for decades in the support of advanced training, K-16 pre-service, and in-service teacher professional development through its short- and long-term Group Projects Abroad in the critical languages.

A further component within this admittedly modest portfolio of US federal support for language and regional studies is the Title VIII program for research and training in Russian, East European, and Eurasian studies, established by the US Congress in 1983 at the State Department (Bureau of Intelligence and Research) as a carefully designed complement to Title VI for the support of independent scholars, including those without US citizenship, as well as of graduate students and postdoctoral and senior scholars for overseas field work, archival research, and advanced language training. Title VIII prioritizes support of policy-relevant research in the humanities and social sciences.

The tragedy of 9/11 and the extended conflicts that followed have brought home to US policy makers, in a way that previous events did not, the reality of the threat to US national security posed by the staggering shortfall across all federal agencies in personnel competent in critical languages and strategic world areas, including the absence within government of a linguistic "surge capacity" for responding to crises in areas of the world not necessarily previously identified as strategic. Concerns about US competitiveness in the global economy contributed to increased public awareness that US economic security is no less central to our national security than the country's ability to respond diplomatically, strategically, and militarily to challenges or threats anywhere in the world. Afghanistan and Iraq brought a heightened awareness of the continuing peril that the nation faces from an array of state and nonstate actors around the globe, players who have proven themselves adept at taking advantage of the linguistic and cultural vulnerabilities of US servicepeople on the battlefield, even as they exercise formidable skills in the manipulation of information and the media worldwide. The distinguished military historian Retired Major General Robert Scales, whose writings are frequently cited by current US policy makers, noted in 2006, "In the Iraq wars a curtain of cultural ignorance continues to separate the good intentions of the American soldier from indigenous peoples of good will. . . . Inability to speak the language and insensitive conduct become real combat vulnerabilities that the enemy has exploited to his advantage."[2] By contrast, competence in the local language(s) empowers and magnifies the professional's capacity (whether uniformed or civilian) for understanding and responding effectively and appropriately when faced with a conflict-ridden situation.

Following a series of hearings convened to examine Defense Department responses to language and cultural issues, a House Armed Services Committee (HASC) subcommittee reached the conclusion that the serious deficit of language skills and cultural expertise in the military is a reflection of a much broader national pattern of neglect of the teaching of foreign languages, and of the less commonly taught languages in particular, in K-12 education. Among other forms of evidence, the subcommittee report noted that very few states require language study for graduation and that this, in turn, has significantly limited the pool from which the Department of Defense can recruit linguistically qualified personnel. In short, the primary solution to the crisis in being able to respond to the growing demands for linguistically and culturally enabled personnel across government agencies was to be found in the nation's K-12 education system. As the report noted,

> The [Defense] Department finds itself in the unlikely position of advancing a national educational agenda that encourages states to recognize the importance of language skills and cultural awareness, not only to meet national security needs, but for the United States to remain competitive in the global marketplace, and for states to provide basic services to their citizens. Today's military establishment, its active duty, reserve, and civilian personnel, must be trained and ready to engage the world with an appreciation of diverse cultures and to communicate directly with local populations.
>
> Professional-level language, cultural, and area skills are no longer a "nice-to-have," nor are they viewed as necessary only to a small cohort of senior analysts and diplomats.[3]

They are central to the military's core mission, and, most importantly, the report concludes, "*These skills save lives.*"[4]

In January 2006, President George W. Bush announced the creation of the National Security Language Initiative (NSLI) in order "to dramatically increase the number of Americans learning critical need foreign languages such as Arabic, Chinese, Farsi, Hindi and others through new and expanded programs from kindergarten through university and into the workforce."[5] The multiagency initiative NSLI represented a portfolio of new or expanded federally supported training programs, including the STARTALK summer domestic programs for K-12 students and teachers of critical languages, funded by the Office of the Director of National Intelligence; major new language-focused State Department exchanges including NSLI-Y[outh] and Critical Language Scholarship (CLS) Program, Fulbright Teaching Fellows, and (K-12) Teachers of Critical Languages (TCLP); and multiple initiatives of the National Security Education Program (NSEP) of the Department of Defense, including the National Language Flagship (initiated in 2003), the National (Civilian) Language Service Corps, Project Global Officer, campus Language Training Centers for in-service military personnel, and support for technologies, assessment, and K-12 partnerships.[6]

The NSLI programs are competitive and open to students of all social, economic, regional, institutional, and academic backgrounds (rather than focusing primarily on language and area studies majors). All programs seek to maximize language and cultural growth by drawing on proven program models, such as domestic summer institutes, intensive summer- and year-long overseas immersion programs, integrated cultural and practical training, and proficiency-based curricula and assessments. Taken together, the newly introduced cluster of federally sponsored NSLI training programs targeted the study of Arabic, Chinese (Mandarin), Hindi, Korean, Persian, Russian, and Turkish, a portfolio that has expanded over the past decade. For example, the CLS Program currently offers summer overseas immersion training in fifteen critical languages: Arabic, Azeri, Bahasa, Bangla, Chinese, Hindi, Japanese, Korean, Persian, Portuguese (Brazilian), Punjabi, Russian, Swahili, Turkish, and Urdu. The Flagship Capstone Program and the African Flagship Language Initiative also support training in multiple languages or dialects for regions where multilingualism is the norm—for example, Modern Standard Arabic as well as Moroccan (and also Egyptian dialect) in Meknes; Kazakh as well as Russian in Almaty; and Wolof as well as Northwest African Francophone in Senegal.

Ten Years Later (2006–16): What Do the Numbers Tell Us?

To date, the NSLI portfolio of programs has supported more than eighty-five thousand K–12 students and teachers and more than fifteen thousand undergraduate and graduate students for domestic and overseas study of critical languages and cultures.[7] Within the context of rising interest in the study of the strategic languages (Chinese in particular), NSLI programming has benefitted significant numbers of US students at critical junctures in their language learning careers: STARTALK and TCLP have created new opportunities for thousands of K–12 students annually to begin or continue the study of a strategic language in hundreds of communities in each of the fifty United States and the District of Columbia.[8]

Participants in NSLI programs are encouraged to consider careers in government, and applicants to these programs frequently cite an interest in government service as informing their decisions to undertake study of the critical languages and participate in the NSLI scholarship programs.[9]

The State Department's NSLI-Y Program provides support to 550 K–12 students each year, 30–40 percent of whom have no prior knowledge of the language, to study for a summer or a full academic year in one of its seven overseas study centers in China, the Middle East, Moldova, Russia, or Taiwan. Post-test results for NSLI-Y summer students, collected over the past decade, reflect levels of end-of-program proficiency in speaking, reading, and listening in the American Council on the Teaching of Foreign Languages (ACTFL) "Intermediate" range, a level consistent with those of most second-year college-level students enrolled in regular through-the-year academic courses.[10]

NSLI-Y year-long participants typically test at the "Advanced" range in speaking and the "Intermediate High" to "Advanced Low" levels in reading and listening upon completion of the nine-month overseas academic programs. As entering freshmen, NSLI-Y students who have spent either the senior year or a gap year abroad in China, Moldova, Morocco, or Taiwan typically place into advanced (junior/senior) college-level target language or content-based courses and frequently continue language studies throughout their college careers, regardless of their choice of a major field.

Graduates of the State Department's eight-week CLS programs typically present test scores one threshold level above the preprogram levels, with most students scoring at the "Intermediate High" or "Advanced Low/Mid" levels at the completion of the program—functional proficiency sufficient for satisfying routine communication and work-level activity in the target culture.[11]

Graduates of the NSEP Language Flagship Capstone Year, students either in their junior or senior year of college, generally attain ILR 3 (ACT-FL "Advanced High/Superior") levels across three or four skills. Until the introduction of the Flagship Program, very few US graduating seniors, including undergraduate language majors (apart from the occasional accomplished heritage speaker), could demonstrate these levels of linguistic and cultural skills. Level 3 proficiencies are required for many language-designated professional positions across dozens of federal agencies, where superior foreign language and cultural skills as well as regional knowledge are critical for performance of the duties of those positions.

While many Language Flagship Capstone graduates go on to serve in the US government (indeed, some apply for Boren Scholarship Awards, which entail a one-year federal service requirement, with hopes of entering government service afterward), many others enter graduate or professional school or take up positions in business, think tanks, or nonprofits as professional-level speakers, prepared to pursue research or full-time graduate study.[12] Flagship alumni also have the opportunity to serve in the National Language Service Corps, a program that makes it possible to pursue civilian careers and still be hired by the US government on a temporary basis as government linguists in times of need, such as during national emergencies or natural disasters.[13]

Over the past ten to fifteen years, Flagship students have formed an expanding pipeline of superior-level L2 speakers with substantial in-country study and professional internship experience, who elect to pursue graduate studies in East Asian, Eurasian, Middle Eastern, or Near Asian studies at Title VI-supported graduate programs, either at the MA or PhD levels. Not surprisingly, many of the major universities that compete successfully to offer Flagship domestic programs also host Title VI National Resource Centers or Language Resource Centers. Indiana University is a prime example: there are currently eleven federally funded Title VI centers on the Bloomington campus, which has also hosted domestic Flagship centers for Arabic, Chinese, Russian, Swahili, and Turkish. The concentration of resources and academic talent available at Indiana University clearly has generated synergies that contribute richly to the research mission of the institution, the educational needs of its students, and the larger policy goals of the US government. Similar government–higher education partnerships supporting both Title VI and Flagship centers can be found at major research universities in Arizona, California, Georgia, Hawaii, Mississippi, North Carolina, Oregon, Texas, Virginia, Washington, and Wisconsin.

US World Language Enrollment Trends: Knowing Where to Look

K-12 enrollment levels in world language study provide a useful, if underutilized, indicator of the state of the educational pipeline for second languages and, indirectly, a sense of the interest levels of a rising generation of US students in other cultures and the outside world. The most recent survey of world language enrollment numbers shows a total of 10.6 million K-12 students in the United States enrolled in the study of languages other than English, a number that is currently 7.5 times greater than the number of students enrolled in world languages (1.3 million) at the nation's two- and four-year colleges for the same school year.[14]

Overall, 19.66 percent of all K-12 students in the United States were enrolled in a foreign language in the 2014–15 school year, while 7.5 percent of tertiary-level students were formally engaged in language study. While higher-education enrollments in foreign language have declined since 2009, K-12 enrollments in languages have grown by 40 percent in absolute numbers over that same period and by an estimated 1.2 percent annually as a percentage of total K-12 enrollments. Both numbers are significant in that world language enrollments do *not* include enrollment data for English language learners, heritage speakers whose numbers over this period have also grown considerably.[15]

Any assessment of the current state of foreign language education in the United States should, therefore, take into account both the K-12 and higher education language enrollment trends, with an understanding that the realities on the ground are, not surprisingly, more complex than these top-line figures might indicate. Investments in K-12 language education vary greatly from one state to another, with as few as 8 percent of students in some states (such as Alabama and New Mexico) enrolled in world languages, to 40-50 percent of all students in other states (such as New Jersey and Maryland, as well as the District of Columbia). District-level differences within a single state and building-level differences within a single school district contribute further to an all-too-predictable pattern of socioeconomic privilege and varying resource levels, which further limit broad access to world language instruction in the United States.

As noted in the American Academy commission report, K-12 world languages are also at the center of one of the most significant innovations affecting US education today: dual language immersion, which is incorporated into 2,500–3,000 programs across the nation as of this writing.[16] Among those states with notably active enrollments in foreign languages are California, Delaware, Georgia, North Carolina, Oregon, and Utah, where state- or district-level 50/50 dual language immersion programs are being implemented at the K-5 and K-8 levels and beyond. Dual language instruction is often linked to the local population demographics, in which Spanish, Chinese, French, Japanese, Russian, and Portuguese are representative of the languages most frequently encountered.[17] Dual language immersion programs may or may not be reflected in state-level foreign language enrollment reporting, given that courses taught in the "partner language" are treated as subject courses rather than foreign language courses.

With Chinese K-12 enrollments doubling at the national level between 2007 and 2015, Japanese and Korean are also registering growth well above the national average, and Arabic, Russian, and Portuguese are more or less holding their own over this same period. In other words, the dynamics of K-12 enrollment change among critical languages is neither zero-sum nor a subtractive process. Although some districts have discontinued world language programming, others have introduced new programs in Arabic, Chinese, Japanese, Korean, or Russian. The data for Russian, for example, are typical: thirty-one states and the District of Columbia showed an increase in enrollments in Russian between 2007 and 2015, while eighteen states showed a decline, and one state remained unchanged. As noted in the 2008 HASC subcommittee report (cited above), the decision by state educational authorities to establish a foreign language requirement for high school graduation affects K-12 enrollments notably, particularly at the senior secondary level. Among those states with positive gains in language enrollments, ten have a graduation requirement, while an additional twenty states "recommend" foreign language study for graduation.[18]

Next Steps: Meeting US Needs, Scaling Up Model Programs

Whether for the production of new knowledge and expertise or the preparation of a globally competent citizenry, US K-20 educational institutions represent the United States' potential for creating the next generation of regional experts, world language teachers, and multilingual analysts, as well as for ensuring the availability of a workforce of internationally connected engineers, scientists, doctors, lawyers, politicians, artists, entrepreneurs, and social workers. While small compared to other federal initiatives, the Title VI and the NSLI program portfolios represent proven models of federal support for US education that can generate high-level expertise in regional affairs, while expanding US national capacity in the strategic languages for service in government and across all the professions.

Expert levels of language and area knowledge are vital for our defense, intelligence, and diplomatic communities, while global security challenges in health, environment, food production, immigration, and cybersecurity rely on professional levels of language and cultural knowledge across virtually all fields. A closely watched Senate hearing in May 2012, convened by the late Senator Daniel Akaka (D-HI), presented public testimony by senior human resource officials of the four major federal agencies dealing with US national security (defense, homeland security, justice, and state) on the current state of linguistic readiness in their respective agencies, to the extent that such information was available.[19] While investments over the decade following 9/11 in the training of new specialists undoubtedly helped to improve these levels, they were, nonetheless, still shockingly low. For example, the success rate in filling advanced-level language-designated positions in the Defense Department in 2012 stood at 28 percent.[20] Only a significantly expanded and sustained joint effort by the government and the US educational community can effectively address the present shortfall.

In the coming decades, the United States will also require heretofore unprecedented numbers of professional- and occupational-level employees competent in foreign languages and capable of ensuring the effective, fair, and equitable operation of our law enforcement, health care, courts, schools, welfare, and social services, as well as in the transportation and consumer spheres here at home. Our research universities and the Title VI centers that support them are the principal source of that expertise, as well as of a new generation of teachers and scholars who will carry the work forward in the future.

"Monolingualism is the illiteracy of the 21st century," a familiar US rallying cry, has now been adopted as well by the British Council and the Royal Academies in their own more recent "Call for Action" in response to the regrettable state of foreign language instruction at all levels in Brexit-era United Kingdom.[21] Thanks to the federal investments in US education represented by Title VI/Fulbright-Hays and the NSLI portfolio of programs, the United States is in a potentially more favorable position regarding world languages than is the United Kingdom. US students can and now do master languages, including the critical languages, at the professional level by the time they graduate from college, with only limited amounts of federal or other external support at key junctures in their learning careers. The twentieth-century anecdotal view of the US student who studied two years of high school French, only later to find no one in France they were able to communicate with, is beginning to give way to a very different image, that of a high-functioning bilingual who combines high-level language study and direct enrollment in content courses at an overseas university, participates in professional internships, and engages in public speaking in the target language on areas of specialization to local audiences.[22]

As is evident from the concurrent trends in K-12 language and dual language enrollment programs around the country, parents (and school districts) are beginning to understand the value of language for their children, very much like parents in virtually all other parts of the world, and are demanding more foreign language study, especially in primary schools. Moreover, the number of US citizens emerging from the public education system, majors and nonmajors, graduates of institutions of various types, with professional-level language and cultural skills in a critical language, demonstrates the broad applicability of the NSLI/Flagship language training model. As the American Academy Commission on Languages makes clear: these models should now be expanded and taken to scale if US education is to meet the myriad linguistic and cultural needs of government, business, research, and the social sector in the decades ahead.

Indiana University possesses a strong institutional model for campus internationalization and the academic leadership essential for preparing a new generation of multilingual, globally competent US citizens. The agenda for the university's next two hundred years will undoubtedly magnify that role many times over, especially if the US succeeds in bringing world language study into our nation's core curriculum alongside English, math, and science, where it already comfortably resides in most other countries of the world.

Notes

1. Commission on Language Learning, *America's Languages*, 27.
2. Scales, "Clausewitz."

3. "Professional-level" is explicitly identified by the Defense Department as Interagency Language Roundtable (ILR) Level 3 in 2002 as the target proficiency necessary for professionals to perform their duties accurately. See Nugent and Slater, "Language Flagship," 10.

4. US House of Representatives, "Building Language Skills," 110-12. Emphasis added.

5. The National Security Education Initiative of 2006 built on the Department of Defense's "Defense Language Transformation Roadmap" of 2005, spearheaded by Dr. David Chu, the Undersecretary of Defense for Personnel and Readiness at that time. The Roadmap served as a blueprint for strengthening US language and regional capabilities based on the principle that "the need for foreign language capability will not abate. Robust foreign language and foreign area expertise are critical to sustaining coalitions, pursuing regional stability, and conducting multi-national missions especially in post-conflict and other than combat security, humanitarian, nation-building, and stability operations." See McGinn, "Foreign Language," 6-8, 9-11.

6. These programs included the National Security Language Initiative for Youth (NSLI-Y) summer and year-long study abroad placements for US high school students in strategic regions of the world; the Critical Language Scholarship Program (CLS), an eight-week overseas immersion summer institute for US undergraduates and graduates; the Fulbright Foreign Language Teaching Assistants (FLTA) Program; and the Teachers of Critical Languages Programs (TCLP), enabling US school districts to host visiting language teachers from China, Egypt, and Morocco. Nugent and Slater, "Language Flagship," 9-28.

7. Total participant numbers are available for the period 2007–19: NSLI-Y Summer, 5,959; NSLI-Y Academic Year, 837; CLS, 6,600; Flagship Capstone Graduates, 1,960; STARTALK, 1,727 programs, 65,680 students, and 14,021 teachers for a combined total of 79,701. See also STARTALK, "Start Talking!," 4.

8. In some cases, these federal domestic study initiatives have led to the introduction of new programs for the study of Arabic, Chinese, and Russian in school districts where they were not previously available.

9. As of 2018, for example, NSEP award recipients have completed work in 3,970 federally funded positions, with approximately 78 percent of those placements in priority agencies, such as the Department of Defense, Department of State, Department of Homeland Security, and the intelligence community. See Defense Language and National Security Office, *2018 Annual Report*.

10. Davidson, "Development of L2 Proficiency," 117–50.

11. CLS programs now operate across fifteen languages, including Arabic, Azeri, Bahasa, Bangla, Chinese, Hindi, Japanese, Korean, Persian, Portuguese (Brazilian), Russian, Swahili, Turkish, and Urdu.

12. NSEP 2019 Annual Report, "Locations of Federal Service by NSEP Awardees," 5; 63–71. https://nsep.gov/sites/default/files/NSEP%202019%20Annual%20Report.pdf.

13. NSEP 2019 Annual Report, "National Language Service Corps," 44–50. https://nsep.gov/sites/default/files/NSEP%202019%20Annual%20Report.pdf.

14. The American Councils for International Education report 10.64 million K-12 foreign language enrollments in the 2014-15 school year in the United States. American Councils for International Education, *National K-12*, 7, table 1. MLA surveys of two- and four-year college enrollments in foreign languages conducted in 2013 and again in 2016, in turn, report aggregate foreign language enrollments of 1.56 million and 1.41 million, respectively. Looney and Lusin, *Enrollments*, 13, table 1.

15. Aggregate numbers as well as state-by-state enrollments in foreign languages illustrate the disparities that exist across the United States in availability for foreign language study in 2009 and in 2015. See American Councils for International Education, *National K-12*; American Council on the Teaching of Foreign Languages, *Foreign Language Enrollments*.

16. American Councils for International Education, "DLI Research Alliance." See also Fausett, "Louisiana Says 'Oui.'"

17. American Academy of Arts and Sciences, "Dual Language Immersion," 15.

18. Education Commission of the States, "High School Graduation Requirements."

19. Senate Committee on Homeland Security and Governmental Affairs, *National Security Crisis*.

20. Ibid.

21. Roberts and Wade, "Monolingualism," 116–18. See also British Academy, "Languages in the UK."

22. Direct enrollment, internships, homestays, and public presentations are a regular part of all overseas Flagship Capstone Programs, which now include thirty-one programs at twenty-three US college and university partners.

Bibliography

American Council on the Teaching of Foreign Languages. *Foreign Language Enrollments in K–12 Public Schools: Are Students Prepared for a Global Society?* Alexandria, VA, 2009. https://www.ced.org/pdf/actfl-k12-foreign-language-for-global-society.pdf.

American Councils for International Education. "DLI Research Alliance." Research and Assessment. Accessed April 20, 2020. https://www.americancouncils.org/research -assessment/dli-research-alliance.

———. *The National K–12 Foreign Language Enrollment Survey Report.* June 2017. https:// www.americancouncils.org/sites/default/files/FLE-report-June17.pdf.

British Academy. *Languages in the UK: A Call for Action.* Policy and Research, London, 2019.

Commission on Language Learning. *America's Languages: Investing in Language Education for the 21st Century.* American Academy of Arts and Sciences, February 2017. https:// www.amacad.org/publication/americas-languages.

———. "Dual Language Immersion." In *America's Languages: Investing in Language Education for the 21st Century.* American Academy of Arts and Sciences, February 2017. https://www.amacad.org/sites/default/files/publication/downloads/Commission-on -Language-Learning_Americas-Languages.pdf.

Davidson, Dan E. "The Development of L2 Proficiency and Literacy within the Context of the Federally Supported Overseas Language Training Programs for Americans." In *To Advanced Proficiency and Beyond: Theory and Methods for Developing Superior Second Language Ability,* edited by Tony Brown and Jennifer Bown, 117–50. Washington, DC: Georgetown University Press, 2014. www.jstor.org/stable/j.ctt13x0djn.12.

Defense Language and National Security Office. *2019 Annual Report: National Security Education Program.* December 10, 2019. https://nsep.gov/sites/default/files/NSEP%20 2019%20Annual%20Report.pdf.

Education Commission of the States. "High School Graduation Requirements." 50-State Comparison. Last modified February 2019. https://coarw235.caspio.com/dp /b7f930000e16e10a822c47b3baa2.

Fausett, Richard. "Louisiana Says 'Oui' to French, amid Explosion in Dual-Language Schools." *New York Times*, August 20, 2019. https://www.nytimes.com/2019/08/21/us /louisiana-french-dual-language.html.

Looney, Dennis, and Natalia Lusin. *Enrollments in Languages Other Than English in United States Institutions of Higher Education, Summer 2016 and Fall 2016: Preliminary Report.* Modern Language Association, New York, February 2018. https://www.mla.org /content/download/83540/2197676/2016-Enrollments-ShortReport.pdf.

McGinn, Gail H. "Foreign Language, Cultural Diplomacy, and Global Security." American Academy of Arts and Sciences Commission on Language Learning: White Papers. Cambridge, MA, 2017. https://www.amacad.org/sites/default/files/media/document /2019–02/Foreign-language-Cultural-Diplomacy-Global-Security.pdf.

Nugent, Michael, and Robert Slater. "The Language Flagship: Creating Expectations and Opportunities for Professional Level Language Learning in Undergraduate Education." In *Exploring the U.S. Language Flagship Program: Professional Competence in a Second Language by Graduation*, edited by Dianna Murphy and Karen Evans-Romaine, 9-28. Bristol, UK: Multilingual Matters, 2016.

Roberts, Gregg, Jamie Leite, and Ofelia Wade. "Monolingualism Is the Illiteracy of the Twenty-First Century." *Hispania* 10, no. 5 (2018): 116–18.

Scales, Major General Robert H. "Clausewitz and World War IV." *Armed Forces Journal*, July 1, 2006. http://armedforcesjournal.com/clausewitz-and-world-war-iv/.

Senate Committee on Homeland Security and Governmental Affairs. *A National Security Crisis: Foreign Language Capabilities in the Federal Government.* May 21, 2012, 112th Cong., 2d sess., S. Hrg. 112–663. https://www.govinfo.gov/content/pkg/CHRG -112shrg75214/html/CHRG-112shrg75214.htm.

STARTALK. "Start Talking! 2017 Longitudinal Impact Report: Student Participants (2007–2016)." National Foreign Language Center, University of Maryland. https://startalk .umd.edu/public/system/files/resources/student_longitudinal_survey_report _2007–2016.pdf.

US House of Representatives, Committee on Armed Services, Subcommittee on Oversight and Investigations. *Building Language Skills and Cultural Competencies in the Military: DOD's Challenge in Today's Educational Environment.* Committee print, November 2008, 110–12. https://apps.dtic.mil/dtic/tr/fulltext/u2/a494470.pdf.

15

MYAAMIAATAWEENKI

The Myaamia Language

Daryl Baldwin

Aya ceeki
    Tipeewe neeyolakakoki oowaaha noonki kaahkiihkwe
    kinwalaniihsia weenswiaani, niila myaamia mihtohseenia
    Mihši-neewe kocimiyiikwi pyaayaani oowaaha aatotamoolakakoki
myaamiaki neehi myaamiaataweenki
    Neewe

These are the words with which I opened my presentation at the bicentennial symposium International Education at the Crossroads, which was the basis for the current chapter. The translation is as follows:

Hello everyone,
    It's good to see you all here today.
    My name is Daryl Baldwin, and I am a citizen of the Miami Tribe of Oklahoma.
    Thank you for asking me to come here and speak with you all about the Myaamia people and our heritage language.
    Thank you.

I wanted to open in my heritage language—primarily because it is the language of the land on which we were gathered. Our heritage, which includes our language and our culture, is deeply embedded within a place and from intergenerational experience. Like many Indigenous people, we still view English as an immigrant language, even though for many of us it is now our first language. Sometimes we need to be reminded that English was not born of this soil as our own Indigenous languages were but was, in fact, brought here from other places. One reason that I chose to point this out is because as Indigenous people, we do not have another country to retreat to in order to speak our language or practice our cultures. If our languages are going to be spoken, they are going to be spoken right here. The challenge for us is to figure out what those community language domains are going to be, how we are going to create those spaces, what resources are needed to sustain them across the generations, and to what extent US citizens are going to support our efforts. That makes the preservation of our language largely a human rights issue—the right and freedom to be who we are in the place that we are from.

My personal work in language and culture revitalization hinges on a larger community effort to reclaim Myaamia ways of knowing and ways of being. Community education is at the core of passing on our Indigenous knowledge system through a language that best reflects that system and promotes not only language but also our cultural practices and value system. This collective educational effort requires many human and financial resources. We do this work to strengthen our heritage and kinship connections to each other and to strengthen the tribal nation as it heals from its past. All of this is accomplished with a mind and heart for the generations that helped preserve our tribal nation through significant hardships. Our recent history has largely shaped what we do and to some degree how we do it. Our survival as a tribal nation through the "making of America" is a testament to our ability to survive and adapt so that we may figure out a way to be in the twenty-first century.

My intent in this piece is to give a brief overview, which might feel like a 10,000-foot view, of what language reconstruction and revitalization looks like for one particular tribe. I do not speak on behalf of other tribes, and I want to acknowledge that there are other tribes besides the Miami that are Indigenous to southern Indiana and that have equal right to claim a history or presence there. We refer to our language as Myaamiaataweenki in our language. Linguists refer to the language as the Miami-Illinois language. It was widely spoken throughout this region, including western Ohio, lower portions of Michigan and Wisconsin, and extending west to the Mississippi River.

In 1830, Congress passed the Removal Act, which called for the removal of tribes east of the Mississippi to reservations west of the Mississippi. Our ancestors resisted removal for as long as they could, but in 1840, they eventually signed a treaty calling for their removal in five years—if not willingly, then by force.

Our ancestors signed the treaty thinking that they would not actually have to leave their beloved homeland, but circumstances produced a situation where a military escort was called in, and in 1846, they were loaded onto three canal boats near present-day Peru, Indiana, and then traveled up to Fort Wayne, where two more canal boats were loaded with people. From Fort Wayne, they began the journey into the Ohio country and down the Miami-Erie Canal system to Cincinnati, where they were then loaded onto steamships and headed west. Five Miami family groups were allowed to remain in Indiana; this forced removal thus fragmented the Miami population. The Miami Nation arrived out on the Unorganized Indian Territory (it wasn't Kansas yet) in November and then walked the last fifty to sixty miles to what would become the 500,000-acre reservation that had been promised to them—and which a survey later determined was only 325,000 acres. They were not there long before the Kansas-Nebraska Act opened that territory up for settlement, and after the US Civil War, the Miami and other tribes that had been relocated to the territory were removed a second time, to Indian Territory, which would later become the state of Oklahoma. Once again, a pocket of Miami people remained behind in Kansas, choosing to stay on their newly built homesteads. By the time their promised reservation in Indian Territory (Oklahoma) had been divided up into approximately 200-acre allotments for each family head, there were sixty-six individuals who remained with the tribal nation. Because of this history, our tribal nation lives in diaspora, with population centers in northeast Oklahoma, where the seat of tribal government resides today; eastern Kansas, including Miami and Linn Counties; and the northern-central part of Indiana in the historic homeland. These historically determined demographics become important in planning language and cultural activities today.

Several early US policies, such as boarding schools and reservation allotments, were strategically designed to break up our sense of community by causing displacement and imposing the idea of individual land ownership. Over the generations, increased pressure to abandon our native language and forced assimilation became too much for community members to resist. These oppressive policies were highly effective and destructive to the people and to our community identity. We emerged into the early twentieth century with significant challenges in maintaining some level of cohesiveness. Broader sociological shifts also affected us, such as the Great Depression, when many tribal members left Oklahoma to find work in other places, in addition to the tremendous cultural pressure during that time to be "American" and speak English only. Sometime during the 1960s and

1970s, we lost the last first-generation speakers of Myaamiaataweenki. It is not entirely clear today when the last speaker passed. What is known is that the event left a huge void in the community and positioned us to need healing in the future.

I was born during the early 1960s, around the time that our last speakers were passing. I would eventually learn that it was my generation that would grow up without ever hearing the language spoken. We would come to be known to some as the "lost generation." The generation before us might have heard the language spoken by grandparents, but my generation was not so fortunate. Many of us knew full well we were Myaamia, but with so much missing during that time, there were more questions than answers.

In 1988, a graduate student named David Costa at the University of California, Berkeley became interested in studying Indigenous languages. He began looking at the Myaamia language because, at the time, there was no one in the field of linguistics who knew much about the language or about what resources were available on the language. Over the years, Costa's research would uncover nearly 270 years of language documentation on what is now known as the Miami-Illinois language. The archival materials begin in the late 1600s and extend through the last speakers of the 1960s and 1970s, and they now serve as the archival sources for today's language revitalization efforts by the Miami Tribe of Oklahoma.

Costa also began the long process of language reconstruction that has lasted over three decades. Much of this early effort to produce learning materials from his work was motivated by a growing base of tribal members within the community who simply wanted their language back and began asking questions about their cultural heritage. It is important to understand that this work began at the grassroots level and was supported by a growing base of community members long before there was any formal tribal support. The beginnings of this effort were as simple and rudimentary as an effort could be.

The passage of the 1990 Native American Languages Act (NALA), although mostly symbolic, began to reshape how Indigenous languages would be viewed at the congressional level. Some initial funding tied to NALA was distributed through grants administered by the Administration for Native Americans. In 1996, the Miami Tribe of Oklahoma applied for this funding and received what would be the first money that we could muster up to begin a more formalized and tribally supported community effort.

Once we began attempting to implement this work of language revitalization more broadly in the community through workshops and evening classes, we quickly realized that as a small tribe in northeast Oklahoma, we simply did not have the resources to promote the language and to carry out the research and educational development necessary to support language revitalization. The Miami Tribe of Oklahoma then turned to our friends at Miami University, with whom we had been developing a relationship since the 1970s, and asked if they would help us create an initiative on campus to support what we were trying to do at the community level. At first, they asked: "Well, what do you want to do?" And we responded: "Well, we're really not sure." They eventually worked with us to develop a short project description that outlined our language needs at that time. We worked with faculty and administrators on campus and eventually arrived at a three-year agreement to establish what was then called the Myaamia Project. In 2001, I was asked to move my family nearer to Oxford, Ohio, where I became the founding director of the Myaamia Project. I think it is important to recognize a certain level of risk that Miami University was willing to take to support such an unprecedented effort. This would likely not have happened without the previously established relationship between the tribe and the university—a relationship that will celebrate fifty years in 2022.

I remember arriving on campus in July 2001, when I was given a small office space that I think was a closet that they had cleaned out up on the third floor of our library. I also remember sitting down upon my arrival and saying to myself: "OK, now what?" On one hand, it was a tremendous opportunity, but on the other hand, there was so much uncertainty about how to move forward because there was no Indigenous revitalization field back then nor any real models for me to follow. There just simply was not much to turn to on the national level to help guide our next steps. This is not to imply that there were not communities struggling and working hard to keep their languages alive in other places across the United States, but in terms of a developed field, with experiences that I could draw from to guide my work at the Myaamia Project, there really wasn't much.

I recall this initial experience as like being in a dark room. We started to poke our way around, to see what we could make happen that would benefit the community. Over time, the effort would continue growing into something the community was ready for. Today, we have a variety of programs that reflect a multipronged approach. Due to our diasporic community, we have outreach workshops for Myaamia populations around the United States. We also develop technologies and make use of social media that help this community reconnect, no matter how far Myaamia people live from the tribal headquarters.

Figure 15.1. Chief's language challenge during Miami Tribe of Oklahoma National Gathering Week in Miami, Oklahoma, June 2019. *Photo by Karen L. Baldwin.*

Over the years, we have developed community-based programs such as the Saakaciweeta Summer Learning Experience, which serves our six- to nine-year-old youth, and the Eewansaapita Summer Learning Experience, which serves our youth of nine to sixteen years; the programs are held in Oklahoma and Indiana, respectively.

In addition to the community-based programs, we have approximately thirty tribe students on Miami University's campus studying under the Myaamia Heritage Program. The Heritage Program supports tribal youth who choose to attend Miami University, with a scholarship and program requirements as part of their collegiate experience. Many of our tribal students attending this university also serve as counselors for our summer youth programs, and since our community programs have been in existence for about fifteen years, some of our incoming freshmen are coming out of our youth programs. This provides a unique opportunity for us as tribal educators to be a part of the cultural education development of our youth from an early age and, potentially, throughout college. The Myaamia Heritage Program not only provides a nice financial incentive for students, but also requires them to take a series of courses in Myaamia language, culture, history, ecological perspectives, and modern issues. During their fourth year, seniors choose a research topic and are encouraged to engage in a project that potentially gives back to the community. For example, one student in engineering designed a stronger traditional lacrosse stick made of synthetic material and another student wrote a children's book in the language for future publication. We are beginning to develop an intergenerational cycle of language and cultural learning between the community and the university, and it has become a very, very rich experience for those who participate.

Our tribal nation today consists of individuals from a wide range of socioeconomic statuses, racial categories, and political and religious affiliations. What holds us together as a distinct people are the strengths of our kinship bonds, our shared history, our ability to govern ourselves as a tribal nation, and our language, culture, and value system. Despite our differences, mentioned above, we are strengthened through our Myaamia identity and tribal/community affiliation. This is important to recognize in the pedagogical development of our learning materials and programs.

Our essential goal is to help community members reconnect and strengthen their identity as Myaamia people through a well-designed and well-executed, community-based educational effort. This is how we engage with the community and how we have managed to support identity development among our youth population, who no longer see themselves as internalizing a single identity. When we hold these bonding agents above our individual differences, we are able to work collectively toward goals that will sustain us into the future. This work draws from our past those things we need to support a healthy, engaged, and knowledgeable generation of tribal youth and community members. Understanding this unique current state of existence allows the kind of flexible learning needed to strengthen the connection that will be essential to the future survival of the tribal nation.

I think it is important to recognize that Miami University essentially created "tribal space" on their campus for us to utilize and to begin exploring how we were going to respond to our community needs around language and cultural education. As much as collaboration and partnerships are important to making something like this happen, the overall community effort needs to be driven by the Miami Tribe. Today, the Myaamia

Center has twelve full- and part-time staff and a mission to help develop the language and cultural educational needs of the Miami Tribe of Oklahoma.

The benefit for Miami University is in our commitment to share our work and experiences on campus through a wide range of activities for faculty, staff, and students. Aside from class visitations, we engage university students in the work of language and cultural development through independent studies, as well as support for several graduate assistantships. The interdisciplinary nature of our work is necessary in order to respond to the broader educational needs of the tribe. Our primary work falls into the broad categories of research and development, education, assessment, and collaboration. Within the realm of research alone, the continued linguistic analysis of our large corpus of language documentation will take at least a couple more generations to work through.

Our relationship with Miami University and the collaborative growth of the Myaamia Center have additionally allowed us to contribute more broadly to the developing field of minority language revitalization throughout North America. In 2015, the Myaamia Center became the institutional home of the National Breath of Life Archival Institute for Indigenous Languages. National Breath of Life is committed to working with endangered language communities to build capacity around methods in archive-based research that support community-directed revitalization programs. National Breath of Life is largely funded by grants from the National Science Foundation's Documenting Endangered Languages program and, more recently, the National Endowment for the Humanities. Since its inception, workshops have trained 117 tribal representatives from fifty-five language communities on how to revitalize endangered or silent languages. More recently, a custom-designed piece of software created through the Myaamia Center called the Indigenous Language Digital Archive has been launched to aid communities in developing digital archives of language materials for revitalization. National Breath of Life has become an important avenue for the Myaamia effort to share tools, technologies, and approaches and to also learn from other tribal efforts through collaborative engagement.

Over the years, we have witnessed growth and increased youth engagement at the community level, and we felt that these changes were being motivated by the overall efforts of revitalization. In order to better understand these changes, we supported the creation of the Nipwaayoni Acquisition and Assessment Team (NAAT) in 2012. The NAAT's initial directive was to gather observational, interview, and survey data on the impact of the

Figure 15.2. Community researcher and linguistic partner working during National Breath of Life Archival Institute for Indigenous Languages Workshop at Miami University, Oxford, Ohio, July 2019. *Photo by Karen L. Baldwin.*

"Myaamia experience" from tribal students attending Miami University, tribal youth attending summer youth camps (Eewansaapita and Saakaciweeta), and through observing community member interactions during annual gatherings. Results of this ongoing study indicate the following:

- Graduation rates have increased among Myaamia tribal students at Miami University after the implementation of Heritage Award classes.
- Through their interactions with the Myaamia Center and in their classes, Miami Tribe students develop an evolving sense of Myaamia identity, as well as culture and language knowledge, that provides a core for their expressed identity.
- Miami Tribe students report that they are better able to cope with the challenges of such topics as mascots and other stereotypes because of the support of the Myaamia Center.
- Miami Tribe students contribute support for intergenerational education about Myaamia culture and language when they return to their families and communities.

- Tribal members are more actively infusing cultural traditions into their lives.
- There is an overall increase in the use of the Myaamia language and involvement in tribal gatherings.
- Over the past four years, there has been an increase of tribal students (upon college completion) choosing careers that directly affect the Miami Nation.

These measurable outcomes are important in shaping our understanding of the role of language and cultural education in the lives of tribal members and the continuation of our national identity as Myaamia people.

Equally important is recognizing that community-based tribal education is expensive and requires a lot of human resources. The federal government's ability and willingness to broadly fund these efforts in any sustainable way does not look promising. The tribe has to provide core funding for stability, which makes tribal economic viability critical. That does not mean that we cannot reach out for grant opportunities and partnerships, such as the one that we have with Miami University, to help us achieve important objectives. But it does mean internal funding, development, and collaboration are what drives this effort in the long run.

I would like to wrap this up with a couple of questions: Why build a community-centered educational effort? Why go through all of this work and effort to revitalize a minority language? Our language may never be important for success in a global economy or for national politics, but it is important to us because it is part of our identity as Myaamia people. Equally important is the fact that our language is the most efficient and effective way for us to communicate our culture and value system to each other and that we strengthen our bonds when we communicate in our heritage language.

We have learned over the years that this effort is important to our youth as well. We are challenged by a new generation who are emerging into the present with very multilayered identities. It may be that three hundred years ago we lived as a village-centered people where our tribal language was the primary mode of communication, but today this is not the case. We are therefore further challenged with figuring out how we, as culturally distinct Myaamia people, are going to survive in a contemporary setting, and that requires us to be flexible and innovative. This effort must connect to and strengthen youth identity formation and make knowing one's language a positive experience for this generation, when it was not a positive

Figure 15.3. Community lacrosse game during Miami Tribe of Oklahoma National Gathering Week in Miami, Oklahoma, June 2019. *Photo by Doug Peconge.*

experience in the past. It's taken us many years to begin filtering out the cultural shame and associated wounding that had built up through the generations. These historically manifested calluses had become so hardened that we struggled to filter out the cultural shame that has built up through the generations, but we're finally beginning to move beyond the demoralizing shackles of our recent past. Language and cultural revitalization are central to that healing process.

After what has now been about three decades of work and effort for us, I am optimistic because I see change, positive change. You would be hard-pressed to find a Myaamia citizen who would tell you that their language is extinct, as some scholars might claim. Although language viability may not compare to what existed in the village-centered life of our past, our language is taking root and finding new purpose among a younger generation. The development of a tribally directed, community-based educational effort is the main force behind promoting not just language but all that affects our identity as Myaamia people. This will continue to develop and create a base for even greater opportunities in the future, and I am honored to be alive at this time to share in this moment of recovery for my tribal nation.

16

NO CHILD LEFT MONOLINGUAL

How and Why to Promote Multilingualism in US Schools

Kim Potowski

A Tale of Two Teenagers

This discussion of language education in the United States begins with two high school students. Rubi is a Mexican American girl born and raised in Chicago, who arrived to kindergarten at age five monolingual in Spanish. Since *Lau v. Nichols* in 1975, all US school districts by law must provide students like Rubi with an instructional program that takes into account her needs as an English learner (EL). The two most common programs are English as a Second Language (ESL) and Transitional Bilingual Education (TBE). ESL programs provide 100 percent of classroom instruction in English, but a portion of it is tailored to the needs of English learners.[1] It is also typically the only option when there are fewer than twenty EL children who speak the same language. Thus, if there are nineteen children who speak Gujarati, in most schools they will receive ESL services.

When there are twenty or more children who speak the same language, at least six states (Connecticut, Illinois, New Jersey, New York, Texas, and Wisconsin) are required by law to offer Transitional Bilingual Education.[2] In TBE programs, a portion of each school day is taught in the children's home language. However, as the name clearly communicates, the goal is to transition students to the mainstream all-English classroom as soon as possible, meaning that the term "bilingual" in the program title refers to a method and not a goal. This typically takes place after three years. In some states, an additional two years in a TBE program can be requested. Given the large number of Spanish speakers in her school, Rubi spent kindergarten through third grade in a Spanish TBE program. She transitioned out on

Table 16.1. Percent of US Schools offering world language instruction

Grades	1997	2008	2015	
K-5	31%	25%	K-12	19%
6-8	75%	58%		

Source: Commission on Language Learning, *America's Language*, 9.

time and began fourth grade in the monolingual mainstream all-English classroom. After June of her third-grade year, Rubi never encountered another book or text written in Spanish; nor did she interact academically with any class content in Spanish.

The other high school student is Rob. When he was five years old, he was enrolled in the mainstream all-English kindergarten classroom in the same school as Rubi. He and his parents speak only English. Rob proceeded with a monolingual English curriculum until he arrived to high school, because his middle school was not one of the 58 percent of those around the country that offers foreign language classes (see table 16.1). World language instruction dropped precipitously shortly after the passage of the No Child Left Behind Act, in effect from 2001 through 2015. Today, some states offer languages to a much larger proportion of K-12 students than others, ranging from 50 percent of schools in New Jersey down to 9 percent in Arkansas.[3]

Not only are the numbers overall relatively low, but the quality of this instruction also varies widely. While some school districts use well-developed curricula with articulated proficiency goals,[4] other classrooms teach only simple material such as vocabulary for colors, numbers, and days of the week, year after year, with no true proficiency goals. In either case, the instruction is designed for second language learners and not for heritage speaking children (like Rubi) who have already acquired communicative proficiency in the language.

When a student like Rubi begins ninth grade, one of two things usually happens. One, she can be placed into a basic Spanish course with students like Rob, who have zero knowledge of the language. There she is bored, sometimes accused of wanting an "easy A" because she already speaks Spanish (a complaint no one levies against English-speaking students in English courses), and often told that the way she speaks Spanish is "incorrect" because it is informal, belongs to a stigmatized dialect, or has English influence. Or two, she can be placed into a "Spanish for heritage speakers" (SHL) class. This is a much better option for students like Rubi because it is specially designed to take her home-developed communicative competence into account. However, in many cases, her Spanish teacher received no training in how to work with heritage speakers, which usually leads to similar frustrations—being erroneously "corrected," having curricular goals that are not a good match for students' skills and interests, and so on. Unfortunately, the most common option is the first, worse one: heritage speakers enrolled in basic Spanish classes, as found by Nancy Rhodes and Ingrid Pufahl in 2010.[5] Specifically, they found that only 9 percent of US high schools offer SHL. Similarly, Kim Potowski and Nancy Domínguez-Fret found that as of 2018, in the state of Illinois, there were thirteen counties with a population that was 10 percent or more Hispanic.[6] Within these counties, the student population in 149 high schools was 10–49 percent Hispanic, and in 61 additional high schools, it was 49–100 percent Hispanic. Many of these schools offered SHL courses, but of the 33 universities in the state that license Spanish teachers, only one, the University of Illinois at Chicago, offered a methods course where pre-service teachers could study best methods in heritage language teaching. So even if separate heritage speaker courses are offered, many teachers aren't properly trained to teach them.

Is teaching heritage speakers that different from teaching second-language learners? Yes, it is, and looking to the field of English can be instructive to understand why. When college undergraduates decide to become English teachers, they must decide whether they want to teach English language arts (ELA) to native/highly-proficient English speakers or English as a Second Language (ESL). These two fields are typically housed in different colleges and have separate degree requirements, state tests, and certifications. This means that a teacher certified in ELA to teach English to native speakers like Rob is not legally permitted to teach ESL to children like Rubi, nor vice versa, because neither is qualified to do so. The strengths and needs of the students are too different. In addition to multiple linguistic differences, second-language learners and heritage speakers also differ in important ways affectively. In the late twentieth century, educators began realizing that Latino students who had learned some Spanish in the home were not well served by traditional foreign language programs, so they began creating Spanish for heritage speakers programs. Yet in high schools and universities across the United States, teachers trained only in teaching Spanish as a second language are regularly called upon to teach SHL.

As for Rob, he enters ninth grade and begins studying Spanish, the language of 50 percent of high school language enrollments.[7] Even though the teacher is relatively young, he was unfortunately trained in traditional second-language teaching pedagogy and also draws from his own outdated high school Spanish experiences. The class is not only carried out in English but also focuses on drilling verb conjugations and completing translations; some teachers claim that they themselves "learned the language just fine this way," when really they learned it in spite of these methods that are empirically proven to be ineffective. They also often supplemented their learning with other experiences and time abroad, given their high levels of interest, which presumably led them to become language teachers. Rob graduates from high school after three years of study of Spanish and can conjugate a number of verbs and form some basic sentences, but he has relatively little communicative competence.

Both of these scenarios are unfortunately very common across the United States. The cases of Rubi and Rob illustrate two problems:

1. Children who arrive to our public schools fluent or even monolingual in Arabic, Chinese, Spanish, Polish, Lithuanian, and a host of other languages do not develop strong levels of proficiency and literacy in them and sometimes lose them completely. These are wasted opportunities to develop our nation's multilingualism and individuals' biliteracy. Figure 16.1 shows how few Hispanics say they can read Spanish "pretty/very well."[8] The proportion is even lower in other groups, particularly in languages that use scripts different from English.[9]

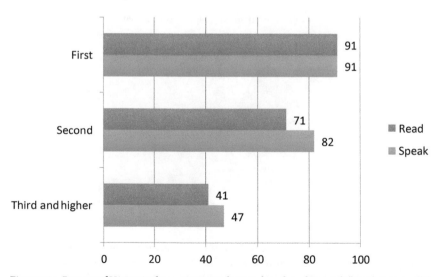

Figure 16.1. Percent of Hispanics by generation who speak and read Spanish "pretty/very well."

2. Children from monolingual English-speaking homes graduate from high school practically monolingual because they begin studying their first new language at age fourteen, despite research showing that earlier language learning is better for many reasons. And even in the 15 percent of public elementary schools that teach languages other than English, they are frequently taught only a few hours per week and with no true curricular goals for developing strong levels of proficiency.[10]

The combination of these problems can be stated another way, using data from the American Academy of Arts and Sciences.[11]

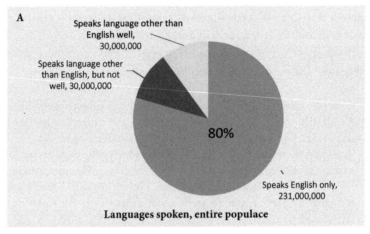

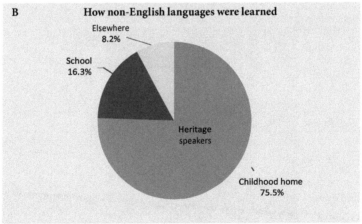

Figure 16.2. Proportion of United Statesians with competence in a language other than English and where they acquired it. Note: The term *United Statesian*, which appears in the *Merriam-Webster Dictionary*, is more accurate than *American*, which includes North America, Central America, and South America.

We can see in figure 16.2a that 80 percent of people in the United States report speaking only English. Of the 20 percent who say they speak a language other than English, half of them say that they do not speak it well. That leaves only 10 percent of the US population who say they speak a language other than English well. How did that 10 percent learn their non-English language? We see this population expanded in the figure 16.2b. Fully 76 percent of them learned it in the home, meaning they are heritage speakers. Only 16 percent of that 10 percent—which totals a mere 1.6 percent of people in this country—have non-English language proficiency that they developed in our schools. I do not believe it is an unfair indictment to say that the United States is doing a very poor job at educating our populace to be bilingual. Even worse is the fact that most of the 80 percent who are monolingual in English actually prefer it that way and express reactions ranging from annoyance ("Why should I have to press 1 to hear English in *my* country?") to physical violence.[12]

Why are we so staunchly, almost pathologically, monolingual in the United States? Part of the answer has its roots in discourses of "one nation, one language" that emerged with the forming of modern nation-states in the nineteenth century. This was particularly relevant for a place like the United States, which received an enormous number of immigrants from many different countries and linguistic backgrounds. A revealing quote comes from a letter written by President Theodore Roosevelt in 1919: "We have room but for one language here and that is the English language, for we intend to see that the crucible turns our people out as Americans, and American nationality, and not as dwellers in a polyglot boarding house; and we have room for but one soul [sic] loyalty, and that loyalty is to the American people."[13]

Roosevelt's term *polyglot boarding house* evokes a sense of transience and poverty; a multilingual nation to him represented a kind of Babelesque slum. A century later, this ideology is still strongly present in many sectors of the country. The nation's recent large-scale immigration coupled with persisting ethnolinguistic stratification and inequality have fueled language policy conflicts and Anglo-American anxieties that English, national unity, and identity are threatened.

While the United States has no official language, every year a member of Congress proposes an amendment giving English that designation. According to James Crawford, "official English" policies are the following:

- Unnecessary: English dominates in all aspects of US life, resulting in a two- to three-generation shift among every single language group that has come here from other countries.[14]
- Punitive: They would immediately cast as non-compliant or criminal anyone who did not have English proficiency.
- Pointless: Such laws in and of themselves offer zero practical assistance to anyone trying to learn English. In fact, they would more likely frustrate that goal by outlawing programs designed to bring immigrants into the mainstream of society.
- Divisive: They could serve as proxies for hostility toward linguistic minorities, Latinos and Asians in particular, exacerbating ethnic tensions.
- Inconsistent with US Values: Such laws have been declared unconstitutional in state and federal courts because they violate guarantees of freedom of speech and equal protection of the laws.
- Self-defeating: Such policies are foolish in an era of globalization when language resources should be conserved and developed, not suppressed.[15]

However, "official English" laws currently exist in thirty-one states, although four of these have one or more additional languages as co-official alongside English.[16] Instead of policies aimed toward "official English" or "English only," what if we as a nation pursued something like "English plus"? What if we provided free, high-quality English instruction to all who sought it, including provisions for transportation and childcare, and also ran our schools such that no child graduated from a US high school monolingual?

A Good Solution: Dual Language Education

A viable solution to both of these problems—the loss of heritage languages and the lack of learning non-English languages among English-speaking United Statesians—is dual language education, also known as *dual immersion*. These programs use the language other than English (LOTE) between 50 and 90 percent of the school day from kindergarten through eighth grade, with the goals of promoting bilingualism, biliteracy, and bicultural appreciation. Most of these programs enroll a balance of children who learned the LOTE at home (many of whom are also ELs) and children who are first learning the LOTE at school. Dual language programs are also designed to address societal power imbalances in that instead of the EL children being the only language learners in the school, the home English speakers are expected to learn the LOTE. In this way, the home LOTE-speaking children are positioned as knowledgeable linguistic and cultural models.

When thinking about EL students, many parents, educators, and laypeople might assume that instruction delivered 100 percent in English would be the best way to help children learn it, given that most things a person seeks to improve are accomplished through time on task. For example, if we want to improve our mountain climbing, we climb more frequently and take lessons at a gym. If we want to become better car mechanics, we spend a lot of time working in garages. But for ELs to learn English more quickly, somewhat counterintuitively, the best results are obtained through quality instruction in the home language. Several nationwide studies have demonstrated this by comparing student outcomes in three different elementary school programs for Spanish-speaking ELs: (1) 100 percent English instruction; (2) transitional bilingual education, which, as already discussed, teaches a portion of the day in Spanish for a maximum of only three years; and (3) dual language immersion, just described. Figure 16.3 compares the English reading scores of California graduates of these program types once they advance to eleventh grade.

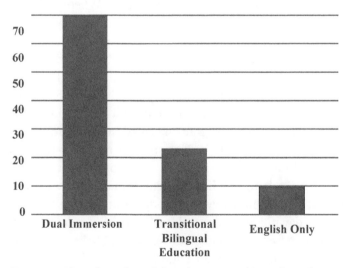

Figure 16.3. Eleventh-grade English reading scores of Spanish-speaking English learners. Source: Lindholm-Leary, *Dual Language Education*.

These findings indicate that the more time spent learning in Spanish, the greater the English language achievement of Spanish-speaking EL students.

Similar findings emerged from a large-scale study in Houston.[17] This is due in part to the fact that there is less chance that EL students will fall behind in their academic subject matter as they gradually develop English proficiency, a gap that usually compounds each year. But children who learn that "dos más dos son cuatro" have learned to add and do not need to relearn "two plus two is four" once they have acquired the English vocabulary. In addition, scientific studies have demonstrated links between bilingualism and general cognitive benefits, reports of which have become increasingly frequent in mainstream media over the past few years. This too may contribute to dual language students' improved educational performance. A third explanation is found in studies suggesting that when children and their languages are positioned as useful resources in the classroom, their self-esteem develops in ways that are conducive to positive school performance. Thinking back to Rubi, in ESL or even in TBE programs, the message is often that students like her are deficient, that if only she did not have her Spanish holding her back, she could be like a regular successful student. In dual immersion, however, for 50 to 90 percent of the school day Rubi can help the half of students who have just begun to learn Spanish; they look to her for assistance when they do not understand Spanish. When students are positioned as successful in such ways, it is more likely that they achieve success.

Not only does Latino students' English benefit in dual immersion; their overall academic achievement, as measured by standardized tests, has also been shown to be higher than in other program types.[18] This too has been reported in mainstream media, including a study of San Francisco schools conducted by faculty at Stanford University and another in Portland, both finding that dual language programs resulted in earlier student reclassification as English proficient as well as stronger academic trajectories over time.[19] A key phrase is "over time." The story of the *Three Little Pigs* can be useful when explaining bilingual dual immersion to skeptical parents and administrators who worry that studying in Spanish for a significant portion of the day might hinder children's English development. Dual language children in first or second grade may appear to have learned less English than their counterparts in all-English programs, but the dual language children are actually like the little pig who built his home out of bricks. It frequently takes longer for them to develop linguistic proficiency, until perhaps fourth or fifth grade, but they eventually develop much stronger systems in both languages. Figure 16.3 makes clear that the children in all-English programs were led to quickly build straw houses that, over time, were unable to sustain high levels of linguistic and academic growth.

What about Latino students' Spanish? It was mentioned earlier that since Rubi attended a TBE program, once she completed third grade she did not read or write in Spanish again. Various studies have documented the erosion of Spanish as children move from elementary grades to middle school.[20] A large-scale study comparing the Spanish of over 250 children found that those in dual language programs developed stronger proficiency than their peers in English-medium programs, and, echoing findings cited earlier, they also scored better on English measures.[21] But if we seek to maximize students' Spanish development, we need focused investigations of what their linguistic systems look like and how they change over time so that we can best calibrate specific language arts instruction. Potowski and Marshall examined the Spanish of two groups of Latino home Spanish-speaking students attending the same K-8 school.[22] Half were enrolled in the mainstream English program (where, if they were classified as ELs, they received ESL services), and half were in the dual language program that taught in Spanish 80 percent of the day in grades K-4, 60 percent in grades 5–6, and 50 percent in grades 7 and 8. The listening comprehension, reading comprehension, and oral production were all higher for the dual language group, but it was in Spanish writing where the biggest differences were found. For readers who can understand Spanish, figures 16.4 and 16.5 compare the writing of two students in first grade and two in fifth grade.

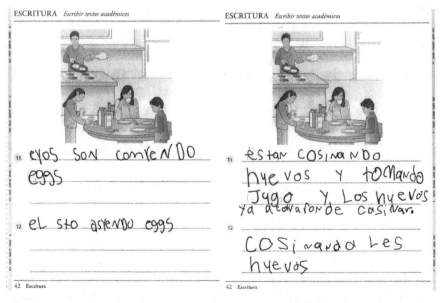

Figures 16.4a and 16.4b. Spanish written production, two first-grade students.

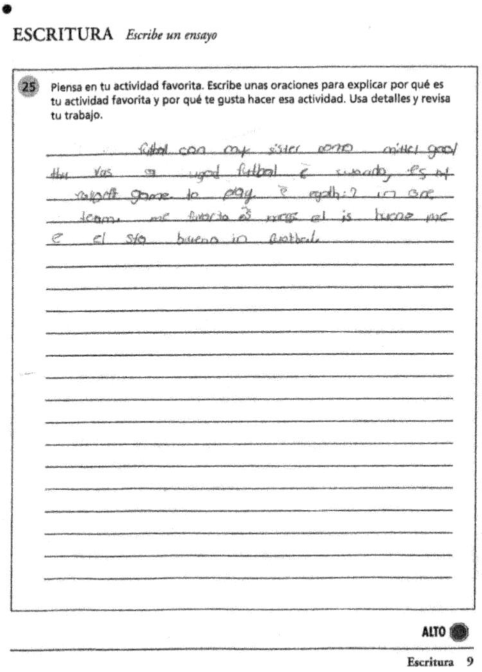

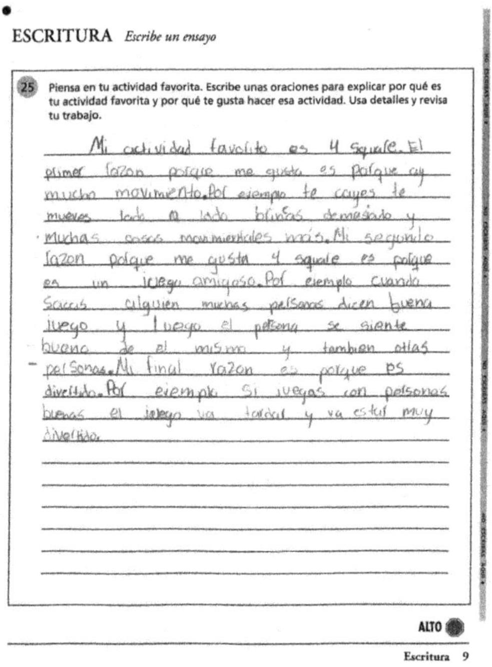

ESCRITURA *Escribe un ensayo*

25 Piensa en tu actividad favorita. Escribe unas oraciones para explicar por qué es tu actividad favorita y por qué te gusta hacer esa actividad. Usa detalles y revisa tu trabajo.

[handwritten student response, partially legible]
Fútbol con my sister como mi mejor goal ... vas a ... fútbol ... cuando, es m ... baloncest game to play. e math? ... con ... me gusta es ... el is bueno ... e el so bueno in football.

ALTO ●

Escritura 9

ESCRITURA *Escribe un ensayo*

25 Piensa en tu actividad favorita. Escribe unas oraciones para explicar por qué es tu actividad favorita y por qué te gusta hacer esa actividad. Usa detalles y revisa tu trabajo.

[handwritten student response]
Mi actividad favorita es 4 square. El primer razón porque me gusta es porque ay mucho movimiento. Por ejemplo te cayes te mueres todo a lado brincas demasiado y muchas cosas mocmuentades más. Mi segundo razón porque me gusta 4 square es porque es un juego amigoso. Por ejemplo cuando sacas alguien muchas personas dicen buena juego y luego el persona se siente buena de el mismo y también otras personas. Mi final razón es porque es divertido. Por ejemplo si juegas con personas buenas el juego va tardar y va estar muy divertido.

ALTO ●

Escritura 9

Figures 16.5a and 16.5b. Spanish written production, two fifth-grade students.

The dual language texts are not only longer; they are also lexically richer and more morphosyntactically complex. And what about the Spanish of the home English-speaking children? Many of them develop very respectable levels of both oral and written proficiency. A child like Rob who starts in kindergarten can be reading *Harry Potter* in Spanish by fifth grade, and at no cost to his English.

Another important consideration is that these programs have been proven suitable for students with many kinds of learning challenges, including those with cognitive difficulties, autism, and speech and hearing issues.[23]

Given the resounding success of dual immersion programs for Latino students' Spanish, English, and overall academic development, educators and families should be fighting to create more of them. Most recently, the number of schools that have registered with the Center for Applied Linguistics as having a dual immersion program was 458, including eight different languages, although 93 percent of them operate in Spanish.[24] However, unofficial estimates place the national number of bilingual dual language schools in the United States between 1,000 and over 2,000, meaning that there are many programs operating that have not filled out the Center for Applied Linguistics survey.[25] There is literature about programs in Albanian, Arabic, Chinese, French, Haitian Creole, Hebrew, Italian, Japanese, Korean, Navajo, Polish, and Russian (see, for example, Fabrice Jaumont's website [https://fabricejaumont.net/] for the growing list of languages offered in dual language programs around New York City), but unfortunately to date no single source documents all of the different languages offered in dual immersion classrooms around the United States.

Stronger Spanish systems can contribute to reducing the Latino achievement gap that currently plagues the United States and, if left unchecked, holds potentially negative consequences for the nation's future.[26] One out of every four school-age students in the United States today is Latino, yet the National Center for Educational Statistics reports that Latino fourth and eighth graders score about two grade levels lower than the national average on tests in math and reading.

However, there are several needs and pitfalls that are important to keep in mind regarding dual immersion education, including the following:[27]

- the need for properly trained dual language teachers, who ideally participate in programs such as the one offered by Dual Language Education of New Mexico[28]
- greater support for dual language programs at the state and community levels
- the "gentrification" of dual language programs, whereby middle-class families' needs take precedence over those of the language minority students[29]

Conclusions and Future Directions

As a nation, the United States could be reaping the collective cognitive advantages of multilingualism along with the rest of the world, where an estimated 50-75 percent of the population is bilingual (compared to an estimated 20 percent in the United States), as well as broader social benefits, including increased possibilities for international diplomacy, commerce, and security.[30] Well-executed Spanish-language curricula in dual language programs may help triage language loss by developing strong proficiency and healthy pride in speaking Spanish among our nation's youth. We find successful examples in other languages. In the early 1980s, fewer than 50 children spoke Hawaiian, but today there are over 18,000 individuals who speak Hawaiian in the home thanks in large part to Hawaiian-medium schooling.[31] Although English is not introduced until fifth grade, students at the Nawah'i immersion school, many from poor and working-class families, outscore their non-immersion peers on English standardized tests, graduate high school at a rate of 100 percent, and attend college at an 80 percent rate. School leaders attribute these successes to an academically challenging curriculum centered on Hawaiian language and culture.[32] Given that 22.5 percent of all school-aged children in the United States speak a language other than English at home and that the number of English language learners is expected to increase by an additional 50 percent by 2025, these programs have critical implications.[33] We also need studies of the linguistic development in dual immersion programs that operate in languages other than Spanish (some of which were listed in note 26).

In addition, the field of foreign/world languages would make an important step toward ensuring that high school heritage learners have properly qualified teachers by convincing state certification/licensure bodies to create an *endorsement* in teaching heritage languages. Endorsements are additional subjects on a teaching license that the holder is authorized to teach and are typically earned through an additional two to four specialized courses. In this way, for high school teachers to be placed in an SHL classroom, they would be legally required to hold the endorsement. Potowski and Domínguez-Fret aim to convince the Illinois State Board of Education to create an endorsement in SHL teaching.[34]

As for college offerings, Sara Beaudrie found that only 40 percent of universities with sufficient Hispanic student enrollment are offering heritage Spanish speaker courses.[35] Several studies document the negative experiences of students like Rubi in nonheritage (basic Spanish) programs.[36] We also need more study abroad programs specifically designed for heritage speakers as well as greater funding to assist them in completing such programs; only 10 percent of students who study abroad are Hispanic, a lower rate than their overall 18 percent representation among college students.[37]

Finally, it may be the case that Anglophone children who study through a language other than English alongside native speaking children end up "inoculated" against negative ideologies that lead to linguistic bullying and other xenophobic and racist ideologies. Dual language programs can thus serve an important social justice mission to increase interethnic and linguistic appreciation among the nation's majority-Anglophone population, while also increasing our nation's multilingualism (currently at only one-fifth) to be more on par with the rest of the world (approximately two-thirds). These programs are currently the most feasible way to ensure that no child in the United States is left monolingual.

Notes

1. I was not able to locate a formal estimate of the percentage of EL children around the country who are enrolled in ESL programs versus the bilingual programs described below.

2. Policies can change very rapidly. As this book goes to press, the current policies for Wisconsin are available at Wisconsin Department of Public Instruction, "Wisconsin Bilingual-Bicultural Programs," https://dpi.wi.gov/english-learners/bilingual-bicultural ?fbclid=IwAR3QEg9i4-t73mBJZTSqIPor5H7GMQ3srsfi7vILZxpUSYXPUnuoJ3srKAw, while those for the other states can be found at US Department of Education, "Dual Language Education Programs: Current State Policies and Practices," 88, https://www.air.org/sites/default /files/downloads/report/Dual-Language-Education-Programs -Current-State-Policies-April-2015-rev.pdf.

3. American Councils for International Education, *National K-12.*

4. See Curtain and Dahlberg, *Languages and Learners.*

5. Rhodes and Pufahl, *Foreign Language Teaching.*

6. Potowski and Domínguez-Fret, "Spanish as a Heritage Language."

7. Looney and Lusin, *Enrollments in Languages.*

8. Taylor et al., *Language Use among Latinos.*

9. Carreira and Kagan, "Results," 40–64.

10. Rhodes and Pufahl, *Foreign Language Teaching.* There is an additional challenge when heritage speakers are enrolled in K-8 world language classes, turning them into de facto heritage language classes, because teachers rarely receive proper preparation to work with these students. Potowski et al., "Spanish for K-8," 25–41.

11. Commission on Language Learning, *America's Languages*, 23.

12. Interested readers can find a video called *Press One for English*, by RivoliRevue (June 8, 2007), at https://www.youtube.com/watch?v=sEJfS1v-fUo; see also http://potowski.org /resources/repression.

13. Roosevelt, "Americanism and Americanization," 82.

14. Exceptions of long-term intergenerational maintenance include Yiddish among the Hasidic Jews and Pennsylvania Dutch among the Amish, two groups that adhere to strict religious and social norms outside of the US mainstream. However, there are also cases of two-generation language shift, resulting in parents and children who cannot communicate with each other.

15. Crawford, "Official English Legislation."

16. New Mexico, Spanish; Louisiana, French; Hawaii, Hawaiian; and Alaska, Native American languages in the area.

17. Lindholm-Leary, *Dual Language Education.*

18. Shown in figure 16.3; see also Lindholm-Leary, *Dual Language Education*; Lindholm-Leary, "Bilingual and Biliteracy Skills," 144–59; and Thomas and Collier, "Astounding Effectiveness."

19. Myers, "Students Learning English"; Manning, "Study: Portland Immersion Students."

20. Merino, "Language Loss," 277–94; Oller and Eilers, *Language and Literacy*.

21. Lindholm-Leary, "Bilingual and Biliteracy Skills," 144–59.

22. Potowski and Marshall, *Spanish Proficiency*.

23. Fortune and Menke, *Struggling Learners*.

24. Center for Applied Linguistics, "Directory." I have read about programs in Albanian, Arabic, Chinese, French, Haitian Creole, Hebrew, Italian, Japanese, Korean, Navajo, Polish, and Russian, but I have not yet located a single source that documents all of the different languages offered in classrooms around the United States.

25. Maxwell, "'Dual' Classes," 16–17; Watanabe, "Dual-Language Immersion Programs."

26. This achievement gap is not always related to language but rather to poverty and other entrenched problems, yet strong levels of bilingualism can play a role in helping these students achieve.

27. Described in greater detail in Potowski, "Elementary School."

28. See Dual Language Education of New Mexico resources, https://www.dlenm.org/what -we-do/.

29. See Freire, Valdez, and Delavan, "(Dis)inclusion," 276–89.

30. Grosjean, "Chasing Down Those 65%."

31. US Census Bureau, "Top 25 Languages," 8.

32. McCarty, "Native American Languages," 47–65.

33. US Census Bureau, "Characteristics of People"; Passel and Cohn, *U.S. Population Projections*.

34. Potowski and Domínguez-Fret, "Spanish as a Heritage Language."

35. Beaudrie, "Research," 203–21.

36. Potowski, "Experiences," 35–42.

37. Institute of International Education, "Profile."

Bibliography

American Council for International Education. *The National K-12 Foreign Language Enrollment Survey Report*, June 2017. https://www.americancouncils.org/sites/default/files /FLE-report-June17.pdf.

Beaudrie, Sara. "Research on University-Based Spanish Heritage Language Programs in the United States: The Current State of Affairs." In *Spanish as a Heritage Language in the United States: State of the Field*, edited by Sara Beaudrie and Marta Fairclough, 203–21. Washington, DC: Georgetown University Press, 2012.

Carreira, Maria, and Olga Kagan. "The Results of the National Heritage Language Survey: Implications for Teaching, Curriculum Design, and Professional Development." *Foreign Language Annals* 44, no. 1 (February 2011): 40–64. https://doi.org/10.1111/j.1944 -9720.2010.01118.x.

Center for Applied Linguistics. "Directory of Two-Way Bilingual Immersion Programs in the U.S." Accessed June 29, 2013. http://www.cal.org/twi/directory.

Collier, Virginia P., and Wayne P. Thomas. "The Astounding Effectiveness of Dual Language Education for All." *NABE Journal of Research and Practice* 2, no. 1 (January 2004): 1–20.

Commission on Language Learning. *America's Languages: Investing in Language Education for the 21st Century.* American Academy of Arts and Sciences, February 2017. https://www.amacad.org/publication/americas-languages.

Crawford, James. "Official English Legislation: Bad for Civil Rights, Bad for America's Interests, and Even Bad for English." Testimony before the House Subcommittee on Education Reform, July 26, 2006. https://www.scribd.com/document/33365093/Crawford-Official-English-legislation-bad-for-civil-rights-bad-for-America-s-interests-and-even-bad-for-English.

Curtain, Helena, and Carol Ann Dahlberg. *Languages and Learners: Making the Match—World Language Instruction in K–8 Classrooms and Beyond.* New York: Pearson, 2015.

Fortune, Tara Williams, and Mandy R. Menke. *Struggling Learners and Language Immersion Education: Research-Based, Practitioner-Informed Responses to Educators' Top Question.* Minneapolis: Center for Advanced Research on Language Acquisition, University of Minnesota, 2010.

Freire, Juan A., Verónica E. Valdez, and M. Garrett Delavan. "The (Dis)inclusion of Latina/o Interests from Utah's Dual Language Education Boom." *Journal of Latinos and Education* 16, no. 4 (November 2016): 276–89. https://doi.org/10.1080/15348431.2016.1229617.

Grosjean, Francois. "Chasing Down Those 65%." *Psychology Today,* November 30, 2014. https://www.psychologytoday.com/us/blog/life-bilingual/201411/chasing-down-those-65.

Institute of International Education. "Profile of U.S. Study Abroad Students from the *Open Doors* Report." Student Profile. Accessed September 9, 2019. https://www.iie.org/Research-and-Insights/Open-Doors/Data/US-Study-Abroad/Student-Profile.

Lindholm-Leary, Katherine. "Bilingual and Biliteracy Skills in Young Spanish-Speaking Low-SES Children: Impact of Instructional Language and Primary Language Proficiency." *International Journal of Bilingual Education and Bilingualism* 17, no. 2 (2014): 144–59. https://doiorg/10.1080/13670050.2013.866625.

———. *Dual Language Education.* Clevedon, UK: Multilingual Matters, 2001.

Looney, Dennis, and Natalia Lusin. *Enrollments in Languages Other Than English in United States Institutions of Higher Education, Summer 2016 and Fall 2016: Preliminary Report.* Modern Language Association, February 2018. https://www.mla.org/content/download/83540/2197676/2016-Enrollments-Short-Report.pdf.

Manning, Rob. "Study: Portland Immersion Students Become Better Readers, English Speakers." *Oregon Public Broadcasting,* November 6, 2015. https://www.opb.org/news/article/study-portland-immersion-students-become-better-readers-english-speakers/.

Maxwell, Lesli A. "'Dual' Classes See Growth in Popularity." *Education Week: Spotlight on Deeper Learning,* March 28, 2012, 16–17. https://secure.edweek.org/media/downloads/files/spotlight-deeper-learning.pdf.

McCarty, Teresa L. "Native American Languages in the USA." In *Language Diversity in the USA,* edited by Kim Potowski, 47–65. Cambridge: Cambridge University Press, 2010.

Merino, Barbara J. "Language Loss in Bilingual Chicano Children." *Journal of Applied Developmental Psychology* 4, no. 3 (July–September 1983): 277–94. https://doi.org/10.1016/0193-3973(83)90023-0.

Myers, Andrew. "Students Learning English Benefit More in Two-Language Instructional Programs Than English Immersion, Stanford Research Finds." Stanford, March 25, 2014. https://news.stanford.edu/news/2014/march/teaching-english-language-032514.html.

Oller, Kimbrough, and Rebecca Eilers, eds. *Language and Literacy in Bilingual Children.* Clevedon, UK: Multilingual Matters, 2002.

Passel, Jeffrey S., and D'Vera Cohn. *U.S. Population Projections: 2005–2050.* Pew Research Center, Social and Demographic Trends, 2008.

Pew Research Center. "Language Use among Latinos." April 4, 2012. https://www.pew research.org/hispanic/2012/04/04/iv-language-use-among-latinos/.

Potowski, Kim. "Experiences of Spanish Heritage Speakers in University Foreign Language Courses and Implications for Teacher Training." *ADFL Bulletin* 33, no. 3 (2002): 35–42.

———. "Elementary School Heritage Language Educational Options." In *The Cambridge Handbook of Heritage Languages and Linguistics*, edited by Marina Polinsky and S. Montrul. Forthcoming.

Potowski, Kim, Jorge Berne, Amy Clark, and Amy Hammerand. "Spanish for K-8 Heritage Speakers: A Standards-based Curriculum Project." *Hispania* 91, no. 1 (March 2008): 25-41. https://www.jstor.org/stable/20063621.

Potowski, Kim, and Nancy Domínguez-Fret. "Spanish as a Heritage Language High School Teacher Preparation in Illinois and Why It Matters for the Rest of the U.S." Forthcoming.

Potowski, Kim, and Megan Marshall. *The Spanish Proficiency of Dual Immersion Students Compared to Peers in All English Programs.* Forthcoming.

Rhodes, Nancy, and Ingrid Pufahl. *Foreign Language Teaching in U.S. Schools: Results of a National Survey.* Washington, DC: Center for Applied Linguistics, 2010.

Roosevelt, Theodore. "Americanism and Americanization: Selections from the Writings of Theodore Roosevelt." *Monthly Bulletin of the Carnegie Library of Pittsburgh* 24, no. 2 (February 1919): 82.

Taylor, Paul, Mark Hugo Lopez, Jessica Martínez, and Gabriel Velasco. *Language Use among Latinos.* Pew Research Center, April 4, 2012. https://www.pewresearch.org/hispanic /2012/04/04/iv-language-use-among-latinos/.

US Census Bureau. "Top 25 Languages Other Than English Spoken at Home for the State of Hawaii." In *Detailed Languages Spoken at Home in the State of Hawaii*, Hawaii State Data Center, March 2016, 8. http://files.hawaii.gov/dbedt/census/acs/Report/Detailed _Language_March2016.pdf.

———. "Characteristics of People by Language Spoken at Home, 2013–2017 American Community Survey 5-Year Estimates." American FactFinder. Accessed September 9, 2019. https://factfinder.census.gov/faces/tableservices/jsf/pages/productview.xhtml?pid =ACS_17_5YR_S1603&prodType=table.

Watanabe, Teresa. "Dual-Language Immersion Programs Growing in Popularity." *Los Angeles Times*, May 8, 2011. https://www.latimes.com/local/la-xpm-2011-may-08-la-me -bilingual-20110508-story.html.

Intersection

17

INTERNATIONAL EDUCATION

Just a Fancy Idea for a Few or a Vital Component
of Higher Education and of Our Future?

Francisco Marmolejo

WE LIVE IN A WORLD that is increasingly interdependent. Today's society and economy are global, highly competitive, constantly changing, technologically driven, and, more importantly, knowledge based. The best way I have to describe how globalized and integrated today's economy and society are—despite sophisticated econometric models—is a bottle of Mexican salsa that I found recently at a supermarket in New Delhi. To my amusement, once I read the label, I learned that it was made in the Netherlands, with ingredients from Morocco, being commercialized by a Chinese company, and ready for consumption for a Mexican guy living in India.

At the same time, today's world is increasingly fascinating, considering the amazing new scientific and technological discoveries occurring throughout all domains of knowledge at such a fast pace that it's hardly even news anymore; it's more interconnected, due to the instantaneous capacity to transmit information—good and bad, true and fake; and it's also increasingly turbulent, due to growing tensions and polarization in societies whose citizens experience anxiety and uncertainty. There is no doubt that the world that our generation is leaving to students currently in college is quite different from the one in which we were brought up. Some may argue that there is nothing new in this phenomenon, but the pace of change being experienced in today's global and local economies and societies is much faster than in the past; it is also magnified by the instantaneity of information, and in a certain way, it is less predictable than ever. And why does that matter? Well, because there is no more room for isolationism, and a more systemic approach is needed. We no longer can ignore others' reality. There is no "us" versus "them" anymore. What will affect us will affect others, and vice versa. We cannot ignore that new, intertwined reality anymore. And indeed, this matters to international higher education.

When I was an adolescent, while reading *Reader's Digest*—a very popular magazine back in those years—I found a "quotable quote" that still is very present in my mind: "When I think about the future, I'm scared about the present." This quote is more than valid in today's context because despite the strong signals in the environment indicating that the world is no longer what it used to be, most of us continue doing things the same way. Such a slow response to clear signals that we need to change in order to face an unknown but different future context is a miscalculation on the part of many of us individually, but it is also the way our colleges and universities currently operate.

The turbulent, contradictory, and intriguing current and future geopolitical environment should be seen as a true wake-up call for higher education and, more specifically, for international higher education. Why? Because in a way, the traditional rationale behind efforts toward the internationalization of colleges and universities is being questioned, probably because it relied on a relatively naive or simplistic vision of the world and of international education. Up until now, the prevalent theory of change is that international higher education enables a transformative educational experience in students that, somewhat magically, will equip them with the tools to become both more competitive and more internationally able and will also make them more tolerant and interculturally sensitive individuals, which consequently will result in more interconnected and less stratified societies. Is that true? I have no doubt that for many students this is what happens and that international education is beneficial to our societies, but in most cases, we do not have evidence beyond anecdotal affirmations to support such statements.

Among other reasons, the aforementioned theory of change has reinforced the idea that the most effective way to provide global exposure to students is by placing emphasis on their international mobility. However, the complex context of today makes it necessary to avoid the tendency to equate international education with student mobility alone—nor should international education be seen as just a commodity in the trade policy of governments or as a compensatory source of funding for higher education institutions. If institutions of higher education are serious about internationalization, they should explicitly adopt a holistic approach aimed at effectively embedding the *glocal* competencies and intercultural awareness throughout the educational experience of all students. In other words, internationalization should transition from being marginal to becoming central to the core mission of higher education. Rather than be seen as "something else" for a few, global awareness and an internationalized academic focus should be a central component of a relevant educational experience for all students.

In today's globalized society, an expanded view of issues and trends influencing education is needed. Consequently, colleges and universities should review and analyze more systematically key macro trends in the local and international environments, not only because they are crucial to ensuring a more meaningful academic experience for students but also because they will affect higher education in general and its internationalization.

Is it relevant for higher education to be aware that, globally, a modest employment growth is being experienced but that in recent years, we missed a great opportunity to spur growth and welfare? Or that while extreme poverty in the world has been reduced, the number of people living in poverty and vulnerable socioeconomic conditions continues to be problematic? Or that the acute disparities existing between graying high-income societies and low-income countries confronted with significant demographic growth is the major incentive for south-north migratory patterns? Or that recent migration trends are feeding strident rhetoric in favor of nationalism and nativism? Or that technology has contributed to the democratization of information and knowledge but at the same time has opened the door for the proliferation of disinformation, misinformation, and mal-information?

It can be argued that some of the aforementioned issues are somewhat distant from the day-to-day work of a typical college or university. Nevertheless, at the same time, these are realities that cannot be ignored, especially because they contribute to the disenchantment and cynicism of regular citizens—including students—in our societies who are skeptical of the response capacity and legitimacy of the social institutions that historically have been in place to address problems and find solutions, such as government, political parties, religions, and even higher education institutions. Even for some, those social institutions are precisely the source of the problems rather than the source of solutions.

On the other hand, interestingly, the world has experienced unimaginable progress connected with a massive amount of innovation and discovery, much of it resulting directly from the research done in the same universities paradoxically being questioned for their usefulness. Further, higher education has experienced at a global level a spectacular growth in enrollment and size, which confirms that, despite criticism and skepticism by some, socially it continues to be seen as the most viable pathway for intergenerational social and economic upward mobility. In fact, studies conducted by the World Bank show that, in general, the economic returns that individuals receive are proportionately higher if they pursue higher education than if they only complete elementary or secondary education.[1] And beyond the economic returns for individuals, there are many associated positive externalities. For instance, we know that people with higher education credentials believe more in democracy than those who have not enjoyed such a privilege; that individuals with higher education studies tend to live longer and healthier lives; and that those benefiting from access to higher education also, in general, have higher levels of intercultural understanding and tolerance, especially if they have participated in international education activities.[2]

In summary, there are plenty of reasons to believe that, against those predicting that colleges and universities are at the risk of extinction, the current and future landscape is fertile ground for more and better higher education and, likewise, for more and better international education. However, it is not easy to predict the degree to which the increased complexity and inherent tensions experienced in our society and economy will affect the way that higher education and international education work. It would be naive to assume that no change is needed or that colleges and universities are somewhat insulated from the outside. The idea of the university as an "ivory tower" is simply not valid.

A good example of the interlinked reality affecting higher education is the issue of demographics. It is known that globally there will be brutal pressure for talent in the near future in which "brain-drain" and "brain-circulation" will be the new normal.[3] The cases of Africa and Europe are obvious: Africa will have by the year 2030 about 40 percent of youth globally, while Europe will experience an overall decline and graying of its total population. In 2030, Africa will have 350 million inhabitants between the ages of fifteen and twenty-four years; in contrast, in Europe the same age cohort will total only 80 million, while the cohort of inhabitants sixty-five years and older will be approximately 170 million.[4]

As expected in the next decade, globally, the stock of individuals with higher education credentials will shift as well: for instance, the United States currently represents 14 percent of the global stock of individuals twenty-five to sixty-four years old with higher education degrees, but its share will be reduced to only 8 percent by the year 2030, while such countries as China and India will increase significantly their proportion.

Paradoxically, higher education, despite spectacular growth in recent years, still is a dream that can be fulfilled by just a few, especially in low- and middle-income countries, which, coincidentally, are the ones experiencing significant demographic growth. At the same time, significant disparities remain in access and completion rates in higher education by socioeconomic and cultural background, gender, location, and so on, in both high-income and lower-income countries.

In other words, if higher education still remains accessible to a small segment of the global society, international education continues to be, unfortunately, an even more elitist component of the higher education experience. The numbers are more than illustrative: international students represent only a mere 3 percent of the total enrollment in higher education globally. Important efforts are being made to increase the number of international students, but just an emphasis on mobility is not enough, because the international experience should become available, viable, and relevant for all students in our higher education institutions.

For this reason, internationalization should be seen as a means rather than a goal. Advocates of internationalization still need to make a stronger case for its importance for relevance, employability, quality, equitable access, and other issues that remain priorities to be addressed by governments and institutions of higher education. Otherwise, internationalization still will be seen as a marginal, costly, elitist, and, in a way, accessory element of higher education.

In summary, it is time to rethink the role of international education in a world with persistent social inequality, demographic shifts, technological transformation, massive information, and ideological polarization. This requires a more systematic assessment of its positive impact while recognizing negative associated connotations (neocolonialism, brain drain, loss of identity), excesses (elitist mobility, commodification), and misinterpretations (mobility as a synonym of internationalization, international rankings as a synonym of quality, signing of memoranda of understanding with international institutional partners as a synonym of internationalization). In other words, more evidence is needed to ascertain and sustain if a more relevant higher education in today's society will result due to, despite, or independently of its internationalization.

In the midst of the significant societal transformation experienced in the world, the words of Paul Valéry are more relevant than ever as we re-think the role of international education: "The trouble with our times is that the future is not what it used to be."[5]

Notes

1. Montenegro and Patrinos, *Returns to Schooling*, 7.
2. World Bank, *World Development Report*, 43.
3. Kerr et al., "Global Talent Flows."
4. Department of Economic and Social Affairs of the United Nations Secretariat, "World Population."
5. Valéry, *Oeuvres*.

Bibliography

Department of Economic and Social Affairs of the United Nations Secretariat. "World Population Prospects 2019." Accessed April 21, 2020. https://population.un.org/wpp/.

Jackson, Jane. *Intercultural Journeys: From Study to Residence Abroad*. London: Palgrave Macmillan, 2010.

Kerr, Sari Pekkala, William Kerr, Çaglar Ozden, and Christopher Parsons. "Global Talent Flows." Policy research working paper no. 7852. Washington, DC: World Bank, October 2016. http://documents.worldbank.org/curated/en/793861475694096298/pdf/WPS7852.pdf.

McGill, Natalie. "Education Attainment Linked to Health throughout Lifespan: Exploring Social Determinants of Health." *Nation's Health* 46, no. 6 (August 2016): 1–19. http://thenationshealth.aphapublications.org/content/46/6/1.3.full.

Montenegro, Claudio E., and Harry Anthony Patrinos. *Returns to Schooling around the World*. Washington, DC: World Bank, 2013.

Valéry, Paul. *Oeuvres*. Paris: Bibliotheque de la Pleaide, 1957.

World Bank. *World Development Report 2018: Learning to Realize Education's Promise*. Washington, DC: World Bank, 2018. https://elibrary.worldbank.org/doi/pdf/10.1596/978-1-4648-1096-1.

CROSSROADS 4

INTERNATIONALIZATION IN PRACTICE

18

FROM INTERNATIONAL TO GLOBAL

Rethinking Worldwide Engagement

Safwan M. Masri

FOR MOST, IF NOT ALL, of us holding positions as senior academic administrators, the concept of international education is not a novel one. Indeed, the need to gain a more enriched understanding of the world, particularly of competitor nations who did not necessarily espouse similar world views to the United States, emerged in the aftermath of World War II. During this time, area studies programs—academic programs whose purpose is to enhance our understanding of a specific geographic location in the world— became an integral part of the fabric of many university campuses.

The first academic center in the United States devoted to the interdisciplinary study of Russia and the Soviet Union was founded as the Russian Institute (now the Harriman Institute) at Columbia University in 1946, with the support of the Rockefeller Foundation. This was twelve years before the National Defense Education Act was signed into law by President Eisenhower, an act that would also provide funding for language and area studies programs through its Title VI statute.

As Title VI grew in size and scope in the mid- to late twentieth century, my generation became both a beneficiary of and participant in this quest for international understanding: first as students and then, for some of us, as university faculty and administrators. We witnessed firsthand the evolution of area studies programs. Take the Harriman Institute, for example: remaining true to its original purpose, the institute's purview has grown to encompass all the states of the former Soviet Union and Eastern Europe, working to directly advance our knowledge of those regions through the coordinated research work of faculty and students. Over time, Columbia, like many other universities, recognized that other parts of the world were equally deserving of such academic focus; the growth in number and breadth of regional institutes—focusing on regions like China, the Middle East, and Latin America—was congruent with increased interest in these locations. Today, Columbia is home to ten such institutes that contribute to our understanding of international affairs and developments around the world.

With the advent of the digital age at the turn of the twenty-first century, we became cognizant of the fact that being international *alone* would no longer suffice. We knew that it was imperative that we reorient our thinking—and ultimately, the university's purpose as a conduit of knowledge—to go beyond the international. It was time for us to become global, too.

These two terms—*international* and *global*—are often used interchangeably. Columbia, however, is of the belief that the two terms carry very distinct meanings with specific implications for both how we understand the concepts and how we gear our actions toward addressing the phenomena that arise from them individually.

International as a term tends to concern itself more with individual nation-states and international relations. The Harriman Institute's work and scope, for example, is an international one. The application of international in such terms reinforces my previous statement: that higher education institutes' foray into the international realm began long before the twenty-first century.

Beyond Title VI's provisions propelling the internationalization of universities' curricular underpinnings and research, technological advancements that have facilitated travel—of ideas, goods, and human beings—have also made universities more international. Institutes of higher education welcomed, over the years, more faculty of diverse nationalities among their ranks—myself, a Jordanian by birth, included. Departments within universities dedicated significant efforts and resources to internationalize their academic programs by providing study abroad opportunities for students, making available funding for students and faculty to conduct research abroad, internationalizing curricula, and, of course, offering instruction in many languages. At Columbia, many of our graduate schools—from the School of International and Public Affairs, to the Mailman School of Public Health, to the Graduate School of Journalism—provide their students with opportunities to fulfill degree requirements in many corners of the world.

Even before setting foot on campus, students are already quite international—our international students, by virtue of the passports they carry and the countries they call home, and our "domestic" students through the number of languages they speak, the diversity of the communities in which they were reared, or simply through their lived experiences.

The term *global*, on the other hand, more aptly describes some of the major shifts we have experienced with the onset of the digital age. By this I mean that the unprecedented pace at which people, money, and ideas now move across the world has made us all inextricably interconnected across boundaries, such that what happens in one corner of the world has a concrete impact in another.

It is no longer possible to study one region of the world without both examining its relations with the rest of the world and appreciating developments in it within a global context. Previously, one could have spent one's entire career studying China without ever having to set foot in Africa; an undergraduate student at Columbia could spend four years in an area studies program without fully comprehending developments in that area from a global perspective.

An example that I cite frequently that illustrates how intertwined our societies have become is the mass displacement of Syrians as a consequence of the ongoing civil war. Until the Syrian crisis, population displacement often occurred on a much more regional scale. Take Palestinian refugees, for example: upon the creation of the state of Israel, displaced Palestinians fled to neighboring countries—namely, Jordan, Lebanon, Syria, and Egypt. But since 2011, the exodus of Syrians from their homeland is not merely a Middle Eastern crisis; it has left its imprint on Europe and North America, not only in terms of how to accommodate the influx of individuals fleeing the violence but also regarding the rising nationalist, populist, and anti-immigrant sentiments that their arrival has stirred.

There are, of course, countless other examples of similar global phenomena that both predate and postdate the Syrian civil war, such as the 2008 financial crisis and the Ebola epidemic, and, at the time this volume goes to press, the COVID-19 pandemic. But the bottom line is that in the early twenty-first century, the way in which we interacted with the world was changing irrevocably, and if universities wanted to remain relevant, our thinking had to change, too.

Upon assuming his role as the nineteenth president of Columbia in 2002, Lee C. Bollinger led the university on a mission to answer pressing questions on how to better engage the world and how we could play an active, participatory role in informing global discourse. We recognized that our existing infrastructure could no longer facilitate a deeper understanding of the world, and it was time to seriously deliberate on how to add a global dimension to the fabric of the university.

Of course, we were neither the first university to grapple with this issue nor the first to take action in addressing it. We were able to consider the many global models that emerged in the late twentieth and early twenty-first centuries, as well as the option of developing our own, unique path.

The most prevalent model, then and now, is that of branch campuses. Education City in Doha, Qatar, launched in 1997 and officially inaugurated in 2003, is a prime example of the application of this model. An initiative of the Qatar Foundation for Education, Science, and Community Development, Education City hosts branch campuses of some of the world's leading universities. American universities with a presence in Doha include Weill Cornell Medical College, Texas A&M, Virginia Commonwealth, Carnegie-Mellon, Georgetown, and Northwestern. One of Education City's primary goals is to provide students from the region and beyond with a world-class education close to home. But it was also conceived as a forum where universities could share their research and forge relationships among one another and with local stakeholders.

Other universities have also embraced the branch campus model, such as New York University (NYU), which has degree-granting portal campuses in both Abu Dhabi and Shanghai, and Duke University, which has a campus in China.

While branch campuses have been embraced by many of our peers, Columbia's reservations about such a model ultimately outweighed its potential benefits. We could not envisage branch campuses enabling us to learn from or engage better with the world. In fact, I consider branch campuses to be somewhat neocolonial; we would simply be going in and transferring our "superior" knowledge to local audiences, with no guarantee that we were building local, sustainable capacities.

We had other reservations about the branch campus model as well. Challenges associated with this model, in terms of hiring faculty of a commensurate quality as those hired by the main campus, as well as risks to the university's reputation, were detracting considerations. Branch campuses are also often encumbered by deep relations with local governments, laws, and practices, which have the potential to impede academic freedom and corrode other values that are fundamental to a US liberal education (which would be deal breakers for us). Take NYU Abu Dhabi, for example: During its construction, the university became entangled in scandals regarding the treatment of laborers by its local partners, in violation of international labor laws. And in the fall of 2017, journalism professors at NYU announced their refusal to teach at the school's Abu Dhabi campus after at least one faculty member was denied an entry visa. In 2018, the temporary detention of a British academic on allegations of spying while he was conducting research in the United Arab Emirates brought negative attention to NYU, raising questions about the potential impact that the country's repressive regime could have on academic freedom.

Whether in China, Singapore, or the United Arab Emirates, a university's branch campus could become subject to local censorship and accused of complicity in a country's clampdown on dissent or its suppression of freedom of expression. When it becomes difficult for a university to justify its existence under such circumstances, it is likely to find that impediments to terminating its presence may be insurmountable, at least in the short term. Heavy investments in brick-and-mortar infrastructure and long-term contractual relationships make it difficult for a university to exit a situation that may have become untenable.

The branch campus model is surely not the only one that has been pursued by a number of universities. Universities in the United States, including Columbia, have countless partnerships and joint-degree programs around the globe. For example, both Columbia's School of International and Public Affairs and its Graduate School of Journalism have joint programs with Sciences Po in France. Columbia, Duke, NYU, and Yale all have partnerships with the National University of Singapore. While certainly effective, such partnerships are typically limited in their scope and scale.

With the limitations and potential high risks of the branch campus model, and the restraining nature of other opportunities for global engagement—be they through joint-degree programs or study abroad opportunities—we at Columbia sought an open-ended, home-grown mechanism for ensuring that all our faculty and students, across the entire campus, have the opportunity and incentive to engage with the world in a meaningful manner. Enter our model of *global centers*.

Our growing network of global centers—currently in nine locations—act as nimble, robust hubs that serve the research and education mission of the entire university. Born of the belief that a global presence is essential to achieving the highest levels of excellence in discovering new knowledge and educating future leaders, the Columbia Global Centers complement existing infrastructures on campus and act as an alternative to more rigid and potentially risky approaches to global education.

Indeed, knowing what we wanted to achieve and to avoid was instrumental in the development and growth of our model. Our vision for the global centers was driven by a motivation to learn *from* and *with* the world—basically, to become less ignorant about the world around us. As it stood, through our area studies programs and regional institutes, we were sitting in our corner in Morningside Heights in Manhattan studying the world. We would travel the world and back, but our perspective remained a North American one. We wanted to challenge this paradigm and develop centers that would be intellectual infrastructures that served as conduits for local, regional, and global knowledge, expertise, and networks. We knew we could neither develop the precise questions nor obtain the correct answers if we did not collaborate with local institutions on the ground, identifying key issues in that region and around the world; doing otherwise would have stifled our learning and impact, in both the short and long term.

And thus, a network of global centers was born. Since our first two centers launched in Amman and Beijing in the spring of 2009, we now have additional physical presences in Istanbul, Mumbai, Nairobi, Paris, Rio de Janeiro, Santiago, and, most recently, Tunis. We do not recruit students or hire faculty into these centers. The global centers are led by individuals—faculty members or accomplished alumni, in most instances—who possess a sophisticated understanding of and networks in their regions, as well as a global mind-set, and they are largely staffed by persons from within the community and region in which they operate.

We encourage our faculty and students, through incentive instruments that we have created on campus, to use the centers in pursuit of their academic projects, often in partnership with local and regional collaborators. The President's Global Innovation Fund, a competitive proposal-funding mechanism, offers financial support for faculty research projects within and across the nine centers, while our Global Scholars Program, another faculty proposal-funding initiative, supports innovative coursework that takes place at and through the centers. Opportunities that exist through the centers cut across the university, schools and academic disciplines, the network of global centers, and international borders.

An innovation that is a favorite of mine, which could not have been conceived or implemented were it not for the existence of the global centers, is a course entitled Democracy and Constitutional Engineering in the Middle East, which was developed by a member of our political science faculty and focuses on the use of data in democratic processes. Rather than offer the course at our campus in New York, the course was delivered on location in Tunis and Istanbul. Leveraging the expertise and networks of the Amman, Istanbul, and Tunis centers, students studied a "democracy in the making" on site in Tunis and then traveled to Istanbul, where they examined a democracy that was, at the time, under stress. The course enrolled Columbia students alongside students from leading universities in the Middle East, North Africa, and Turkey, offering students the opportunity to learn from each other's perspectives and experiences.

The centers also focus on community engagement, be it by hosting speaker series that seek to spark dialogue in the community on issues ranging from public policy to the arts, or through workshops organized by Columbia faculty and schools in partnership with local stakeholders.

Undoubtedly, venturing into relatively uncharted territory comes with its own risks. From the outset, we were aware that this would be a process of trial and error and that we would have to learn from our mistakes along the way and adjust accordingly. Simple in its concept and modest in terms of the resources that it required, we knew nonetheless that the ambitious journey we were embarking on was akin to the kind of transformation universities went through in the nineteenth and early twentieth centuries in evolving from local teaching colleges into international research universities.

In the decade since we launched our first centers, our strategy in developing and expanding the network has evolved as our engagement with and consequent understanding of the world and global dynamics have increased. For example, our centers were originally defined regionally; we had the Columbia Global Centers: Middle East in Amman, the Columbia Global Centers: Europe in Paris, and so on. As the network expanded and collaborations grew among the centers, the question of how a region was defined became a relevant and important one. For example, Paris is just as intertwined with Europe as it is with its former colonies in West and North Africa. Istanbul is quite literally at the crossroads between Asia and Europe and is just as intertwined with the Middle East as Amman is. Africa is too large, important, and diverse a continent to be represented by what was, at the time, a single center in Nairobi called the Africa Center.

Regional designations were thus dropped from the centers' titles, to allow for a more fluid and organic integration among existing and future centers and to ensure that no center's work or scope was restricted by a geographic designation.

Our expanding presence abroad has also very much informed how we think of ourselves at home. Our president, Lee C. Bollinger, has been quite focused on utilizing our increased engagement with the world not just as a means to expand our global reach and engagement but also to ensure that we reflect our global approach in how we define and try to solve global problems. Columbia World Projects, a recent initiative that attempts to accomplish this objective, was founded with the aim of funding projects that bring academics and outside partners together to solve real-world problems. Three to four forums are convened every year around a specific global challenge, bringing together experts from within and outside the university, including from governments and NGOs, to develop ideas for proposals for research projects that would offer implementable solutions in a three- to five-year time frame. Recent forums have focused on energy, inequality, and cybersecurity, at home in the United States and around the world.

In 2018, we welcomed our inaugural cohort of Obama Foundation Scholars at Columbia, under the auspices of the Columbia World Projects. The program brings together emerging young leaders from across the globe who have demonstrated their commitment to addressing the most difficult challenges facing their communities, countries, and regions. Over the course of an academic year, in a program designed by Columbia in consultation with the Obama Foundation, these scholars are provided with opportunities to expand their knowledge and skill sets and to develop new networks and abilities that, we hope, will serve to strengthen their impact in their home regions.

Columbia Global Centers celebrated their tenth anniversary in 2019. Looking back at the past decade, we have attained many of the goals we set out to achieve, as our network of nine global centers actively promotes and facilitates collaborative and impactful engagement between faculty, students, alumni, and the world.

Our centers have demonstrated that they are well immersed in their local regions and are positioned to further leverage contacts, networks, and expertise on behalf of the Columbia community. With every passing day, the centers' roles of acting as conduits of understanding, addressing global challenges, and advancing knowledge and its exchange are becoming inextricably woven into the constitution of our university.

The Columbia Global Centers have formed the core of the university's global strategy, which, in addition to the network's own expansion, has seen Columbia's global engagement expand to other initiatives such as the Columbia World Projects. Our global foray represented a major shift in how we think of ourselves as a university. We hoped then and believe now that we are setting an ever-rising benchmark for institutions of higher education to engage with an ever-globalizing world and to remain relevant in a twenty-first-century context.

19

GLOBAL EDUCATION, EDUCATING GLOBALLY

Caroline Levander

A RECENT ANALYSIS OF INTERNATIONALIZATION and higher education in the *Economist* concluded, "The top level of academia is perhaps the world's most international community, and the world benefits from the growth of this productive international body of scholars and students."[1] And their reasoning is sound: research is getting more global, with researchers working together across borders on borderless problems from climate change to artificial intelligence.

And yet we know that this is not the whole story. International research collaboration does not occur equally with all university partners across the globe but tends to further privilege the premiere institutions in those countries that have stable economic and political infrastructure—hence a gated international community.

And within the United States, there is a similar growing divide because of universities' decisions to engage internationally. Those elite US research universities with visibility abroad and resources for active recruitment efforts (including visa application support) report increases in international student enrollments and research scholars. And they do so at a time when the social and political environment in the United States and growing competition from institutions in other countries have created, in 2018 alone, a 2 percent decline in international student enrollment in the United States. The net result of this uneven internationalization success is a further differentiation between the haves and the have-nots among institutions within the United States.

As we can see from table 19.1, from the UNESCO Institute for Statistics, a substantial percentage of the total number of bachelor's degree and advanced degree students in the world today actively seek international education. And these numbers do not include the students who pursue international immersion opportunities through study abroad, programs such as the ERASMUS student exchange in Europe, or fellowships and other awards that explicitly promote international educational experiences.

The Fulbright Association, for example, has sent over 140,000 students and scholars on international fellowships as part of its mission to stimulate international education and exchange with the goal of promoting greater peace and understanding in the world. And the Fulbright alumni network further reinforces this mission by fostering lifelong connections among these 140,000 people. As a Fulbright Association Board member and alumna, I have seen firsthand the power of this network and the deep hunger that students and those in higher education have for opportunities to learn through immersion in international contexts.

Table 19.1. Location of the world's students by continent (millions)

Asia	91	S America	16
Europe	27	Africa	11
N America	19	Oceania	19

Where the Students Go:	Inbound Students	Where the Students Come From:	Outbound Students
1. United States	907,000	1. China	791,000
2. United Kingdom	429,000	2. India	234,000
3. Australia	266,000	3. Germany	116,000
4. France	235,000	4. Republic of Korea	108,000
5. Germany	229,000	5. Saudi Arabia	85,000
6. Russian Federation	213,000	6. France	79,000
7. Canada	151,000	7. Nigeria	71,000
8. Japan	133,000	8. United States	67,000
9. China	123,000	9. Kazakhstan	67,000
10. Italy	88,000	10. Malaysia	65,000

Source: UNESCO Institute for Statistics, Enrollment by Level, Levels 6–8, Outbound and Internationally Mobile Students by Country of Origin, 2015.

But these numbers are the tip of the iceberg. They do not reflect the many millions of students and would-be students who need, arguably as never before, the education and periodic re-education offered by the world's best universities. Universities in many parts of the world face continuing challenges around cost, access, relevance, and educational quality. Compounding these factors, the needs of learners are evolving rapidly as a result of social, economic, and technological changes, not to mention the changing nature of work and careers and the impact of artificial intelligence and data science on intellectual and commercial practices. For those in the many parts of the world with limited ability to attend universities due to infrastructure, access, and economic constraints, a university education, if it is to happen at all, must come from outside their country of origin. And yet herein lies the rub: the education needed to improve a would-be student's socioeconomic situation, to lift local communities out of poverty and disease, and to begin to solve the world's most pressing problems has thus far been out of that student's reach.

And so, when we think about educating globally, we quickly find ourselves moving beyond our typical student communities and grappling with the fundamental question of how best to educate people around the world so that we can endure and thrive as a planet.

With this very big question in mind, I secured funding in 2018 from the Rockefeller Foundation to host a summit aimed at envisioning a new form of global university. My co-conveners and I invited a small group of education experts and leaders from around the world to design a new university model that would overcome existing impediments to worldwide learning, global problem solving, and applied research collaboration.

Participants included senior leaders from the Education Outcomes Fund for Africa and the Middle East, the Chan Zuckerberg Initiative, Edraak, the African Leadership Academy, Macmillan Learning, and presidents and university leaders from Imperial College London, Stanford, Ecuador's Escuela Superior Politécnica del Litoral, Rice, India's new SRM University, Andhra Pradesh, the University of Chicago, Delft University of Technology (TU Delft), and Harvard.

And we began with a simple but potentially profound idea: acting in competitive isolation, the lone university has reached the limit of its impact as a force of educational good, both nationally and globally. Acting together, however, universities can realize a collective power sorely needed and thus far unrealized in modern times. And this collective power has the potential to transform how we conceive of international education and university cultures.

There are, of course, historic reasons for universities' competitive isolation. Universities have largely developed as singular institutions or regional networks, such as state public university systems. These separate institutions often compete beyond their region for faculty and students. However, they are typically physically isolated in an archaic manner reflecting the predigital era in which books, scholars, and learners needed to be physically co-located. Most importantly, universities with virtually identical goals and challenges have not generally collaborated on defining goals, setting or evaluating strategies, or finding the resources needed to collectively address the pressing world need for advancement and learning.

But history need not be destiny. Universities exhibit ample evidence of collaborative capability. Responding to the needs and priorities of funding agencies, research universities typically support and encourage interinstitutional research collaboration. In addition, many colleges and universities offer student exchange opportunities and accept the Common Application, as well as Advanced Placement and transfer credit, among other coordinated efforts. There are many examples of dual-degree programs between complementary partnered universities.

Moving beyond these limited collaborations, we began to develop a new model of the globally engaged university, one that is formed as collaborative networks that share best practices, support necessary advances, leverage complementary expertise, and realize economies of scale. This new model, which we called the New Global University (NGU), therefore, seeks to be a networked "university of universities" enabling educational institutions to collaboratively innovate pedagogy, link more diverse groups of learners, leverage new learning tools and technologies, and develop new modes of learning. In the NGU, collaboration activates and sustains the network. The network, in turn, brings together communities of students for shared problem solving and team-based learning. The NGU is thus an educational ecosystem characterized by collaborative community among faculty, students, and institutions. These new universities of universities have the potential to enhance the value of existing institutions, support local identity and culture, and offer meaningful learning opportunities on a much-needed global scale.

This new model differs significantly from delivery platform organizations such as edX or Coursera, associations such as the Association of American Colleges and Universities (AAC&U), or external supporting private enterprises such as Workday or McKinsey. Delivery platforms of so-called online program managers (OPMs) provide shared course content with a broader public but still assume single institutional partners and leverage university brand power. Focusing on platform development and the reuse of content, OPMs reinforce the institutional status quo. They do not offer new forms of interinstitutional community, develop interinstitutional infrastructure, or broadly support new models of collaborative pedagogy made possible by technological advances. On the other hand, such long-standing organizations as the AAC&U put forward a shared vision, such as "liberal education," and provide a forum for some forms of collective problem solving but do not support collective action at a strategic, curricular, or operational level across the larger higher education ecosystem. Nor do they leverage the power of recently available educational technologies to build new forms of academic community and educational opportunity. Looking forward, quality education requires innovative collaboration at all steps of the education process, from curricular development to educational delivery methods to new student markets. Recognizing this, the NGU model leverages new tools to create a collaborative network that, in conception, operation, and social impact, supports and enables quality education at scale.

The benefits of collaborative networks are evident. While individual institutions are locked in competition with their peers, a network looking beyond this competitive dynamic allows universities to support and extend their traditional mission with new and collaboratively sourced methods and tools. In doing so, each institution partners with others to move beyond traditional boundaries for the shared and common good, while reinforcing its own mission and identity. Networks can share advances and best practices in pedagogy, reinforcing innovation at one site with validation and faculty support from another. By linking student bodies, learners at one form of regional or targeted institution can learn from the experience, insight, and perspective of those at another. This key connection at the student level is an important step toward global awareness, global community, and global learning.

From an operational standpoint, many aspects of such a new networked university are becoming an economic and pragmatic necessity; shared infrastructure is already advancing through the efforts of commercial vendors to colleges and universities who are intrinsically motivated by economies of scale. Vendors of admissions platforms, student tracking systems, learning management systems, and other support structures already impose uniformity and regularity out of economic necessity. Going even further beyond the operation of universities, such organizations as the private testing services in the United States have tremendous influence over admissions, without any real transparency, accountability, or need to conform to academic values of specific institutions. The effective consolidation of practice will be driven by for-profit providers. It is up to academic leadership to take control of the process and drive the academic enterprise toward mutually beneficial shared goals.

Economies of scale will also drive aspects of pedagogy and curriculum. These changes are inevitable and well underway at certain kinds of institutions. Over time, digital smart textbooks are gradually replacing paper, partly because of reduced cost and partly because sophisticated research-based learning activities and routine aspects of courses can be automated, raising the floor and giving the best teachers the opportunity to focus on what they do best. This will happen first, over the coming half decade, in standardized courses with the highest collective enrollment across a wide spectrum of institutions (i.e., basic required courses such as expository writing, college algebra, introductory psychology, economics, computing, and physical sciences). Modern advances offer the outstanding benefit of low incremental cost per learner, at a high fixed-development cost for the platform, tool, method, and its validation. As digital platforms and data science become increasingly effective, they will structure admissions, student pathways, learner feedback and grading, retention and learning success, financial modeling and accounting, alumni tracking, and such areas as the competency-based assessment of returning professional learners.

The custom platform developed and used by a single university has already become outdated and impractical. The infrastructure supporting and enabling the New Global University will not only support collaborative sourcing but will also enable a community to realize the highest-caliber education possible by adapting, customizing, and specializing educational opportunities to meet local needs and support a diverse range of communities and cultural needs.

Our goal was not to converge on a single new global university or select a single model. Rather, the aim was to explore design choices that arise in adopting new ways of approaching worldwide engagement and find ways for a new university of universities (or new partnerships between portions of existing universities) to constructively and successfully approach these choices.

But what might this networked concept look like in practice?

At Rice University, we have undertaken a Global Scholars pilot program that connects students at nine universities around the world through a shared online course catalog. These courses were developed independently through various platforms, including edX, Coursera, and Canvas, and were already being offered for credit to students matriculated at the home university. The universities that you see in figure 19.1 agreed to experiment with internationalizing our online classrooms by offering our existing online for-credit courses to all students matriculated at the university network partners. Recognizing that ideas transcend nations and that international immersions are an essential component of a Rice education, this program enables our students to join a global community of learning. While it's not the same as on-premise study abroad, this virtual study abroad means that Rice students taking our online Computer Science 140 course, for example, will now have students from top-tier research universities around the world in their class. Study abroad now is integrated into our campus, whether or not students actively choose to take a semester away from campus. And it is a multinational classroom because of our networked approach to our online curriculum.

You might imagine that for this pilot the devil is in the details, and you are right. Coordinating administrative details, coming to a shared understanding of best practices, and learning to speak a common language around credit hours, exam protocols, and time zone expectations were all substantial endeavors involving the coordination and commitment of all the universities' registrars, relevant academic departments, bursars, and student advising teams. We bracketed the financials by agreeing for the time being to a quid pro quo arrangement when it comes to student numbers. Thus far, no money has changed institutional hands; nor have students paid network partners any tuition, other than their home institution.

We are beginning our third year of the pilot, and so we have some initial findings. First, students find the experience of being in an international, transcontinental classroom exhilarating and daunting. For those Rice students who might decide, for example, to take a course from École polytechnique fédérale de Lausanne or TU Delft, best results come when students are focused, ambitious, and deeply interested in the subject. Second, students taking classes in this shared catalog (whether they register for a class at their home university or a class with one of the network partners) may not have thought that global immersion would be part of their undergraduate education but relish the networked learning environment. Third, because students are subject to the norms of the university offering the course, learning the culture is a significant part of the students' opportunity. Rice, for example, has an honor code, and so we developed an online orientation to ensure that everyone in the class knew the rules of the pedagogic game they were playing. While I have focused here on the student experience, it is clear that faculty across the network are beginning to explore developing multi-institutional areas of disciplinary focus, leveraging faculty strength across the partnership to build curriculum.

Figure 19.1. Map of Rice University Global Scholar locations.

This network has been an important proof of concept for Rice's development of global strategy more generally. Our vision is to develop an international network with academic partners in order to achieve deeper collaborations among faculty and meaningful student opportunities at the graduate and undergraduate levels. Key to this vision is a commitment to build international engagement that is bi- and multidirectional, integrative, and that enables international engagement both at home and abroad.

Because many pressing problems affect us all, there is a need for universities around the world to come together to set research priorities and build learning communities that tackle borderless problems. Rice's approach to global engagement begins with the recognition that we live in an era when many of our biggest challenges are global in scope. As such, they demand new collaborative approaches to research and education—approaches that move beyond the competitive isolation and national frameworks in which universities have historically operated.

And so the international network that we are developing with a select number of academic partners accelerates collaboration and discovery around research questions of global importance. This network is comprised of hubs of educational and research activity at partner universities in our network. Instead of building campuses, we are co-creating hubs of shared research interest. Key to the success of our approach is multidirectional academic traffic, with students and faculty from both institutions spending time on the partner university's campus. To facilitate this bilateral approach, we are establishing a home hub on our campus that supports the global network and its research and education programs. This approach is characterized by nimbleness and flexibility. These dynamic multiyear global pop-ups allow us to activate research opportunity and educational innovation as global challenges evolve, as our faculty seizes new research fields, and as the world changes. Our faculty bring a rich variety of international backgrounds that we leverage at the level of strategy: over 30 percent of Rice faculty are foreign nationals, and the vast majority of our faculty have international research collaborations.

With its focus on grand challenges, this approach enables us to have an outsize impact on solving problems for the betterment of our world. Our goal is to advance and dynamize research that grapples with the world's most pressing problems by building a powerful research and education accelerator—an international incubator of sorts. While this approach does not grow our student body per se, it does expand the impact of our research and educational enterprise, making those activities meaningful for many who have never heard of our university.

This may sound like a lofty goal, and it is. But then, universities have a long history of this kind of thinking. Over the centuries, universities have had three major functions: (1) to advance knowledge through research and scholarship, (2) to serve the personal and professional development of learners, and (3) to sustain communities of experts who contribute to public service and the private sector. Universities seeking global engagement must collectively support and enable these three functions using the tools, methods, and organizational structures that will be most effective in the coming decades. Doing so will ensure the ongoing dynamism, vitality, and innovation of diverse university communities in the decades to come.

Note

1. "Degrees of Success," *Economist*.

Bibliography

"Degrees of Success: How Global University Rankings Are Changing Higher Education." *Economist*, May 19, 2018. https://www.economist.com/international/2018/05/19/how -global-university-rankings-are-changing-higher-education.

20

GROWING GLOBAL COMPETENCE IN UNDERGRADUATE AND PROFESSIONAL EDUCATION

Kathleen Claussen

IN THIS CHAPTER, I'LL DISCUSS how my experience at Indiana University (IU) has informed my career, as well as some of the unexpected consequences of the work that I did at IU on my future trajectory. I'll also examine the ways that I see global and international education having a role in professional schools, drawing on my experiences as a law student, a lawyer, and, now, a legal academic.

My experience with the IU Center for the Study of Global Change, which has since become part of the Hamilton Lugar School of Global and International Studies, began as a high school student, when I participated in the International Studies Summer Institute at Foster Quad. The experience served as a launch pad for me, attracting me to the work of the center when I started at IU. I also came to IU to study Spanish. Certainly, living in Miami now, Spanish is critical to my daily life.

While at IU, I had the opportunity to work in Costa Rica, supported by my Herman B Wells Scholarship. Additionally, IU sent me to Mexico to participate in courses in the graduate school at the Benemérita Universidad Autónoma de Puebla, with which IU had a partnership. That course work gave me an opportunity to study and write in Spanish and to think more about the future of the public sector from a Latin American perspective. It was that skill set that helped me land a position at the Office of the US Trade Representative (USTR) in 2014, as the lead lawyer on a case against the government of Guatemala. The case involved Guatemala's failure to effectively enforce its labor laws. My role entailed going to Guatemala, where we interviewed workers, and putting together the legal arguments in Spanish and

English that we then presented to an international arbitral panel. Without the skills that I honed at IU, this work would not have been possible.

Other unexpected consequences of my pursuit of international studies involved the USTR sending me to Denmark, Ireland, and the Netherlands to engage those governments to join the United States in an innovative trade policy matter. I was dispatched there because I had contacts with those governments—contacts that I had developed during my time at IU, when I had studied and worked in those countries.

Throughout my international work, sometimes IU's global connections helped in less professional but even more critical ways: for example, when I secured an internship at the International Criminal Court in The Hague, a generous IU alum helped me secure housing.

Additionally, beginning in 2015, I spent two years working with international counterparts of the Federal Bureau of Investigation, Central Intelligence Agency, and National Security Agency to develop strategies to deal with international cyberthreats. I was tasked with this role because my colleagues believed I had the cultural competence to engage with our allies on delicate diplomatic issues.

Lately, I have also drawn on my upbringing in southern Indiana to better understand some of the Midwest-focused policy-making strategies employed by the Trump administration. While I was still in government, my IU training served me well by helping me bridge what sometimes felt like a divide among perspectives. This personal experience reflects larger conversations at the heart of contemporary discussions about international education: there are communities within this country that are foreign to one another, and bridging these gaps likewise ought to be part of global education and communicating across barriers.

I could go on about the many other ways that the global-to-local linkages in which IU excels have enriched my life, professionally and personally, but space would not permit such a lengthy list.

I turn now to the place of global and international education within professional schools. I focus my comments on two primary manifestations that I see in law schools, but I suspect that other professional schools face similar situations. The questions that I examine here link up to the paradigmatic debate that runs deep in legal education reform—and, I think, across other areas of curricular reform—namely, whether to integrate global and international education across the curriculum or to include it in a separate track focused exclusively on that area. In my own opinion, these are not mutually exclusive tracks, but they are often discussed as such. On one hand, some argue in favor of a curricular concentration on international and transnational law. Such a concentration allows students to focus their studies on a variety of general and specialized courses in international law—a discipline near and dear to my heart—and also comparative law. Comparative law is, I believe, falling by the wayside in many law schools. You will not find candidates on the entry-level market for academic positions who would put it as their first teaching choice, for it will not get them hired in the present environment—one where law schools find themselves under financial constraints that force them to hire largely in the subject areas that are tested on the bar exam.

The second manifestation of this field in law schools is what I will refer to as global competence. This area is, I think, less understood, and I believe that the issue is particularly acute in professional schools. I've certainly seen it in my own experience teaching at law school. Global competence is an integral part of professional competence—that is, it is essential to our engagement with the world in many ways, such as writing a professional email or knowing how to handle a complicated situation. Those are strengths that I believe are deeply connected to an understanding of the world. They require an understanding of one's audience and a sensitivity to certain topics and words. They require figuratively meeting one's collaborator where he or she is—not just asking of oneself, "How do I engage in interpersonal skills?" They are central to what it is to be a lawyer today. When talking with other practitioners, trying to assess the skills and skill sets that we want junior lawyers to have, a frequent response is that junior lawyers should have more training in area and global studies, regardless of one's future practice area, because all of law practice has some cross-border element these days.

Problem-solving skills form part of the repertoire of professional global competences that we are training our lawyers to have. Every class session that I teach includes some sort of problem-solving exercise. In fact, the University of Miami did something very interesting beginning in fall 2018 that I think could be a model for all law schools: it organized a legal hackathon. We brought in members of the large practice community in Miami who spent a day working with first-year students, organized into groups, trying to solve global legal problems. It was an amazing experience.

Another skill that practitioners identify as important is anticipating potential challenges. This often involves situating legal issues in a larger picture, from domestic to global and beyond. It also involves communication skills, which include, but are not limited to, language abilities, familiarity with cultures other than one's own, the ability to cooperate effectively, and teamwork among people from very different backgrounds. It has been said that the language of the global economy is English, which I find true in some respects yet not true in others. In fact, in recent years, the most-needed language competence at the USTR has been Indonesian. Why is this the case? Because the global economy is changing, and as it changes, so too does the need for closely scrutinizing the acts, policies, and practices of our trading partners to enforce international trade rules.

To be able to do this, in addition to legal training, a valuable trade lawyer must have language skills, international experience, and the ability to communicate and understand across cultural and linguistic barriers. Such nontransparent issues in international affairs thus benefit very deeply from practitioners who have been trained in global and international issues. And, of course, there are other languages that are pertinent: in the context of international dispute settlement proceedings at present, Russian and Chinese are necessary, but so are many others. So, as we think about new directions for Title VI in professional schools, we need to make the case that global and international studies are a part of professional competence to which training devised and supported by Title VI programs may contribute.

I'd like to return to an earlier theme and make one final point, addressing the intersection of the international and domestic, or the global and the local, and the role of technology. Title VI funding originated as a legal response to a national security threat. Today, the definition of "national security" and US management of it is evolving. But if you asked many civil servants or lawmakers on Capitol Hill how to handle these international challenges, at least some of them are likely to say that part of the answer lies in local and domestic policies: infrastructure policy, tax policy, and education policy, to name a few. To address those would help deal with the underlying causes and larger issues, rather than the symptoms, of our global economic grievances. Likewise, as a student at IU, I wanted to engage the people of Indiana in global affairs, and so, with the help of the Center for the Study of Global Change, and especially Deb Hutton, the center's outreach coordinator at that time, I created a videoconference program, Conversations About Service and Engagement (CASE). Back in 2003, when videoconference technology was not as prevalent as it is today, CASE operationalized this medium to allow students who could not afford to go abroad to engage with communities in other places. IU and its able and visionary leaders made this work happen. It is absolutely crucial that we as educators make connections and reach students where they are. So, again, as we think about the future of Title VI and professional schools in particular, I think paramount to that brainstorming session ought to be questions of design: shaping an approach that empowers professionals to engage from local to global and back again.

21

A VIEW FROM SOMEWHERE

Takyiwaa Manuh

I ARRIVED AT INDIANA UNIVERSITY (IU) Bloomington in March 1992 for a six-week fellowship and was invited back in August 1992 as a visiting lecturer for an initial period of one year in what was then the Department of Afro-American Studies. I ended up staying for another five years and earned a PhD in the process, while continuing to teach courses in Afro-American studies. I had come to IU from a position as a senior research fellow in the Institute of African Studies at the University of Ghana, Legon. The Institute of African Studies has a particular history, which I have written about elsewhere.[1] Suffice it to say that African studies at universities in Ghana is not considered as area studies but as essential in excavating, recovering, and restoring African knowledges and agencies and was envisioned to build active bridges between scholarship and practice of various kinds in Africa and its diasporas. At the Institute of African Studies at the University of Ghana, I had worked in an interdisciplinary milieu where scholars of religion, history, anthropology, gender studies, and politics interacted with music and dance scholars and practitioners, linguistics and language experts, and environmental scholars. Unfortunately, the active scholarly exchanges and interactions with other African universities and research centers that had been built in at the institute's establishment in 1963 had been increasingly curtailed as a result of continued economic austerity from the mid-1970s and Ghana's changed foreign policy focus and outreach within Africa after 1966.[2] That notwithstanding, the institute's vision and mission aspired toward realizing the hopes encapsulated in its founding charter. It continued to serve as the University of Ghana's beacon to the world, long before the establishment of an International Programs Office with its own dean in the late 1990s and early 2000s, welcoming students and faculty from around Africa, the Caribbean, Europe, and North America for short and extended periods of study in Ghana.

I was not a typical student and came to Indiana as a midcareer academic, with my African lens on the world. I had practiced as a lawyer in Ghana, was a member of the women's movement there, was part of a network of scholars in the social sciences in Africa, and had an established record of publications. I had language skills in French, from living in a closely interconnected West African region where many of our neighbors are French speaking, and was also fluent in Akan and several other languages of the multilingual communities in Ghana. My two-year master's program in Tanzania had also afforded me the opportunity to live in another African country and to appreciate the commonalities as well as the diversities around Africa. I had also participated in a one-year United Nations University program in 1986–87, studying at both the University of Chicago and the Universidad de los Andes in Bogotá, Colombia, where I gained a smattering of Spanish while living in the country at a particularly difficult time in its history.

But arriving at an institution like IU that had both a mission and enormous intellectual and financial resources was like tinder for the spark that was in me. It was left to me to make use of those extraordinary resources and opportunities to further develop myself and to forge my career as I interacted with my professors and the highly driven crops of younger students from different backgrounds and interests that I took courses with. The Department of Anthropology, where I was based as a student, gave me the space to hone my social science skills as I immersed myself in the threefold organization of the discipline into sociocultural, linguistic, and bioanthropology. Inevitably for me, there were also courses in legal anthropology that I took with Carol Greenhouse, who was also my PhD advisor and generous with her time and interest. I recall in particular a course on Africa's vulnerability to environmental change that I took with Emilio Moran, which has stuck with me with me all these years for its prescience in foreshadowing many of the current issues in climate change, especially for Africa. I also remember the courses that I took with Michael Jackson in the phenomenological tradition that opened up and enabled conversations from the particular to the universal in a shared humanity.

My minor in African studies, including a course on bibliographic resources available for studying Africa and the weekly seminar series, exposed me to different topics and perspectives and deepened my understanding and training. The many Title VI conferences that I attended provided opportunities for scholarly engagement and interactions with K-12 instructors from around Indiana. I also audited some courses in the School of Public and Environmental Affairs and occasionally went over to the Law School.

I had been a member of the African Studies Association before arriving at IU, but it was from Indiana that I participated more actively, receiving grants and invitations to attend conferences both in the United States and abroad, to present my work or to comment on the work of others. I took advantage of IU's rich array of events, conferences, distinguished lecture series; its concert programs; the outstanding IU faculty; the Teaching Resources Center (now the Center for Innovative Teaching and Learning), which helped me balance my responsibilities as a student and an instructor on the move; and, of course, the library and all its resources, to enrich my brain and to drink from the cup of the new knowledges and viewpoints that I was encountering. I felt supported in my own endeavors and believed that my insights and opinions were also valued and enriched through the interactions I had. I was invited to contribute a chapter to the third edition of the textbook *Africa*, edited by Phyllis Martin and Patrick O'Meara, and my scholarly output grew during the time I spent at IU.[3] I was able, therefore, to apply for promotion in my home institution just around the time I defended my doctoral dissertation.

Initially, I had assumed that my PhD dissertation would be on an aspect of women's rights and citizenship in Ghana and Africa, in line with my earlier research interests and scholarship, but I ended up working on Ghanaian migrants in Toronto, Canada, and their increasingly transnational lives. To be sure, gendered constructions, practices, and relations among the migrants would constitute a key focus of my investigations, as would notions of citizenship, rights, and identities, all within my comfort zones of gender studies, law, and the texts I had read in my anthropology courses on Caribbean and Hispanic immigrant lives in New York or Florida. But my immersion in migration studies arose from my existential condition of living as a migrant, albeit a privileged one, in the United States and from participating in various Ghanaian communities both virtually and in real time. My fieldwork in Toronto and Ghana was facilitated by travel grants from the African Studies Program, the Department of Anthropology, and the Office of International Programs, after I failed to convince the foundation I had applied to about the usefulness of a transnational perspective for studying African migrants. The theories, debates, and insights I had gained from my courses and readings would be put to the test and challenged as I began to study communities of Ghanaians that I thought I knew at one level but did not know so well in their translated states. As a trained lawyer, I was to confront migrants' views on the uses and limitations of citizenship, of laws and their efficacies, contestations around culture and rights (particularly as they pertained to gender and intergenerational relations), and their notions of the "good life"—the dichotomy between what they termed "living" and "existing." While in Canada they merely existed, it was in Ghana that they believed they could live. But migrants were also conscious of global power, wealth gulfs, and inequities that both shaped and constrained their lives and preferences. They appreciated the mobility that possessing Canadian citizenship and a Canadian passport gave them, enabling them to move as they pleased, as the "few" years they had initially planned to stay abroad stretched into decades, as they waited for their kids to complete college, and so on, or to build the coveted house back "home" in Ghana.

I returned to the University of Ghana almost immediately after my PhD studies. More than anything, my time in Indiana helped me build on what I knew and what I had done, to give me cultural and global competence and confidence. The influences I came under and the connections and relationships they engendered ensured that when I returned to the University of Ghana, I had become a much more rounded academic, ready to assume a senior position in the university and to shape some of its choices and orientations.

Having earned my promotion, I was soon catapulted into the role of deputy director of the Institute of African Studies and to director after another three years. In between the two positions, I was elected as a professorial member of the University Council for two terms. As director of the institute, I became part of the senior management team of the university and was able to draw on my experiences at IU as my university and indeed several other universities around Africa recharted their paths following the decades of austerity and neglect that they had undergone.[4] As donors and foundations rethought their stances and funding for African higher education institutions, I became team leader of the Ghana research team of the Partnership for Higher Education in Africa, which supported the revitalization of African universities from 2000 to 2010.[5] I also became part of UNESCO's Working Group for Higher Education in Africa and was for many years a board member of UNESCO's International Institute for Educational Planning.

The importance of strong institutions, including higher education institutions, for building sustainable and resilient societies and economies is universally recognized. Through their teaching, research, and outreach functions, higher education institutions impart knowledge and develop critical thinking and problem-solving skills, as well as their students' capacity for innovation and engagement with society and their ability to impact their societies through these activities. With specific reference to international education, strong universities and partnerships are fundamental for the quality of exchanges and collaborations, as you cannot exchange what you do not have. There would be no point in sending students or faculty abroad to impoverished and nonfunctioning institutions where people hardly have time to teach or do research. Without a doubt, the renewed attention to higher education in Africa by foundations and governments has led to improvements in teaching, learning, and research as more resources become available and greater investments are made. Students and faculty exude greater confidence about their own competencies and skills, about their possible contributions to knowledge production and its applications to the societies in which they live. This has also strengthened the quality and scale of collaborations, partnerships, and exchanges, both locally and internationally, and helped to make the experience more valuable for both the universities and their partners. As director of the Institute of African Studies, I was able to shape some of these exchanges and to ensure that our faculty and students, as well as students from lesser-endowed Ghanaian universities, could participate meaningfully in some of these exchanges and make their own contributions.

The revitalization of institutions has also contributed to the mobility of scholars in both directions. One of the things that has become clear to me over the years is that as an intellectual you need to be mobile—not just physically but also virtually—to be able to connect to other scholars and to be in constant dialogue even when you may not share the same perspectives or work in the same discipline. These connections become more salient when they are based on respectful and mutually supportive relationships, especially for academics in constrained environments.

My growing seniority and contributions to the university also positioned me to be an institution builder. I refer specifically to my role in spearheading the formalization of a long-standing teaching, research, and advocacy program on women's and gender studies, mainly through the Institute of African Studies into a university-wide Center on Gender Studies and Advocacy that has its own director. Spending almost all of my adult life in the women's movement in Ghana has helped break down some of the tensions between scholarship and practice and to use that in our teaching, research, advocacy, and alliance building.

The insights that I gained from studying the Ghanaian community in Toronto and their transnational world shaped my understanding of migration and the partnerships I have formed through it. As the subject of migration has become increasingly politicized, muddled, and emotive, local understandings and contributions to both theory and practice are imperative and invaluable for clarifying definitions and concepts, contextualizing issues, and adding historical depth and nuance, as well as forging consensus on more fruitful paths for global understanding and progress. In the current paranoia around migrants, slippage often occurs. Refugees and displaced persons can be reclassified as migrants at will, and sensationalist media coverage makes it seem that whole populations and continents are on the move, when indeed the proportion of migrants in world populations has not increased. Particularly in Africa, where movement is more likely to be internal or regional and has formed part of livelihood strategies for generations, it is important for scholarship to be able to influence and shape public discourse to prevent state actions and xenophobic attacks on noncitizens that can ultimately be damaging. It is also important to recall that many African countries host large numbers of refugees and displaced persons; poor countries such as Uganda have shared their meager resources with their guests and integrated them in their educational and social systems, while also providing land for them to till. Such examples in intercultural practice bear retelling and could inform the actions of more prosperous societies intent on shutting the door in the face of needy neighbors.

I was instrumental in establishing the interdisciplinary Center for Migration Studies at the University of Ghana in 2007, much to the opposition of some demographers in the university, one of whom informed me thus: "Migration is the third leg of demography." My response was, "When you have a third leg and you don't use it, it falls off." So this one has fallen off, and the center that we managed to create is not necessarily the kind of center the demographers would have created. The center includes demographers as well as legal scholars, geographers, sociologists, gender theorists, and others. And we participate actively with staff from the Ghana Immigration Service, some of whom have now obtained doctoral degrees through the center. The center has developed partnerships with policy makers in Ghana and with centers, institutes, and programs around Africa and Europe, as it studies African mobilities and migrations from the perspectives of Africans.

In Ghana, I am a public intellectual. I have been passionate and critical about issues and causes dear to me: women's rights and gender justice, higher education, African migrations, transformative social policy, and a just and fair society. I have been recognized and consulted on many national issues, even if I have not always been successful in positively influencing a course of action. I have served on several national, continental, and international boards and committees. I challenge myself and those I come into contact with, be they students, colleagues, or ordinary citizens, to start from and reflect on their local contexts and also to be open to the world and to constantly learn and have a questioning mind. In the methods and approaches that I use, I draw on my cultural competencies as well as broader and more universalistic criteria that reflect the learnings, lessons, and exposures that have come my way, including the seven years that I spent at IU.

But I want to end on the power of strong institutions. Indiana University is great because of all its centers, because of all the grants that it attracts, because of its staff, because of its students. And therefore, if international education is to succeed, it needs to build on these strong institutions. International education is ultimately about exchange and ideas. And this is built on the excellence of institutions. So, in conclusion, I would like to ask the question: How do we use international education and exchange to build up institutions, including in far-off places, such that exchanges can be truly mutual?

Notes

In this brief contribution, I wish to highlight the importance of place, position, and gender to what we contribute as well as take from the opportunities that become available to us. The phrase "a view from somewhere," used by my co-panelist Eric Hershberg captures for me that essence.

1. Manuh, "Building Institutions."

2. After the military coup in Ghana in 1966, much criticism was leveled at President Nkrumah and his involvements around Africa, which were regarded as a waste of Ghana's resources.

3. I also contributed a chapter to the fourth edition of *Africa*, edited by Maria Grosz-Ngate and Patrick O'Meara (Bloomington: Indiana University Press, 2014), long after I had left IU.

4. Manuh and Singh, "Contribution."

5. See Manuh, Gariba, and Budu, *Change and Transformation*. According to the MacArthur Foundation website, "The Partnership for Higher Education in Africa was a joint project of the Carnegie Corporation of New York, Ford Foundation, John D. and Catherine T. MacArthur Foundation, Rockefeller Foundation, William and Flora Hewlett Foundation,

Andrew W. Mellon Foundation, and Kresge Foundation. The Partnership represented both a belief in the importance and viability of higher education in Africa and a mechanism to provide meaningful assistance to its renaissance. From 2000 to 2010, the Partnership awarded more than $439.9 million to support African higher education." Bello, "Partnership."

Bibliography

Bello, Muhammad Yahuza. "The Partnership for Higher Education in Africa: A Conversation with Muhammad Yahuza Bello." Interview by the MacArthur Foundation, May 22, 2018. https://www.macfound.org/press/40-years-40-stories/partnership-higher-education-africa-conversation-muhammad-yahuza-bello/.

Manuh, Takyiwaa. "Building Institutions for the New Africa: The Institute of African Studies at the University of Ghana." In *Modernization as Spectacle in Africa*, edited by Peter Jason Bloom, Stephen Miescher, and Takyiwaa Manuh, 268–86. Bloomington: Indiana University Press, 2014.

Manuh, Takyiwaa, Sulley Gariba, and Joseph Budu. *Change and Transformation in Ghana's Publicly Funded Universities*. Accra, Ghana, and Oxford: Woeli Publishing Services and James Currey, 2007.

Singh, Mala, and Takyiwaa Manuh. "The Contribution of Higher Education to National Education Systems: Current Challenges in Africa—Overview Paper." In *The Contribution of Higher Education to National Education Systems: Current Challenges in Africa*. Proceedings of the UNESCO Forum on Higher Education, Research and Knowledge Research Seminar, Paris, 2008.

Intersection

22

LESSONS FROM HISTORY . . . MADE IN INDIANA

Allan E. Goodman

THE BICENTENNIAL SYMPOSIUM INTERNATIONAL EDUCATION at the Crossroads, which was held at Indiana University Bloomington in 2018, invited us to reflect on lessons learned and what we need to do over the next one hundred years. Twenty years ago, the position of senior internationalization officer did not exist on most campuses; however, many of our partnering colleges and universities established their own foreign policies by the beginning of the twentieth century, and some, as is the case of Indiana University, have specific offices dedicated to serving international students and faculty.

Indiana University marked the seventy-fifth anniversary of the Office of International Services a few weeks after our symposium. Indiana University president Michael A. McRobbie expressed his gratitude to the office's staff, fondly remembering when he was a new faculty member and how thankful he was to the office for assisting him as he applied to renew his green card and later for US citizenship as he transitioned into American academic life.

The importance of highlighting both milestones is that it underscores how deeply embedded international students and faculty are in the DNA of many universities. As McRobbie stated at the symposium, the aim of international education is to "instill in all our students an international understanding."[1]

Indeed, you can instill an international understanding in many ways, from being open to hiring a professor from another culture, to assisting a student to get their first passport, to creating multiple opportunities for study abroad. It is also more necessary than ever to instill an international understanding in students who don't study abroad so that by the time of the next centennial, our profession will have made international education a part of everyone's education.

Many of the speakers and guests at the International Education at the Crossroads Symposium referred to the impact of the National Defense Education Act of 1958. Some years ago, I approached Congressman John Brademas (D-IN, 1959–81) to suggest that we co-author a second National Defense Education Act. He pulled out of his desk something called the International Education Act, which he did in fact author and which passed Congress with a very high bipartisan vote. I read his legislation and said, "Boy, this is exactly what we need in the wake of 9/11. It is a twenty-first-century National Defense Education Act." To which he responded, "What matters is passing an appropriation. Focus on burnishing the programs that you have, including the language programs. Focus on individual appropriators, and focus on building continually broad bipartisan support, and that's how you'll get the twenty-first-century equivalent of a National Defense Education Act." As he taught me, just passing a really good authorization act without assuring that funds get appropriated by passing a spending bill means that all those good ideas and intentions will end up as a few pages of paper in a desk drawer.

His wisdom really shaped our strategy and still does. I think that by continuing to build the bipartisan support to fund all the programs that were discussed at the symposium and continuing to make sure that faculty are engaged in nurturing the critical skills and tools that language and area studies programs provide, we are going to be able, as McRobbie said, to provide the opportunities to instill in all our students an international understanding.

What we have been finding since World War I is that there are multiple ways to enact mobility, multiple resources on campuses, in the private sector, and in government to promote that mobility. And it takes a paradigm shift, a culture shift, so that faculty regardless of discipline become the engines of getting all students a passport and guiding them to make plans to use it.

In sum, IU's two hundred years of history and the Institute of International Education's one hundred years offer those of us working in international education at least three lessons.

First, international education works in all weathers, situations, and geographies. It has a place on every campus and in practically every age, especially those divided by "isms" that seek to exclude others and extol the virtues of isolation.

Second, the university is just as much a destination as any country.

And third, colleges as well as countries need a foreign policy. And a very sound start for us all is what university president Herman B Wells declared about one hundred years ago: "Bring the world to Indiana and Indiana to the world." Indeed, Hoosier values and Hoosier hospitality might just make the world we share today a less dangerous place. It has happened before.

Note

1. McRobbie, "Introduction."

Bibliography

McRobbie, Michael A. "Introduction to Keynote Lecture by Jonathan Fanton." Bicentennial Symposium, International Education at the Crossroads, Indiana University Bloomington, October 26, 2018.

CROSSROADS 5

AGENCIES, MECHANISMS, AND A NATION

23

REFLECTIONS ON TITLE VI FROM
A NATIONAL PERSPECTIVE

Dawn Michele Whitehead

TITLE VI HAS SERVED AS an influential vehicle in my personal and professional development while also serving as a powerful force for advancing international education at the campus level during my work at Indiana University–Purdue University Indianapolis (IUPUI). When I was a high school teacher in Indianapolis, Indiana, revising the curriculum for our multicultural studies course, I realized the importance of including international perspectives in multicultural studies and the need for my students to engage with people from different parts of the world. Although our school was very diverse, some of my students had not taken time to speak with one of our many international students in a meaningful way. Thanks to the wonderful outreach of Indiana University's African Studies and East Asian Studies Centers, my students had multiple opportunities over the years to hear directly from individuals from these parts of the world. It helped to shatter existing stereotypes, present diverse communities as contemporaries, and provide students who might never travel outside the United States with an opportunity to directly engage with individuals from other parts of the world. When I left the high school teaching ranks to become a graduate student at Indiana University, Title VI Foreign Language and Area Studies (FLAS) Fellowships program funding allowed me to study Twi and adopt a concentration in African studies as a part of my interdisciplinary program.

Indiana University president Michael McRobbie spoke about the IU-Kenya partnership on the first day of the International Education at the Crossroads Symposium. It is a long-standing, truly reciprocal partnership between Indiana University and Moi University in Eldoret, Kenya, which started as a partnership between two medical schools, and over the years the partnership has expanded to touch all the schools on the IUPUI campus.

Title VI played a major role as we attempted to expand involvement across the campus. Without funding from the Fulbright-Hays Group Projects Abroad Program, we would not have been able to take IUPUI faculty and staff and teachers from our local school district to Kenya to gain deeper understanding of the nation's cultural, historical, and political context. This was critical as Kenya was a strategic partner for our campus, and we sought to extend these connections to our local school partners, but many of our faculty had limited knowledge about Kenya. We felt it was irresponsible to engage with colleagues at Moi University without providing cultural, intellectual, and institutional support. We had many faculty, staff, and students on campus who wanted to be involved in the partnership, but they did not know anything about Kenya. Through the visionary leadership at IUPUI, we said, "What is it that we can do to make sure that faculty and staff across disciplines and departments can engage in this project in a respectful way?" The Fulbright-Hays Group Projects Abroad Program provided us with the resources to do this.

However, my contribution to this publication is not based on my personal experiences; rather, I was invited to share a national perspective on why international education matters. As the leading national association dedicated to advancing the vitality and public standing of liberal education by making quality and equity the foundations for excellence in undergraduate education in service to democracy, the Association of American Colleges and Universities (AAC&U) has just over fourteen hundred member institutions. Our membership reflects the great diversity of higher education. We have institutions of all types: two-year colleges, four-year colleges, predominantly white institutions, historically black colleges, tribal colleges, and both public and private institutions. Admission standards for these institutions run the gamut from open access to highly selective. Regardless of type, quality liberal education and equity are at the foundation of their work. When we say liberal education, we are not saying every student should major in anthropology, history, or another liberal arts field. What we are talking about is broad and in-depth knowledge of a student's field of interest. The AAC&U views liberal education as, "An approach to learning that empowers individuals and prepares them to deal with complexity, diversity, and change. It provides students with broad knowledge of the wider world as well as in-depth study in a specific area of interest. A liberal education helps students develop a sense of social responsibility as well as strong and transferable intellectual and practical skills such as communication, analytical and problem-solving skills, and a demonstrated ability to apply knowledge and skills in real-world settings."[1] One might ask, "What in the world does that have to do with global learning or international education?" Global learning is one of the strongest examples of liberal education. Our member institutions, in collaboration with our leadership, think about what liberal education means and how this best prepares students for life, work, and citizenship.

AAC&U works with engineering programs, health science programs, video production programs, and many others at both two- and four-year levels to help institutions figure out how they can offer students a strong liberal education. In his keynote lecture at the IU symposium, Jonathan Fanton, the president emeritus of the American Academy of Arts and Sciences, said, "Students educated in the broadest possible sense will lead us into a bright future."[2] And that is exactly what a quality liberal education does.

In order to ensure that all students have access to international education, it is critical to look at who the college students of today and tomorrow are and will be. Changes are occurring in the composition of who attends college around the world. In the context of the United States, the college student population is changing, but the K-12 student population is also changing, which indicates a shift for more colleges and universities in the coming years. The K-12 sector is becoming more and more diverse in the US context, and institutions of higher education need to be ready for these changes. Two-year colleges are already seeing greater change than some of our four-year institutions, but we need to be ready for what many are calling "new majority students," which include students of color, students from low-income backgrounds, students who are returning from the military or are still in the military, and nontraditional college-age students. We also need to look at whether our colleges are student-ready, to use part of the title of my colleague Tia Brown McNair's co-authored book, *Becoming a Student-Ready College: A New Culture of Leadership for Student Success*, and how we are engaging these students in international education.[3]

Some may question why this changing student population matters. As our institutional populations become more reflective of our overall populations, we must ensure our students are prepared to engage with serious societal challenges, such as the aftermath of the murder of George Floyd on May 25, 2020. There were national and global protests and a push for an examination of systemic racism and racial bias in the criminal justice system, and today's students should be prepared to contribute to these conversations. It also matters because we need to make sure that our colleges are ready for these students and that we are meeting their needs. Estela Bensimon's work at the University of Southern California's Rossier Center for Urban Education is an excellent guide to prepare an institution for a more diverse population that has historically been underrepresented in colleges and universities for both curricular and cocurricular dimensions. Bensimon and her colleagues have developed a framework that has been used to advance equity work with the AAC&U and many institutions. The equity-minded framework heightens awareness of the historical context of exclusionary practices, both intentional and unintentional, that have affected participation in higher education for people from a wide range of backgrounds. When institutional leaders are willing to examine their own practices and how they may have contributed to inequities and to look at things from the perspectives of those who have not always been at the center, then institutions are better positioned to make changes to ensure that all students are included in initiatives. I have spent time with a number of institutions talking about this framework and how international education fits into it. One recurring theme is the narrative that many students of color do not participate in study abroad because of financial reasons. While that may be true for some, some researchers have explored factors that hinder the participation of affluent African American students as well. When money is not an issue, why is it that students are not participating more in study abroad programs? Is it about changing perspectives and telling parents that we are expecting their students to participate in international education? That sort of shift in thinking and unpacking of the issues of participation pushes us to look at the practices we need to adopt to ensure that we have more equitable participation in international education, including education abroad.

The notion of employment and preparing students for work is another contemporary issue facing institutions of all types. Our philosophy focuses on preparing all students for life, work, and society, but many of these skills are applicable in all three areas.

The AAC&U conducts employer surveys every few years.[4] For our survey in 2015, we worked with Hart Research and Associates, and over four hundred executives were interviewed and surveyed from both private-sector and nonprofit organizations. One thing we found was that employers are increasingly globally connected and that they placed more emphasis on hiring candidates with global knowledge. We found that 70 percent of employers in our survey said they were globally connected. This did not mean that the employers necessarily had operations overseas but rather that they were connected to suppliers and clients outside the United States. So, for me, as a Hoosier, that means that students from the state of Indiana—rural, suburban, and urban students—as well as students all across the United States and the world, need to graduate with global perspectives and awareness in order to be prepared to meet the expectations that they will face in the workplace. We do students a disservice if we do not provide them with global knowledge and experience and prepare them to be able to communicate in a variety of ways with people who are a phone call or an email away and will be a part of their occupations.

In the AAC&U survey, employers also reported that students should be prepared to collaborate with diverse people in the workplace, and 96 percent of employers agreed or strongly agreed that all students should have experiences that train them to solve problems with people whose views are different from their own. This ability would be useful right now, as so many of us are dealing with a lack of understanding and an inability to engage with different perspectives on our campuses. Finally, 78 percent of employers surveyed also agreed or strongly agreed that college students should gain intercultural skills and an understanding of societies and countries outside the United States.[5]

These skills and expectations are useful to prepare students to be good members of society, and they also prepare them for the workforce. When we provide these types of opportunities for a small number of students, and not all students, we are doing a disservice to the majority of students who are not able or willing to opt in to these specific global-learning-focused programs. It is important to build on the work of Title VI programs and courses, but institutions must also provide opportunities for global learning beyond Title VI. An increasing number of institutions are reaching out to Title VI programs, for their resources as well as models, to find out how to develop programs that give more, if not all, students access to internationalized experiences across campuses and curricula.

Since education abroad remains a very prominent practice of international education, it is important to have conversations about how education abroad programs are structured. The number of short-term study abroad programs is growing, and for both short-term and long-term programs, it is essential that learning outcomes and key skills that students need—that are prioritized by the faculty and the institution—are intentionally and transparently integrated into the programs. The program can be an engineering program but can still incorporate elements of cultural competence and global learning knowledge. It is also critical to make sure that we identify ways to provide these experiences for students who are unable to go abroad. All students should engage in rich learning experiences where they gain global knowledge and perspectives and learn how to put these ideas in a global context.

High-impact practices (HIPs) are educational practices that have been found to benefit all students in terms of their success, engagement, retention, and learning, and they also especially benefit students of color, first-generation students, and other new majority students.[6] The 2013 National Survey of Student Engagement report on HIPs demonstrates that there are only a couple of areas where students of color participate at the same level or higher than their white counterparts: of the eleven HIPs, those areas are service learning and learning communities.[7] These areas are typically integrated into the broader curriculum; all students might be expected to participate in a learning community or to engage in service learning as a component of specific courses. When a HIP is linked to the curriculum, more students tend to participate. Some institutions are finding that participation in multiple HIPs, even simultaneously, increases their benefit to students. For example, some study abroad programs integrate community-based learning components to more meaningfully engage with the world. Students are solving problems with people in the community from different educational levels and backgrounds and are collectively learning how to apply these principles.

McRobbie has shared that individuals from the IU-Kenya partnership had learned about infant mortality and were bringing what they had learned back to the local community in Indianapolis. This is exactly what we are encouraging people to do when they are blending global learning with other high-impact practices. True global education is not just about what is going on outside or in another place but also about local applications of global knowledge: How does what you saw and learned affect you when you come back to your own community?

Finally, national organizations are also working to expand participation in HIPs. For example, the leadership of TRIO Programs, federal programs for outreach and student services to help students from disadvantaged backgrounds in their pursuit of college degrees, have collaborated with leaders of the AAC&U to explore ways to integrate high-impact practices, including global learning, in their experiences.[8] We have been looking at developing community-based global learning experiences in curricular and cocurricular spaces to provide students with opportunities to go into the community and work with people from different parts of the world who may have been in the community for thirty years or three weeks. These experiences with people who are culturally different, both in the local community and more distant communities, allow students with less global engagement to gain a cultural education without leaving the country. It starts to level the playing field between those with access to global experiences and those who are not able to travel abroad. Indiana University is not the only institution to do this, but its Office of Diversity, Equity, and Multicultural Affairs created several education abroad programs for first-generation students, students of color, and students from low-income backgrounds. The office collaborated closely with Kathleen Sideli, the associate vice president for the Office of Overseas Study at IU, who provided guidance and assistance in developing programs to take student cohorts abroad. Some of those students plan to participate in additional programs in the future. Once again, working with partners across campus contributes to expanded access to international education.

The founding fathers are often evoked when one explores the history of US engagement with the world, but I want to offer a different perspective on the founding fathers than what is regularly shared. *Hamilton: An American Musical* is a show on Broadway.[9] I want to share two things about it, the first of which is that students all over our nation need to have access to these types of global experiences and perspectives. My cousin, Christopher Jackson, who grew up near Cairo, Illinois, which is not an urban or metropolitan area, ended up studying theater in New York, where he lived, worked, and studied alongside many people who grew up differently than he did and were from a number of places he had never visited. He developed an impressively global perspective, and we always joke about how he gained this perspective in the heartland, not on one of the coasts. Even as children, we talked about the importance of being aware of the world. He was the original George Washington in the cast of *Hamilton*.

Hamilton is near and dear to my heart because of his experience. But I think the other thing about *Hamilton* that is really fascinating is the music. I am a novice student of hip-hop, and the show uses many different styles of rap and hip-hop throughout—that's what makes it great. It also draws on reggaeton, which has roots in the Caribbean and in the United States.

The inclusion of this very international, global music is telling. But there is one song in particular that connects to the work that we are currently undertaking as we consider how to connect area studies to other areas of international education. It is a song called "In the Room Where It Happens," which references the room in which the decision was made to move the US capital to Washington, DC—a room in which there were only a handful of people. This happens often when we think about trying to spread out international education: we do not welcome everyone who should be in the room into the room. The next time you think about how to expand international education, keep in mind *Hamilton* and the founding fathers. We need many people in the room.

Notes

1. Association of American Colleges and Universities, "What Is Liberal Education?"
2. Fanton, "The Broadest Possible Education."
3. McNair et al., *Becoming a Student-Ready College.*
4. Association of American Colleges and Universities, "Employer Surveys."
5. Hart Research Associates, "Falling Short?," 1–13.
6. Kuh, *High-Impact Educational Practices*, 9–11.
7. National Survey of Student Engagement, *NSSE 2013.*
8. Council for Opportunity in Education, "TRIO."
9. Miranda, *Hamilton: An American Musical.*

Bibliography

Association of American Colleges and Universities. "Employer Surveys and Economic Trend Research." Publications and Research. Accessed April 21, 2020. https://www.aacu.org/leap/public-opinion-research.

———. "What Is Liberal Education?" Accessed April 21, 2020. https://www.aacu.org/leap/what-is-liberal-education.

Council for Opportunity in Education. "TRIO." Resources. Accessed April 21, 2020. http://www.coenet.org/trio.shtml.

Fanton, Jonathan. "The Broadest Possible Education: The Future of Global and International Studies." Paper presented at International Education at the Crossroads, Indiana University Bloomington, October 2018.

Hart Research Associates. "Falling Short? College Learning and Career Success." Association of American Colleges and Universities, January 2015, 1–13. https://www.aacu.org/leap/public-opinion-research/2015-survey-results.

Kuh, George D. *High-Impact Educational Practices: What They Are, Who Has Access to Them, and Why They Matter.* Washington, DC: AAC&U, 2008. https://www.aacu.org/leap/hips.

McNair, Tia Brown, Susan Albertine, Michelle Asha Cooper, Nicole McDonald, and Thomas Major Jr. *Becoming a Student-Ready College: A New Culture of Leadership for Student Success.* San Francisco: Jossey-Bass, 2016.

Miranda, Lin-Manuel. *Hamilton: An American Musical.* Atlantic Records, 2015, MP3.

National Survey of Student Engagement. *NSSE 2013 High-Impact Practices.* Accessed April 21, 2020. http://nsse.iub.edu/2013_institutional_report/pdf/HIPTables/HIP.pdf.

24

US DEPARTMENT OF EDUCATION INTERNATIONAL AND FOREIGN LANGUAGE EDUCATION PROGRAMS

Pathways to Expertise, Access, and Global Competitiveness

Cheryl E. Gibbs

THE US DEPARTMENT OF EDUCATION (the Department) plays a unique role among federal agencies as a provider of area studies, international studies, and modern foreign language training programs. This wide range of programs supports the infrastructure and pathways that enable institutions of higher education to prepare multiple sectors to successfully navigate the ever-evolving landscapes of education, international business, the global economy and workforce preparation, foreign language and cross-cultural communication, and national needs. Specifically, the domestic programs authorized by the National Defense Education Act of 1958 and, subsequently, Title VI of the Higher Education Act of 1965, as amended, and the overseas programs authorized by the Mutual Educational and Cultural Exchange Act of 1961 (Fulbright-Hays) (F-H) strengthen American education, teaching, outreach, and interdisciplinary research via institutionally based grants that provide the resources and training to foster and enhance global competencies, world region expertise, and advanced proficiency in world languages. Our capacity to provide transformative instruction and research opportunities to diverse sectors distinguishes us from other federal agencies engaged in the enterprise of the internationalization of American education. The Title VI and F-H programs represent deliberate, diverse, and interconnected pathways that are specifically intended to lead to area studies and foreign language expertise, access to training, and global competitiveness.

Global Education and Global Competencies through Legislative Lenses

The Title VI and F-H program legislations and the constituencies they serve are the lenses through which our agency defines global education and global competencies.[1] From the Title VI perspective, a global education is needed because our nation's security and our academic, technological, research, and economic vitality depend on it. To that end, the Title VI programs provide resources to produce US experts in and citizens knowledgeable about world regions, foreign languages, and international affairs, as well as a strong research background in these areas. From the F-H perspective, a global education is needed to enable teachers, administrators, and researchers to strengthen US K-16 curricula and graduate research, by providing resources that encourage US participants to engage with other cultures to promote mutual understanding or to conduct research overseas. It is also necessary to note that the grant projects conducted under the seven Title VI programs and four F-H programs (Group Projects Abroad [short-term and long-term], Seminars Abroad, and Doctoral Dissertation Research Abroad) are directly relevant to the Department's mission "to promote student achievement and preparation for global competitiveness by fostering educational excellence and ensuring equal access."[2] International education is for all students.

The current numbers of 272 Title VI institutional grants and 149 F-H grants to institutions and individual participants take their cues from the legislation as well and define global competencies as knowledge of world regions and languages, and cross-cultural and critical-thinking skills that contribute to one's self-understanding and understanding of other cultures and diverse perspectives. Acquiring global competencies through disciplinary and interdisciplinary study and engagement allows participants in these programs to develop and hone their skill sets to investigate the world beyond their immediate environment and experiences. This may involve identifying key issues, generating questions, and explaining the significance of those issues; using less commonly taught languages and sources to identify and weigh relevant evidence; analyzing, integrating, and synthesizing information; recognizing and expressing one's perspectives and being open to others' perspectives; applying new ideas and perspectives to specific actions; and communicating more effectively within and across cultures. Working collaboratively with grantees, the International and Foreign Language Education (IFLE) office ensures that grant projects are working collectively and individually to prepare graduates with global competencies.

To be successful in today's interconnected world, students, teachers, administrators, business leaders, and employees all need to be equipped with global competencies, such as critical thinking, communication, socio-emotional, and the foreign language skills to work effectively with their counterparts in the United States and other countries and world regions. The Department's international strategy outlined in *Succeeding Globally through International Education and Engagement* (revised in 2018) and its *Framework for Developing Global and Cultural Competencies to Advance Equity, Excellence and Economic Competitiveness* (2017) recognize the importance of discipline-specific knowledge and foreign language proficiency among the competencies required to address the nation's ongoing global needs.[3] The international strategy acknowledges that IFLE is the only office in the Department that offers international education programs. Considering that the projected number of people in the global labor force will reach over 3.1 billion by 2030, the value and significance of the course development, teacher training, international business, outreach, instructional materials development, and cultural engagement activities conducted under the various Title VI and F-H programs cannot be underestimated. Our grantees understand and take seriously the mission of these programs and are guided by the reality that program graduates are less likely to work in only one location, country, or culture throughout their careers. All students must acquire the skills, attitudes, and behaviors that will enable them to work across cultures and adapt to changes. These attributes are in high demand from prospective employers because these qualities translate into global competitiveness—that is, the potential productivity of an economy.

IFLE Competition Priorities to Influence Internationalization and Diversity

To ensure that IFLE's international education programs are accessible to a more diverse institutional demographic, IFLE uses competitive preference priorities to increase the participation of and collaboration with community colleges and minority-serving institutions (MSIs).

The legislation for a limited number of Title VI programs, such as the Business and International Education Program, the Institute for International and Public Policy (currently inactive), and the active Undergraduate International Studies and Foreign Language Education Program, requires the participation of community colleges and MSIs as eligible applicants. Historically, the projects supported under these programs have been very successful in demonstrating the value and impact of diversity in the Department's international education programs. IFLE recognized that concerted and consistent efforts were needed to close the gap between traditional and nontraditional applicants to IFLE's annual and four-year grant competitions. Effective with the 2014 grant competitions, IFLE used competition priorities to appeal to and hopefully expand the number of underserved and underrepresented institutions that receive Title VI and F-H grant awards. Additional qualitative points were awarded based on the potential success of the proposed activities to be conducted in collaboration with community colleges and MSIs. The priorities focused on incorporating international, intercultural, or global dimensions into the curricula at a community college or MSI. The activities could include foreign language instruction, faculty professional development, study abroad, teacher training, international business, and course development.

The information we receive in annual performance reports and the stories we solicit for the IFLE newsletter reveal compelling evidence that these priorities have made and continue to make a difference in institutional strategizing, teaching, and research and in preparing students for today's workforce, as exemplified by grantees in the following programs.

National Resource Centers

The Ohio State University's (OSU) East Asian Studies Center (EASC) is partnering with Ohio-based Japanese facilities to train students in professional interpretation.

In order to increase students' readiness for Japan-related careers after graduation, the EASC—with support from a Title VI National Resource Center fiscal years 2018–2021 grant and in partnership with local industry—has developed a portfolio of professionalization programs for students studying the Japanese language. From career talks to conferences, from demonstrations to job shadowing, and from internships to skill-based coursework, these initiatives are aimed at preparing students to succeed in the workforce, particularly in the area of interpretation. "Following a year-long focus and series of events on the topic in 2016–17, including a week-long interpretation workshop and the 28th International Japanese-English Translation Conference hosted at OSU, we identified an interest in interpretation among our students, a strong demand for these skills in industry, and great expertise in our community," said EASC director Etsuyo Yuasa.[4]

In Ohio, where Japan is the top foreign investor, "the demand for Japanese-English interpreters is high, with 484 Japanese facilities, including Honda of America Manufacturing, Inc., creating more than 77,000 jobs, 98 percent of which are held by Ohioans, according to the Consulate General of Japan in Detroit's '2017 Japanese Direct Investment Survey.'"[5] The EASC has worked with many of these facilities, including Honda R&D America, Inc., which in 2018 delivered a Japanese Interpretation Demonstration at OSU and later hosted students on-site to observe interpretation in practice. It has also worked with THK Manufacturing of America, Inc., which offered a panel discussion on campus on the topic of "Working for a Japanese Company: How to Prepare? What to Expect?" and hosted groups of OSU students studying Japanese at their manufacturing facility in Ohio, as well as in Japan. Based on the relationships formed with local companies and the momentum created on campus and in the community, in spring 2019, EASC launched its first course on Japanese interpretation.[6]

Centers for International Business Education

The Center for International Business Education and Research (CIBER) at the University of South Carolina Darla Moore School of Business has formed a CIBER Minority Serving Institutions / Community College Consortium (CMCC) that includes eight additional CIBERs currently funded by the Title VI Centers for International Business Education program. The CMCC comprises Brigham Young University, Florida International University, The George Washington University, Georgia Institute of Technology, Indiana University, San Diego State University, the University of Maryland, and the University of Washington.

The consortium provides funding opportunities and academic support to previously underserved and underrepresented faculty, staff, and students from MSIs and community colleges (MSI/CC). The four-year academic and business outreach program—collectively funded with $40,000 from each of the nine CMCC members during the four-year grant cycle (2018–22)—will provide funding and support in the international business (IB) areas of research, curriculum, and program development, student study abroad, student internships and work studies, faculty and professional development programs, and business foreign language training to many of the more than three thousand MSI/CC institutions throughout the United States. The CMCC allocates funds each year to numerous MSI/CC awardees based on quarterly scheduled competitive calls for proposals submitted to the CIBER consortium.

In the first year of the CIBER grant cycle (2018–19), the CMCC awarded approximately $90,000 in awards to forty faculty leaders, administrators, and students at MSI/CC institutions (at an average of more than $3,000 per project). Some of the cutting-edge international business activities funded in 2019 include Morgan State University and Edmonds Community College for the development of IB courses and curricula; Alabama A&M and Governors State universities for a study abroad program design and implementation; Montgomery College and Eastern New Mexico University for faculty professional development programs and seminars; and Howard University and Morgan State University for international business research projects.

Undergraduate International Studies and Foreign Language Education

Cornell University and Tomkins Community College received an Undergraduate International Studies and Foreign Language Education grant to support the integration of science, humanities, and social science training into their respective programs. The institutions are using new field-based and engaged learning opportunities on their campuses as well as in Latin America and the Caribbean. The project seeks to enrich undergraduate laboratory and classroom learning through diverse international research and internship opportunities.

Synergies and Intersections to Promote Global Education

IFLE engages with the various White House initiatives and the Office of Career and Technical Education to share information about the IFLE international education programs that are relevant to their constituencies. We also target our technical assistance at community colleges and MSIs and give presentations at international education conferences, area studies association meetings, and higher education organization meetings to reach and assist underserved and underrepresented institutions of higher education seeking technical assistance and funding for campus internationalization projects.

Conclusion: International Education and the US Department of Education: Resilient, Relevant, Responsive

The US Department of Education Office of International Affairs and the International and Foreign Language Education office are committed to promoting the Department's mission of increasing the global and cultural competencies of all US students, teachers, and other stakeholders. Through its discretionary grant programs, IFLE is committed to its mission of increasing the number of graduates from institutions of higher education who are highly prepared for careers in education, diplomacy, defense, business, public health, and other sectors to meet our national needs. Throughout the more than sixty-year histories of the Title VI and Fulbright-Hays programs, we have witnessed these programs' capacity to pivot and respond with integrity and resolve to our national needs and make a difference on the international education training landscape at any given time. This capacity enables the US Department of Education to fill a unique niche among other federal agencies that cannot be duplicated in its reach and impact.

Notes

1. See program descriptions at "Programs," International Resource Information System, https://iris.ed.gov/programs.
2. The seven Title VI programs are National Resource Centers, Foreign Language and Area Studies Fellowships, Centers for International Business Education, Language Resource Centers, International Research and Studies, American Overseas Research Centers, and Undergraduate International Studies and Foreign Language. The four Fulbright-Hays programs are Doctoral Dissertation Research Abroad, Group Projects Abroad (Short-term Projects), Group Projects Abroad (Long-term Language Projects), and Seminars Abroad.
3. US Department of Education, *Succeeding Globally*; US Department of Education, *Framework*.
4. East Asian Studies Center, "EASC Partners with Ohio-based Japanese Facilities."
5. Ibid.
6. Ibid.

Bibliography

East Asian Studies Center. "EASC Partners with Ohio-based Japanese Facilities to Train Students in Professional Interpretation." The Ohio State University, May 30, 2019. https://easc.osu.edu/news/easc-partners-ohio-based-japanese-facilities-train-students-professional-interpretation.

US Department of Education. *Framework for Developing Cultural and Global Competencies to Achieve Equity and Excellence.* Washington, DC: US Department of Education, International Affairs Office, January 2017.

——. *Succeeding Globally through International Education and Engagement.* Washington, DC: US Department of Education, International Affairs Office, November 2018.

25

INTERNATIONAL EDUCATION AND EXCHANGES OFFER EFFECTIVE EDUCATION DIPLOMACY FOR THE UNITED STATES

Anthony Koliha

State Department Bureau Advances People-to-People Diplomacy Efforts

The US Department of State is the lead US government agency on foreign affairs and foreign policy, including government-to-government relations. The State Department's Bureau of Educational and Cultural Affairs (ECA) supports the department's public diplomacy efforts through people-to-people exchanges in support of foreign policy objectives. Exchanges are further bolstered by ECA efforts to encourage more US citizens to study abroad and greater numbers of qualified international students to pursue studies in the United States, working in partnership with US higher education and other stakeholders.

The ECA receives strategic direction on foreign policy from the secretary of state, as well as the White House and Congress, and embraces goals that represent the highest priorities of policy makers, as reflected in the National Security Strategy and the Department of State / USAID Joint Strategic Plan. Secretary of State Michael Pompeo stated that "educational exchanges, whether it's Americans going overseas or foreigners coming to the United States, are among the most important tools in our diplomatic arsenal. They maintain America's competitive edge, preserve our leadership in the world. The success of our foreign policy priorities depends on it."[1]

Under the legislative mandate of the Fulbright-Hays Act of 1961, the ECA funds and administers dozens of educational and cultural exchange programs for US and foreign citizens, with the goal of "[enabling] the

Government of the United States to increase mutual understanding between the people of the United States and the people of other countries by means of educational and cultural exchange . . . and thus to assist in the development of friendly, sympathetic, and peaceful relations between the United States and the other countries of the world."[2]

More than one million people, including four hundred thousand US citizens, have participated in an ECA exchange program across a broad array of sectors, including academia, business, politics, culture, civil society, and sports. Currently, one in three foreign government leaders, as well as many leaders in other sectors, are alumni of an ECA exchange program. These alumni contribute all across the world to advancing mutual understanding and respect between the people of the United States and the people of other countries.

Successful people-to-people exchanges bolster national security, strengthen the economy, enhance US academic and research collaboration, and further US diplomatic standing in the world.

State Department Supports Thousands of Academic Exchanges Each Year

The US Department of State supports more than 55,000 exchange participants annually, including 15,000 US citizens. The Fulbright Program, funded by the US Congress at an all-time high of over $270 million in the 2019 fiscal year, is the flagship international educational exchange program sponsored by the US government through the ECA. Since 1946, the Fulbright Program has provided more than 380,000 US and international students, scholars, teachers, and other professionals from the United States and more than 160 other countries with the opportunity to study, teach and conduct research, exchange ideas, and contribute to finding solutions to shared global challenges. Fulbright is so valued by foreign governments, higher education partners, and the private sector that these sources collectively contribute an additional $150 million annually.

Faculty play a key role in internationalizing teaching and research, as well as in international student mobility. Fulbright scholar exchanges support the international exchange of faculty and researchers between institutions. Fulbright scholars infuse cross-cultural perspectives into curricula, revitalize teaching methods, and contribute to faculty research and professional development. They often initiate and grow international partnerships between US and foreign campuses that help sustain teaching and research collaborations, student and faculty mobility programs, and other important relationships. Given the outsized impact of US Fulbright scholars both on their host communities abroad and back home in the United States, the ECA is constantly adjusting the program to ensure the broadest possible participation by US faculty members and higher education institutions and thereby contributing to broader internationalization efforts on US university campuses across the country. For instance, Fulbright Administrator and Scholar Programs, as well as the Fulbright Scholar-in-Residence Program and the Fulbright Specialist Program, actively recruit from and engage with US community colleges to ensure that the Fulbright Program is accessible to and benefits a wide array of diverse institutions.

Together, the Fulbright Program, the Benjamin A. Gilman International Scholarship Program, Critical Language Scholarships, and youth exchanges annually support approximately seven thousand US students from high school through the university and graduate levels to go abroad. The efforts of faculty and administrators across the United States further contribute to the more than 330,000 US students who study abroad each year. State Department EducationUSA global advising centers and activities and USA Study Abroad capacity-building efforts, in collaboration with US higher education institutions, further bolster US and international student mobility to and from the United States.

The Number of US Students Studying Abroad Continues to Rise

One of the goals of the US government is to ensure that the United States remains a global leader in all fields. US national security hinges on peaceful and productive foreign relations and continued economic prosperity and competitiveness. To achieve these goals in the twenty-first century, it is imperative that our country's next generation of leaders understands and is able to operate within the global political and economic landscape.

The US Department of State has supported US study abroad for decades through such programs as Fulbright, Gilman, and Critical Language Scholarships. In 2015, we expanded our focus on US student mobility with the creation of a US Study Abroad branch within the Bureau of Educational and Cultural Affairs. Its establishment emphasized the importance of US student mobility for the State Department's foreign affairs goals, including national security and economic prosperity.

Studying abroad provides US students with the skills they need to be competitive in today's global marketplace. These skills include "hard" skills, such as developing proficiency in a foreign language and knowledge of other regions, and "soft" skills, such as adaptability and resilience, both of which foster creativity and innovation. During their time abroad, US students learn foreign languages, expand their horizons, gain critical skills, and establish personal and professional networks. They also become unofficial ambassadors for the United States, sharing US viewpoints and perspectives and dispelling myths about the United States.

US study abroad is at an all-time high, with 332,727 US students having studied abroad for academic credit in 2016-17.[3] However, only 10 percent of US undergraduate students will benefit from a study abroad experience prior to graduation.[4] We must strive to expand the study abroad participation rate, so the next generation of leaders in business, government, the sciences, technology, and the arts has the knowledge and networks to succeed in their careers and contribute to the United States' global competitiveness.

As mentioned, US Department of State programs directly support study abroad for approximately seven thousand US students from the high school through the university and graduate levels, who take part in such programs as the National Security Language Initiative for Youth (NSLI-Y), the Benjamin A. Gilman International Scholarship Program, the Critical Language Scholarship Program, and the Fulbright US Student Program. Through these programs and other capacity-building initiatives, the State Department provides broad support to study abroad efforts by US colleges and universities and builds the capacity of foreign higher education institutions to host US students studying abroad.

US Hosts Record Number of International Students

US higher education remains highly sought after around the world and is one of the United States' greatest public diplomacy assets. International students choose to study in the United States due to the quality of education, world-class laboratories and facilities, emphasis on critical thinking and interactive classrooms, the appeal of US culture, and the value of a degree from a US higher education institution for future studies and employment.

According to the most recent *Open Doors Report*, an annual report published by the Institute of International Education and funded by the US Department of State, the United States hosted 1,094,792 international students in 2017–18, an increase of 1.5 percent from the previous year and a record high.[5]

International students contributed nearly $45 billion to the US economy in 2018 and generated an estimated 450,000 jobs.[6] They also internationalized classrooms and communities across the United States. While studying in the United States, international students gain exposure to and appreciation for US culture and values, and they forge lifelong relationships with US friends and peers. Likewise, for US students who do not have the opportunity to study or travel abroad, international students, scholars, and faculty may offer the most direct exposure to a wide range of ideas and cultures that enhance their ability to compete globally.

The State Department's EducationUSA global network of educational advisers and advising centers is the official source about US higher education around the world, providing prospective international students with the necessary information to find the US college or university that fits their needs from our 4,700 accredited higher education institutions. EducationUSA has over 430 advising centers and 550 advisers in more than 180 countries around the world. Through individual and group advising, in-person and online resources, and student recruitment fairs and other signature events, EducationUSA works with US colleges and universities and international students to ensure that the United States remains the top destination for international students.

In 2018 alone, EducationUSA advising services concluded over 19 million contacts through in-center advising, public trainings and events, and an increasing virtual presence, including the use of social media. Advisers provided individual or group sessions for nearly 300,000 prospective students, offering free advising services and walking students through the EducationUSA "5 Steps to US Study."[7] Over 630,000 individuals attended an EducationUSA student recruitment fair to explore study options in the United States through direct engagement with a diverse array of US colleges and universities.[8] EducationUSA also works closely with the US higher education community, through our overseas fairs and regional forums, at our annual Washington, DC, forum, and through increased domestic outreach. In early 2019, EducationUSA partnered with the University of Wisconsin-Madison for our first in a series of seminars designed to position successful US host institutions to share experiences and best practices with US colleges and universities looking to build or expand their international student recruitment efforts. Additional outreach seminars will take place in partnership with other US colleges and universities at locations across the country. With expanded domestic outreach and enhanced digital marketing tools, the State Department is committed, through EducationUSA, to communicating the value of a US higher education to prospective students the world over.

Never Too Early to Start Internationalizing Classrooms

International student exchanges and mobility are enormously beneficial for university students; however, for younger students, taking part in an international exchange program, coming in contact with an international exchange visitor, or gaining knowledge and understanding of the world from a teacher in elementary or high school can also have an important impact. Learning about and gaining interest in the world at an early age can open a pipeline of opportunities as a young person progresses into college and a career.

The US Department of State offers high school youth exchange programs for both US and international students, including such programs as NSLI-Y, the Kennedy-Lugar Youth Exchange and Study, the Congress Bundestag Youth Exchange, and the Future Leaders Exchange. For youth from underserved sectors abroad, the State Department's in-country English Access Microscholarship Program teaches English language and US culture through after-school programs, preparing young people for future educational, employment, and exchange opportunities.

State Department teacher exchange programs bring the world to US classrooms and US values to classrooms around the world. ECA teacher exchanges provide professional development opportunities for approximately four hundred K-12 teachers on an annual basis, primarily through a suite of Fulbright-affiliated teacher exchanges. These exchanges build teaching capacity and internationalize curricula and allow teachers to share global best practices; when the four hundred teachers return to their home classrooms, they will reach approximately sixty-five thousand schoolchildren annually with their increased knowledge. Over time, the four hundred alumni from a single year may reach as many as one million students, in addition to sharing their knowledge and experiences with fellow teachers and school administrators.

US alumni of teacher exchanges return to their classrooms with new lesson plans and teaching methodologies. They also implement new approaches both in and out of the classroom to provide students with international and global skills and to help address such issues as the racial and ethnic achievement gap in the United States or how to more effectively teach STEM education. Coupled with such outreach events as the State Department's annual Global Teaching Dialogue and a relatively new online teacher training program, Global Ed 101, teacher exchanges are internationalizing classrooms for US schoolchildren across the United States.

Toward More Inclusive International Educational Opportunities

International education provides participants with skills, knowledge, and understanding for success in a global society. An international educational experience can also position individuals for academic success, career readiness, and social and economic advancement. We promote the goal of access to international education for all US students, as well as maximizing opportunities for international students to study in the United States. The Department of State is dedicated to providing exchange opportunities to a broad array of talented individuals who represent the rich diversity of the United States and the world.

The profile of US students studying abroad has become more inclusive over time. In 2005–06, just 17 percent of study abroad students identified as racial or ethnic minorities, and by 2016–17 the percentage had grown to 29 percent.[9] While this is progress, 29 percent remains well below the approximately 45 percent of students representing racial and ethnic minorities enrolled in US higher education overall.

The State Department's Benjamin A. Gilman International Scholarship Program has determined an effective model for increasing opportunities for a wide array of US students to study or intern abroad. With a congressional mandate to increase the number of US undergraduates with limited financial means who pursue study abroad, the Gilman program has also successfully expanded opportunities for individuals from all backgrounds. In 2017–18, 47 percent of Gilman scholars reported being the first to attend college in their families. African American students studied abroad through Gilman at three times the rate of participation by African American students in study abroad overall, while Hispanic students participated at nearly two and a half times the rate for study abroad overall. Similarly impressive statistics show that 8 percent of Gilman participants who studied abroad in 2017–18 identified as having a disability, which is far higher than the percentage of US students with disabilities in study abroad overall.

ECA programs, like the Gilman program, actively seek candidates from a broad array of backgrounds, including racial and ethnic minorities as well as individuals with disabilities, and individuals from colleges and universities large and small, including minority-serving institutions and community colleges. By working directly with community colleges and supporting flexible offerings such as short-term programs, Gilman and other ECA programs have successfully increased participation by community college students, faculty, and administrators.

Community colleges can be important resources to expand the number of international students studying in the United States and diversify the institutions and communities where they study. By offering a combination of quality and affordability, together with options to transfer to and complete degrees at four-year institutions, community colleges provide options for study in the United States to prospective international students who, due to cost, may not have considered the United States as a viable destination.

Of the more than one million international students in the United States, approximately 70 percent study at only 200 of the more than 4,700 US colleges and universities.[10] International students currently comprise only 5.5 percent of the total number of students enrolled in US higher education, so there is ample capacity to expand the number of international students studying in the United States, including at community colleges, branch campuses, and small- and medium-sized public and private colleges and universities across the United States.[11]

The State Department's EducationUSA advising network works to ensure that international students and their families, as well as foreign governments, understand the broad array of quality study options in the United States, providing information about accreditation and quality assurance, testing and admissions processes, and financing and affordability. Many prospective international students and their families are unaware of the vast array of quality colleges and universities in the United States, and EducationUSA advisers promote all accredited US higher education institutions, explaining such options as liberal arts colleges, minority-serving institutions, and community colleges. For instance, EducationUSA actively promotes the "two-plus-two model," whereby an international student may complete the first two years of an undergraduate degree at a US community college before successfully transferring to a four-year college or university to complete a bachelor's degree. These students benefit from a quality US education at an affordable price, while building lifelong connections with US peers in two locations.

International Education Builds Better International Relations

As President Trump stated in his National Security Strategy, we must "facilitate the cultural, educational, and people-to-people exchanges that create the networks of current and future political, civil society, and educational leaders who will extend a free and prosperous world."[12]

International education opens minds, builds connections, and enhances knowledge, awareness, and skills. International education provides meaningful understanding and skills to individuals, preparing them for successful studies and rewarding careers. The knowledge and connections created through international education contribute to the State Department's public diplomacy efforts and US foreign policy by building mutual understanding between people and nations. Funded by the US Congress at an all-time high of $730 million in fiscal year 2019, the ECA remains dedicated to promoting US public diplomacy through an array of successful people-to-people exchanges, including the Fulbright Program, the Gilman scholarship, and our EducationUSA advising services.

The US Department of State is the US government's lead foreign affairs agency, but international education benefits both foreign and domestic policy. International education contributes to and supports US economic competitiveness and economic prosperity here at home as well as stability and progress around the world. In addition to the 450,000 jobs created in the United States from the economic benefits of international students, Americans who study abroad gain critical skills to succeed in science and innovation and to contribute in the global marketplace. US campuses and communities gain exposure to international networks of future professionals while exporting US values abroad. International education is a critical investment in our collective future.

Notes

1. Pompeo, "Secretary Pompeo."
2. Public Law 87–256, Sept. 21, 1961, 75 Stat. 527, as amended, known as the Mutual Educational and Cultural Exchange Act of 1961.
3. Baer et al., *Open Doors 2018*.
4. Ibid.
5. Ibid.
6. Bureau of Economic Analysis, "Table 3.1"; "NAFSA International Student."
7. EducationUSA, "Your 5 Steps."
8. EducationUSA, *Global Guide 2019*, 6.
9. Baer et al., *Open Doors 2018*.
10. Ibid.
11. National Center for Education Statistics, "Table 303.10."
12. Trump, *National Security Strategy*, 33.

Bibliography

Baer, Julie, Rajika Bhandari, Natalya Andrejko, and Leah Mason. *Open Doors 2018 Report on International Educational Exchange*. New York: Institute of International Education, 2018.

Bureau of Economic Analysis. "Table 3.1: US International Trade in Services." Washington, DC: US Department of Commerce, June 20, 2019. https://apps.bea.gov/iTable/iTable .cfm?ReqID=62&step=1.

EducationUSA. *Global Guide 2019*. Washington, DC: US Bureau of Educational and Cultural Affairs and the Institute of International Education. https://educationusa.state.gov /sites/default/files/2019_educationusa_global_guide.pdf.

———. "Your 5 Steps to US Study." US Department of State. Accessed April 22, 2020. https:// educationusa.state.gov/your-5-steps-us-study.

NAFSA: Association of International Educators. "NAFSA International Student Economic Value Tool." Last updated 2017–18 academic year. Accessed April 22, 2020. https:// www.nafsa.org/policy-and-advocacy/policy-resources/nafsa-international-student -economic-value-tool.

National Center for Education Statistics. "Table 303.10: Total Fall Enrollment in Degree-Granting Postsecondary Institutions, by Attendance Status, Sex of Student, and Control of Institution; Selected Years, 1947 through 2028." Washington, DC: US Department of Education, March 2019. https://nces.ed.gov/programs/digest/d18/tables /dt18_303.10.asp.

Pompeo, Michael R. "Secretary Pompeo on International Education Week." US Department of State. Streamed live on November 13, 2018. YouTube video, 1:29. https://www .youtube.com/watch?v=Q4YwN_oRow8.

Trump, President Donald J. *National Security Strategy of the United States of America*. December 18, 2017. https://www.whitehouse.gov/wp-content/uploads/2017/12/NSS -Final-12-18-2017-0905-2.pdf.

26

FOREIGN LANGUAGE AND INTERNATIONAL EDUCATION—A CRITICAL REQUIREMENT

A Practitioner's View

General Gene Renuart, USAF (Ret.)

AS I PREPARED TO PARTICIPATE in a panel at the International Education at the Crossroads Symposium that reflected on the importance of language, culture, and international educational opportunities in the world today, I tried to look back at my career and capture the events that underlined the importance of those international experiences and how they might have been influenced by more focused and in-depth international education. Having completed thirty-nine years of military service in twenty-three countries on five continents, I was struck with how little I had known of any of those places and people before I encountered them and how I would have benefitted from more focused preparation in making the key decisions required in my profession. With this in mind, I have shaped my contribution around the very real and strategic military, diplomatic, and business imperatives that surround the leadership role the United States faces in the world today.

By way of background, I grew up in Miami during the height of the Cuban Missile Crisis and the migration of thousands of Cuban refugees to south Florida and, specifically, Miami. This was my first experience with a large-scale influx of non-English-speaking families who were, in many cases, influential, affluent members of Cuban society arriving in the United States with very little but the clothes on their back and trying to find a way to integrate into a new culture. Unfortunately, my high school language education was Latin rather than the obvious Spanish or even the French that was my family heritage. While it was certainly valuable to learn the historic language spoken across much of the Christian world, it did little to connect me to the culture that was growing right outside of my doorstep. Later, in my university days, my four years of Latin fulfilled my college language requirement, and my degrees in production management and industrial engineering had neither room nor requirement for international education or cultural study. So, as I began my Air Force career, I was culturally ignorant and language deprived in a career path that I soon learned was dependent on partnerships with friends and allies from across the globe. I quickly learned that familiarity with language and cultural perspective was going to be critical to my approach as an Air Force and Department of Defense (DoD) leader.

My first assignment for flight training was to Laredo Air Force Base in Laredo, Texas, a border town with Mexico. Little did I know then that the understanding of the cultural sensitivities and close Mexican relations that both my wife (a fluent Spanish speaker, courtesy of Indiana University) and I would develop there would be central to my last assignment as commander of the North American Aerospace Defense Command and US Northern Command, which was responsible for US military strategy with Mexico, as I will discuss below.

When I graduated from Indiana University in 1971, my business education was almost completely focused on a future tied to US manufacturing and sales, with no real anticipation of the growth in global economies we have seen in the last fifteen to twenty years. We manufactured for the US market and sold almost exclusively to the US market, and any international initiatives were a distant second to the engine that was this nation. We harvested our own raw materials, processed and refined them to US-made rough stock (steel, lumber, plastics, etc.) and then made products for our own market. Those realities have changed by orders of magnitude! The digital market was a dream, and information management was an internal function that moved at rotary-dial speed. Record keeping was done on hard copy, and no one forecast the digital information access we see today. Much of that change has been driven by the overseas entry of products and services into the global economy. Today, raw materials are sent from the United States all over the world for processing, refining, and manufacturing and then sent back to the United States for consumer purchase. Virtually every product used in our homes and our businesses is sourced offshore, and their production and distribution require day-to-day interaction with businesses at every corner of the globe. The global economy drives virtually every business decision we make. From energy to microelectronics, to consumer products, to travel, to space travel, we rely on our trading partners to fulfill the demands of our citizens.

Similarly, in my career in the US military, I have seen significant changes in the way we consider military operations and the way in which we reach out to allies, friends, and potential partners. In the bipolar world of the Cold War, we focused all military interactions through NATO and focused on the Soviet bloc. Our cultural awareness and much of our military language training was intelligence related and primarily Russian focused, allowing the United States to monitor Russian intentions. There was very little emphasis on other language training and very few officers involved in area studies, other than through direct assignments as defense attachés. Our nation's first major conflict since Vietnam, Desert Storm, necessitated an expanding group of military partners as we began what would become a twenty-seven-year involvement in the Middle East. The discovery of large oil reserves in Saudi Arabia, Iran, and Iraq, as well as natural gas reserves in Qatar and the United Arab Emirates, also contributed to very active engagement by US and Western businesses in that region. In sum, these activities demonstrated why we must invest more in our military, diplomatic, and business awareness in the culture and, especially, the languages of this important region.

Like many Cold War veterans, my first international experience was an assignment to the NATO theater as part of the US contribution to the defense of our European allies against the Soviet Union. While this was planned to be a three-year assignment to the United Kingdom, that relationship turned into twelve and a half years of leadership experience with every nation in the alliance. Understanding the very real cultural differences among NATO nations was crucial to the success of the military activities of the alliance. From Turkey and its historical differences with Greece to the post–World War II sensitivities of a divided Germany and the proximity of the Nordic nations to the Russian border, each of the nations of NATO had very real differences in their perspective of threat and interaction among other NATO partners. When the Soviet Union dissolved in the late 1980s and early 1990s, that dissolution opened up historical ethnic and religious divides that we, in NATO, did not fully understand and were not prepared to address. Bosnia-Herzegovina, the breakup of Serbia, the establishment of new nations such as Slovenia, and the split of others such as Slovakia and the Czech Republic highlighted the long-standing religious and political wounds that were overshadowed by the occupation of Russian forces underpinning totalitarian regimes. The breakup of the Soviet Union brought all of those divides to the surface, and the West was not educated enough in the history or sensitive enough to the divisions to diplomatically deal with these challenges. In-depth study of regional history, familiarity with the language, and cultural awareness might have alleviated some of the difficulties the United States encountered.

September 11, 2001, added yet another reason for reliance on leaders with the ability to interact with a variety of governments and cultures around the world. As the director of operations for the US Central Command (responsible for the region from Egypt to Pakistan and from the Seychelles to the southern border of Russia), we were tasked to build a broad coalition to combat the violent extremists responsible for the attacks in the United States. Ultimately, we built a "Coalition of the Willing" consisting of seventy-two nations: some as small as Estonia, others as large as Canada, and with nontraditional partners like Mongolia, Tajikistan, Poland, Qatar, Japan, and many others. Each nation came willingly to the team with a series of national concerns and national political restrictions, and unless we fully understood their view of their relationship with the United States, their view of other partners in the region, and the internal political dynamics they dealt with at home, we could not adequately incorporate them into our planning efforts. To help with this, we formed a coalition study group that spent hundreds of hours analyzing the dynamics of each contributing nation and briefing me daily as we prepared for a thrice-weekly coalition meeting with senior national representatives from each of the seventy-two nations in the coalition. This was incredibly helpful as we dealt with ticklish political scenarios. Imagine if we had had some of this exposure much earlier in our careers; we might have avoided a number of learning missteps. Interestingly, at this same time, there were fewer than ten speakers of such Central Asian languages as Pashtu or Urdu in all of the DoD, and not many more in the Department of State. The other interesting dynamic at the outset of our efforts was that the United States had no military and few diplomatic relations with any nation surrounding Afghanistan and no overfly or landing rights with any of those nations either. The fact that the United States had essentially abandoned Pakistan and Afghanistan and the Central Asian nations after the Russians left Afghanistan a few years earlier complicated critical negotiations, underlining the importance of constant US engagement across the globe and of understanding the political and cultural dynamics in areas that we often choose to ignore. Solutions to these military problems required an extensive diplomatic, intelligence, and military outreach effort to allow the basing and overflight rights we needed. More expertise in these critical political dynamics would have greatly enhanced our early negotiations.

Similarly, as the United States began planning for and executing military operations in Iraq, the availability of experts in the cultural dynamics of the Sunni, Shia, and Kurdish sects was virtually nonexistent and led to assumptions and, ultimately, decisions on strategy in those operations that were flawed. Had we known more of the depth of Shia oppression by the Sunni ruling class in Iraq, I believe we would have had a very different strategy and, certainly, postcombat governance. At the very least, we would have had evidential conviction for the paths we chose.

As my career focus shifted to the Pacific in 2003, I sought out experts in the region assigned to the Asia Pacific Center for Strategic Studies (APCSS) to assist me as I prepared to engage with military and civilian leaders of the fifty-four Asian nations in that region. While language was going to be too challenging to learn in the short preparation period I had, I focused on the historical and cultural differences among the nations in that region. From India to Korea and Australia to Mongolia, the differences were stark, and the relations the United States had with each were developing, prickly, or adversarial. What made the situation more difficult was that the relations and history between and among each of these nations were fraught with historical divide and interdependency. To say the environment was complicated is an understatement. The value to me of regional experts was that they had detailed perspectives on the nations with which I would engage and, importantly, on the leadership in each of those countries. This became extremely helpful during responses to such major natural disasters as the earthquake in Pakistan and earthquake/tsunami response in Indonesia and Thailand in late 2004 and early 2005. We could reach leaders in these stricken nations directly and effect humanitarian assistance very quickly and with region-changing results. The relationships built by military from the United States and the host nations, formed at our centers like APCSS and at our senior service schools like the National War College, served us incredibly well as we worked with national leaders in the region to gain access and move relief supplies rapidly through traditional bureaucratic red tape at light speed. The result of that regional relationship and rapid aid was also pivotal in reversing a separatist movement in the Aceh region of Indonesia as recovery ensued.

For me, regional relationships and history have been critically important as I have navigated the variety of international assignments that made my military career. Fortunately, our military services have begun to demonstrate a commitment to this same experience, and today, we see many young officers taking advantage of this emphasis.

An example of the growing importance that the DoD places on this cultural and regional education is the fact that the US military has placed a premium on the training of a number of its officers as so-called foreign area officers, or FAOs. The department has recognized this important skill and has actively supported the awarding of Olmsted Scholarships in the early stages of its officer corps. This program is described in the Olmsted Scholar course summary as follows:

> Since 1959, the Olmsted Scholar Program has challenged young military officers to learn a foreign language and pursue graduate studies in that language at a foreign university . . . a life-changing experience for our Scholars and their families. . . . Many describe it as the best time of their lives. The life-changing experience comes from the cultural immersion. . . . Living as aliens delivers two years of constant surprises. Scholars remember "being thrown into the deep end of the pool" but then rising to the surface and thriving.
>
> Olmsted candidates come from different military branches, educational backgrounds, nationalities and temperaments. Scholars are promoted to leadership positions. Some become Generals and Admirals. Whether working as an astronaut on the International Space Station or as National Security Advisors in the White House, Scholars aspire to positions of great responsibility and public service. Whether nuclear physicists, military strategists at the Army War College, or CEOs of international corporations, the most senior leaders recognize Olmsted Scholars as the kind of performers they want on their teams.[1]

The value of regional and cultural awareness followed me in my career in the military roles I had to support the Joint Chiefs of Staff as the director of strategic plans and policy, or J-5 in DoD-speak. In that role, our team was responsible for all international policy recommendations to the chairman of the Joint Chiefs. I also served as the US military representative to the Office of Security Cooperation in Europe in Vienna, as well as the chairman's representative to the National Security Council's Deputies Committee, carrying international military policy recommendations to the president's national security advisor. In those roles, I routinely interfaced not only with the most senior leaders in the Department of State and other departments of the US government but also the most senior military leaders of more than seventy-five nations around the world.

As senior military assistant to two secretaries of defense, I routinely traveled with the secretary and assisted in the preparation for and meetings with heads of state and ministers of defense and foreign affairs, and I participated in discussions at such world forums as Davos and Shangri La. Without the deep understanding of regional and cultural issues and perspectives that I gained in my career, success in these roles would have been impossible. It is critical that we require and inspire our new generations of leaders to invest themselves in that same immersive experience.

As the husband of a fluent Spanish, French, and German speaker, and the father of two men who have lived in more than twenty US states and foreign countries and traveled extensively as part of their military family upbringing, I have seen the deep personal experiences we have all benefited from and how that exposure to the cultures and customs of so many has enriched our lives and enabled all of us to be better citizens. Today, my oldest son serves in the US Department of State, and my younger son is a physician with extensive international medical experience and a strong supporter of Doctors without Borders. Our family is a great example of the impact of language, cultural, and historical study.

Note

1. Olmsted Foundation, "Olmsted Story."

Bibliography

Olmsted Foundation. "The Olmsted Story." Who We Are. Accessed April 22, 2020. http://www.olmstedfoundation.org/who-we-are/.

INDEX

Page numbers in *italics* refer to figures; page numbers in **bold** refer to tables.

Nipwaayoni Acquisition and Assessment
Team (NAAT), 152–54
No Child Left Behind Act (2001), 157
Noorda, Sijbolt, 53
North Carolina, 139
Northwestern University, 186

Obama Foundation, 190
Office of Career and Technical Education,
237–38
Office of Diversity, Equity, and Multicultural
Affairs (Indiana University), 229
Office of International Programs (Indiana
University), 209
Office of International Services (Indiana
University), 217
Office of Overseas Study (Indiana University), 229
Office of the Director of National Intelligence, 135
"official English" policies, 161–62
Ohio, 235–36
Ohio State University (OSU), 235–36
Olmsted Scholar Program, 255
Olson, Mancur, 73
O'Meara, Patrick, 209
online program managers (OPMs), 195–96, 198
Open Doors, 113
Open Doors Report (Institute of International Education), 243–44
open educational resources (OERs), 90
Oregon, 139
Orientalism (Said), 96
Orientalism, 96, 99
orientation, 30

Page, Larry, 20
Pakistan, 253–54
Palestine, 26
Palestinian refugees, 185
pandemics, 20, 117, 185
Panetta, Leon, 61
Paris Institute of Political Studies (Sciences
Po), 187
Parker, William Riley, 8–9
Partnership for Higher Education in Africa, 210

partnerships: faculty and, 241–42; funding
of, 82–83, 84; future directions for, 53–55;
importance and benefits of, 3, 5, 22–23,
29–31, 51–53, 186–91, 211; Indiana University and, 8, 10–11, 223–24; less commonly
taught languages and, 25; New Global
University model and, 195–200
Pashto (language), 71–72, 253
Peak, Michael, 44
Pell Grants, 75
Pennsylvania, 88
Pennsylvania Dutch (language), 169n14
Persian (language), 124–25, 142n11
Pew Research Center, 112
Pinto Baleisan, Carolina, 41
political polarization, 74
Pompeo, Michael, 240
populism, 25–26, 36, 51, 112
Portuguese (language), 124–25, 139, 142n11
postcolonialism and postcolonial studies,
43–44, 96, 99
postcommunist studies, 71
postconflict settings, 40–41
postsocialist studies, 94–100
poststructuralism, 96, 97, 99
Potowski, Kim, 158, 165, 168
President's Global Innovation Fund, 188
Price, David, 60
problem-solving skills, 204, 211
professional education, 202–6, 235–36
Project Global Officer, 135
protectionism, 51
Pufahl, Ingrid, 158

Qatar, 186, 252
Qatar Foundation for Education, Science,
and Community Development, 186

Ramírez Sánchez, Carlos, 41
Rampersad, David, 43
Reader's Digest (magazine), 176
refugees, 40, 49, 185, 250
Regulska, Joanna, 32
research: American Academy of Arts and
Sciences and, 58–65; Department of Education and, 232–38; Fulbright Program
and, 241–42; funding of, 74–77, 81–90;

CONTRIBUTORS

DARYL BALDWIN is Director of the Myaamia Center at Miami University. He has been actively involved in language revitalization efforts for Myaamia, as well as other Native American languages throughout North America. His efforts have earned him a MacArthur Award and, most recently, a grant from the National Endowment for the Humanities.

KATHLEEN CLAUSSEN is Associate Professor at the University of Miami School of Law. She is author of more than twenty articles, book chapters, and books on topics related to international law, particularly international economic law. She is a graduate of the Yale Law School, Queen's University Belfast, and Indiana University Bloomington (IUB), where she was a Wells Scholar.

DEBORAH N. COHN is Provost Professor in the Department of Spanish and Portuguese and Associate Director of the College Arts and Humanities Institute at IUB. She is author of *The Latin American Literary Boom and U.S. Nationalism during the Cold War* (2012) and *History and Memory in the Two Souths: Recent Southern and Spanish American Fiction* (1999). She has received awards from the National Endowment for the Humanities, the Harry Ransom Center, the Rockefeller Archive Center, and others.

KENNETH M. COLEMAN is Director for Partner Programs at the Association of American Universities. Formerly a faculty member at the Universities of Kentucky, New Mexico, and North Carolina, he held Fulbright Awards in Mexico, Venezuela, and Nicaragua. He is author with Charles L. Davis of *Politics and Culture in Mexico* (1988).

MARY SUE COLEMAN is a past president of the Association of American Universities (AAU). Prior to joining the AAU, she was President of the University of Michigan from 2002 to 2014 and President of the University of Iowa from 1995 to 2002. *Time* magazine named her one of the nation's "10 best college presidents," and the American Council on Education honored her with its Lifetime Achievement Award in 2014.

DAN E. DAVIDSON is Director of the American Councils Research Center and Emeritus President, American Councils for International Education, Washington, DC, and Emeritus Professor of Russian and Second Language Acquisition on the Myra T. Cooley Lectureship at Bryn Mawr College. Davidson is author/editor of twenty-four books and sixty-five scholarly articles on language, culture, and educational development. He is co-editor of and contributor to *Transformative Language Learning and Teaching* (2020) and served on the American Academy of Arts and Sciences Commission on Language Learning and Commission Working Group.

HANS DE WIT is Director of the Center for International Higher Education and Professor of Practice at the Lynch School of Education and Human Development, Boston College. He is founding editor of the *Journal of Studies in International Higher Education*, consulting editor of the journal *Policy Review in Higher Education*, and associate editor of the journal *International Higher Education*. He has published widely about international higher education, including as editor, with Kara A. Godwin, of *Intelligent Internationalization, the Shape of Things to Come* (2019).

BRIAN T. EDWARDS is Dean of the School of Liberal Arts at Tulane University, where he oversees thirty-four departments and programs in fields from the social sciences, humanities, and fine and performing arts. Prior to moving to Tulane in 2018, he was Crown Professor in Middle East Studies and Professor of English and Comparative Literary Studies at Northwestern University, where he was also Founding Director of the Program in Middle East and North African Studies; in 2016–17, he served on the American Academy of Arts and Sciences Commission on Language Learning. His books include *Globalizing American Studies* (co-edited, 2010) and *After the American Century: The Ends of U.S. Culture in the Middle East* (2016).

EVA EGRON-POLAK is Senior Fellow and Former Secretary General of the International Association of Universities. She also served as Vice President, International and Canadian Programs at Universities Canada. She authored *Internationalization of Higher Education* (2015) and *Internationalization of Higher Education—Growing Expectations, Fundamental Values* (2014).

JONATHAN F. FANTON served as President of the American Academy of Arts and Sciences from 2014 to 2019. Previously, he was Interim Director of the Roosevelt House Public Policy Institute at Hunter College, President of the John D. and Catherine T. MacArthur Foundation, and President of the New School for Social Research. He is author of *Foundations and Civil Society*, volumes 1 and 2 (2008), and *The University and Civil Society*, volumes 1 and 2 (1995, 2002).

ROSEMARY G. FEAL is Executive Director Emerita of the Modern Language Association and Professor Emerita of Spanish at the State University of New York at Buffalo. In 2018–19, she was Wilbur Marvin Visiting Scholar at the David Rockefeller Center for Latin American Studies at Harvard University, and in 2017–18 she was Mary L. Cornille Distinguished Visiting Professor in the Humanities at Wellesley College. Her books include *Isabel Allende Today* (2002), *Painting on the Page: Interartistic Approaches to Modern Hispanic Texts* (co-author, 1995), and *Novel Lives: The Fictional Autobiographies of Guillermo Cabrera Infante and Mario Vargas Llosa* (1986).

CHERYL E. GIBBS is Senior Director of the International and Foreign Language Education office in the Office of Postsecondary Education at the US Department of Education, Washington, DC. She oversees the policies and grants for area studies, international studies, and modern foreign language training programs authorized under Title VI of the Higher Education Act of 1965, as amended, and the Mutual and Cultural Exchange Act of 1961 (Fulbright-Hays). These programs strengthen the capacity at US institutions of higher education to meet the national need for global competitiveness.

ZSUZSA GILLE is Professor of Sociology and Director of Global Studies at the University of Illinois at Urbana-Champaign. She is author of *From the Cult of Waste to the Trash Heap of History: The Politics of Waste in Socialist and Postsocialist Hungary* (2007) and co-editor of *The Socialist Good Life: Desire, Development, and Standards of Living in Eastern Europe* (2020).

ALLAN E. GOODMAN is the sixth President and Chief Executive Officer of the Institute of International Education (IIE), which was founded in 1919. Dr. Goodman is the author of books on international relations published by IIE, Princeton, Harvard, and Yale University Presses.

STEPHEN E. HANSON is Vice Provost for International Affairs, Director of the Wendy and Emery Reves Center for International Studies, and Lettie Pate Evans Professor in the Department of Government at the College of William & Mary. At William & Mary, Hanson is responsible for strategic management of international teaching, research, and outreach initiatives across the university. Hanson is a noted specialist in Russian and postcommunist politics and author of numerous scholarly publications concerning Russian, East European, and Eurasian affairs.

ROBIN MATROSS HELMS is Deputy Chief Innovation Officer and Principal Internationalization Strategist at the American Council on Education. Her research and writing focus on college and university internationalization and global higher education issues.

ELSPETH JONES is Emerita Professor of the Internationalisation of Higher Education at Leeds Beckett University, United Kingdom, and Honorary Visiting Fellow at the Centre for Higher Education Internationalisation, Università Cattolica del Sacro Cuore, Milan. She is founding editor of the book series Internationalization in Higher Education and has published widely. She is past chair of the European Association for International Education's (EAIE) Expert Community on Internationalisation at Home and winner of the EAIE Award for Excellence in Research.

HILARY E. KAHN is Associate Vice Chancellor for International Affairs at Indiana University–Purdue University Indianapolis (IUPUI), Associate Vice President for International Affairs at Indiana University, and Associate Professor of Anthropology at IUPUI. She is a past president of the Association of International Education Administrators, and she serves on the advisory board for Diversity and Democracy and the Global Learning Advisory Council of the Association of American Colleges and Universities. She is author of *Seeing and Being Seen: The Q'eqchi' Maya of Livingston Guatemala and Beyond* (2006), *Framing the Global: Entry Points for Research* (2014), and *On Islam: Muslims and the Media* (edited with Rosemary Pennington, 2018).

SEUNG-KYUNG KIM is Korea Foundation Professor in the Department of East Asian Languages and Cultures and Director of the Institute for Korean Studies at IUB. She is author of *Class Struggle or Family Struggle? Lives of*

Women Factory Workers in South Korea (2009), *The Korean Women's Movement and the State: Bargaining for Change* (2016), and co-editor of *Feminist Theory Reader: Local and Global Perspectives* (2016).

ANTHONY KOLIHA is Director of the Office of Global Educational Programs, Bureau of Educational and Cultural Affairs, US Department of State. Koliha oversees a portfolio of international teacher, professional, and global mobility programs and services for US and foreign students. He previously held positions including Director of International Programs, College of Arts and Sciences at IUB, Director of the Fulbright Program in Russia, and other positions with the Institute of International Education, American Councils for International Education, and the Social Science Research Council.

CAROLINE LEVANDER is Carlson Professor in the Humanities, Professor of English, and Vice President for Global and Digital Strategy at Rice University; she also is on the Board of Directors of the Fulbright Association. She is author of *Where Is American Literature?* (2013) and *Hotel Life* (2016) and is currently at work on a book entitled "Undisciplined," which tells the story of how scientific innovators of the digital age imagined a future out of the collective wisdom, practices, and ideas of other disciplines, most particularly the literary and creative arts as well as philosophy, religion, and history. She was funded by the Rockefeller Foundation to lead an international summit on the Future Global University in 2018.

TAKYIWAA MANUH is Emerita Professor of African Studies at the University of Ghana, Legon, Ghana, where she also served as the director from 2002–2009. She also served as Director of the Social Development Policy Division at the United Nations Economic Commission for Africa (UNECA) in Addis Ababa, Ethiopia, from 2014–2017. She has published widely in the fields of African development, gender and women's rights in Africa, higher education in Africa, contemporary African migrations, and social policy in Africa.

FRANCISCO MARMOLEJO is Education Advisor of Qatar Foundation. Previously, he served as Global Higher Education Coordinator of the World Bank, and also as Lead Higher Education Specialist in India and South Asia. From 1995 to 2012, he served as Founding Executive Director of the

Consortium for North American Higher Education Collaboration at the University of Arizona.

SAFWAN M. MASRI is Executive Vice President for Global Centers and Global Development at Columbia University and a senior research scholar at Columbia's School of International and Public Affairs. He is author of *Tunisia: An Arab Anomaly* (2017), which examines why Tunisia was the only country to emerge from the Arab Spring as a democracy. Masri is a lifetime member of the Council on Foreign Relations and an honorary fellow of the Foreign Policy Association.

MICHAEL A. MCROBBIE is the eighteenth President of Indiana University, which was founded in 1820 and is one of the largest universities in the United States. He is also past chair of the Board of Directors of the Association of American Universities, whose members are the sixty leading research universities in the United States and two in Canada, and Vice Chair of the Board of Directors of the Indiana University Health System, one of the largest and most highly regarded hospital systems in the United States. In 2016, he received the International Citizen of the Year Award from the International Center for outstanding contributions to the globalization of Indiana.

KRIS OLDS is Professor in the Department of Geography, University of Wisconsin–Madison. He is also affiliated with the Department of Planning and Landscape Architecture and the Department of Educational Policy Studies. His most recent book is the co-edited volume *Global Regionalisms and Higher Education: Projects, Processes, Politics* (2016).

PATRICK O'MEARA is Special Advisor to the President of Indiana University, Vice President Emeritus for International Affairs, Professor of Public and Environmental Affairs, and Professor of Political Science. He has published books and articles on southern African politics, globalization, development, and international higher education. *Africa*, originally edited with Phyllis M. Martin, has been adopted by nearly one hundred universities and colleges throughout the United States; the fourth edition, edited with Maria Grosz-Ngate and John Hanson, appeared in 2014.

KIM POTOWSKI is Professor of Linguistics at the University of Illinois at Chicago. She is author of *Language and Identity in a Dual Immersion School* (2007) and *"Mexi-Rican" Spanish and Identity in Chicago* (2016).

GENERAL GENE RENUART, USAF (Ret.), is Chairman of the Indiana Innovation Institute, a state-supported applied research institute bringing research and advanced technology from Indiana University, Purdue, and Notre Dame to bear on the Department of Defense's most pressing challenges. General Renuart's Air Force career culminated as Commander of North American Aerospace Defense Command and US Northern Command, where he was responsible for providing for the homeland defense and defense support to civilian authorities for the United States, and for partnering with Canada and Mexico in broader security issues for North America. General Renuart is a member of the Military Advisory Group of the US Global Leadership Coalition, a member of the Council on Foreign Relations, and a dean's advisor at Indiana University's Hamilton Lugar School of Global and International Studies.

DAWN MICHELE WHITEHEAD is Vice President of the Office of Global Citizenship for Campus, Community, and Careers at the Association of American Colleges and Universities. She is author of *Essential Global Learning* (2016).